Cambridge Studies in Cultural Systems

Human spirits:

A cultural account of trance in Mayotte

Cambridge Studies in Cultural Systems

Clifford Geertz, Editor

Human spirits:
A cultural account of
trance in Mayotte

MICHAEL LAMBEK

Department of Anthropology
University of Toronto

avec amitiés
Michael Lambek

CAMBRIDGE UNIVERSITY PRESS

Cambridge
London   New York   New Rochelle
Melbourne   Sydney

Published by the Press Syndicate of the University of Cambridge
The Pitt Building, Trumpington Street, Cambridge CB2 1RP
32 East 57th Street, New York, NY 10022, USA
296 Beaconsfield Parade, Middle Park, Melbourne 3206, Australia

First published 1981

Printed in the United States of America

Library of Congress Cataloging in Publication Data
Lambek, Michael.
Human spirits.
(Cambridge studies in cultural systems; 6)
Bibliography: p.
Includes index.
1. Comoro Islands – Religion.   2. Spirit possession.
3. Trance.   I. Title.   II. Title: Mayotte.   III. Series.
BL2470.C56L35   306'.6   81–1842
ISBN 0 521 23844 7 hard covers   AACR1
ISBN 0 521 28255 1 paperback

In memory of Jane Katherine Sallade, 1949–1979

In the object which he contemplates, therefore, man becomes acquainted with himself; consciousness of the objective is the self-consciousness of man. We know the man by the object, by his conception of what is external to himself; in it his nature becomes evident.

Ludwig Feuerbach, *The Essence of Christianity*

A work does not only mirror its time, but it opens up a world which it bears within itself.

Paul Ricoeur, "The Model of the Text: Meaningful Action Considered as a Text"

Contents

Tables and figures

Cultural zero

Lombeni, Mayotte, Comoro Islands, July 6. It was the heart of the winter season, when the sun shone all day and the older people complained of chill at night. During the day, children and anthropologist continually had to be reminded to stay out of the direct sunshine, but in the evenings everyone settled on mats spread wide under the clear and perfect sky to enjoy a leisurely dinner and conversation.

Tonight I was eating in the compound of Tumbu and Mohedja, in the other section of the village from which my own house lay. A young man whom I did not know had reached the climax of some amusing incident and, with barely a pause to deliver a last spoonful of rice to his mouth, began another. Tumbu, conscious of his responsibility as host, quickly turned to me and inquired whether I had understood the story. I returned my gaze from the stars and replied that it had been too difficult. "Which word didn't you understand?" demanded Tumbu. "There are still so many of them –" I began. "Well, if you don't stop and ask questions," replied Tumbu, "how will you ever learn anything?" I smiled at this, remembering all the times I had been told not to ask so many questions during meals. In truth, tonight my silence had not been out of consideration (the anthropologist who is too considerate about these matters is, as Tumbu realized, lost), but from exhaustion after a long and busy day. I had been in the village of Malagasy speakers for only a little more than a month, and my concentration in conversations that were not of my own construction was destined to falter for several more months to come. Furthermore, I was trying to keep my wits in reserve for whatever I was to face later that evening, a meeting that I anticipated with curiosity but without the slightest idea of what would happen or what would be expected of me: I was to meet my first spirit.

The assignation had come about in the following way. Before moving to Lombeni I had learned that there existed a belief in what the French colonials called *diables*, that these 'devils' or 'spirits' tended to establish ties with particular individuals, and that no one ever seemed to admit being party to such a relationship. Upon moving to Lombeni, I had decided to wait until the villagers themselves chose to bring up the subject.

It happened quite by accident. In the hot hours of the early afternoon I came upon my friends Tumbu and Mohedja sitting together on a mat spread in the narrow patch of shade cast between the badly decaying wall of their small wattle and daub hut and the larger, taller, and airier two-room house of raffia poles they had built for their married daughter Nuriaty. Tumbu invited me to join him in the typical noon meal of *batabata* – boiled green bananas and manioc. The fishermen had been unlucky that night, so we had to be content to dip the starchy food into a relish of freshly crushed black pepper and sour tomato. There was nothing unusual in the encounter; perhaps I was contemplating a year of eating *batabata* for lunch. Mohedja sat beside us sewing strips of red material onto a fringed, bright blue cloth unlike any piece of clothing I had ever seen before. Idly, with no great interest, I asked about it. To my surprise, both Mohedja and Tumbu responded with embarrassed and quite uncharacteristic giggles. They said the cloth belonged to Tumbu's *fundi,* his 'teacher' or 'master.' Who was that? I asked. Tumbu replied that Mohedja wished to give a gift to his spirit. It soon appeared that the spirit itself had requested the cloth and that Tumbu had just returned from an excursion to purchase it. They planned to give the spirit the cloth that evening, after dinner, when everyone would have left the compound.

Somewhat more hesitantly, I inquired if I might stay to watch. They appeared to be incredulous. Did I really want to see a spirit, they asked, as if nothing could have been expected to be of less interest to me. I did, if it was possible. For an instant they paused and looked down at the ground. With hindsight I can surmise that they were foreseeing and considering the implications this would have for our relationship. Eventually they replied with a single word, *mety* 'permissible.' They were being very kind but were clearly inclined to drop the subject. I was excited but willing, too, to drop the conversation and wait. I fantasized that at last I would be able to see the "real" world at motion there, behind the facade of everyday domestic concerns, of sleepy afternoons and boiled bananas.

And so, some eight hours later, I rejoined them. Tonight the neighbors and sons-in-law seem slower than usual to retire to their homes. It strikes me that I am the only one present to know of Tumbu and Mohedja's plans. The invocation of the spirit is to be a private affair between husband and wife; even their close kin are excluded. One by one our friends disperse – even Tumbu retires to the hut – until only Mohedja and I are left behind. Mohedja acknowledges my presence with a dry, "What, are you still here?" I realize they have been assuming I would forget or lose heart to stay on. Clearly, they were not planning to remind me. But now Mohedja scoops up some embers from the dying cooking fire into an empty coconut shell and motions for me to follow her into the hut.

It is late, the village dark and absolutely silent; the small, low, rectangular room is lit by a single, flickering kerosene lamp constructed from an empty beer can discarded by a Frenchman on the far side of the island. We are all cold and very tired. Tumbu sits with his legs up on one of the small beds. Mohedja motions me to a place just across from him, at the foot of the other bed, upon which their baby son lies fast asleep. Mohedja herself crouches on a block of wood on the floor between us, huddled from the cold and facing Tumbu. She places the coconut shell by her feet and adds a piece of incense to the embers. As the smoke curls up, Tumbu silently rubs his shins and forearms, from the cold, I believe. I wait for something to happen. Tumbu's motions appear a bit obsessive. He starts to breathe heavily; now and then he snorts. I begin to wish I were back in my own house, safely ensconced within sleeping bag and mosquito net and escaping into my current bedtime reading of Simone de Beauvoir's autobiography – into the orderly world of bourgeois French childhood, of clean, hard-edged rationality.

Tumbu now closes his eyes and tenses, as though in pain. He emits a few low whistling noises. This lasts some minutes, intensifying and then subsiding. He opens his eyes and slowly looks about. The eyes start with a peculiar intensity. I have the strong feeling that this is no longer the Tumbu I know but someone quite different, perhaps a little mad. What is a spirit? What do spirits do? Do spirits like foreigners? It is the middle of the night; no one else in the village knows that I have come to this house to meet a spirit; the tiny flame of the lamp flickers over the narrow, shoulder-high mud walls; I am apprehensive.

The spirit (who has replaced Tumbu) reaches out to shake our hands, addressing Mohedja directly by name and asking us, in the form appropriate for a person of higher status addressing someone of lower status, how we are. I reply automatically, "fine." The spirit asks me who I am and bids me welcome, reassuring me. Its attention switches back and forth rapidly between Mohedja and myself. It inquires if indeed I come from very far away, a question that is commonly among the first asked me by new acquaintances in Mayotte, and then brags that it can go to Canada and back in a day, that it will one day soon. Its speed is like that of an airplane, the spirit says. It tells me that I have letters from my mother and father, with photographs in them, awaiting me in the post office. A kind thought from a spirit for a perhaps lonely anthropologist who has traveled so far; I recognize Tumbu's considerate nature behind the intense gaze, the abrupt manner, and the bravado of the spirit. As if reading my thoughts, the spirit adds that it is a good spirit, that it doesn't fight, that it likes human beings.

I am no longer frightened, but still uncertain. How does one talk to a spirit? Which of its bodily movements are significant and which of its remarks require formalized responses? What is the proper etiquette? I have no idea. Mohedja is of no help. She sits, staring at the floor, listening carefully to the spirit when it addresses her and answering in an even tone. I try to maintain a friendly and frank manner. The spirit continues to sit up on the bed, looking about with a sometimes vacant, sometimes piercing, stare. It appears to be enjoying itself; occasionally, for no apparent reason, it grins broadly or laughs. The spirit takes down the new cloth from where it has been hanging on the rafters and wraps it around its head like a turban. Then it winds it around its neck. The spirit smiles, strokes the scarf, and tells Mohedja it is pleased with it. It asks for some cologne to drink. Mohedja replies that there is hardly any cologne in the house. The spirit insists, and she fetches a small bottle with less than half an inch of liquid. The spirit drinks some of this, with exaggerated smacking noises, pours some on its hair, and then gulps the rest, assuring me that spirits love cologne. I wonder whether it really drank any or poured all the cologne on its hair.

For the first time since my arrival on the island I feel entirely within a foreign culture: without knowledge; without even intuition for what the appropriate conventions might be; for what, after all, it is I am after; for what we are supposed to be doing together here in this dark room in the middle of the night. I am even at a loss for questions; I am totally confused. Then an idea creeps into the back of my mind. This is the experience that is supposed to lie at the base of the anthropological venture, the experience that validates the world view of my profession and marks the real beginning of my own enterprise. A month ago I put on weights and jumped into a strange ocean. For a month I have been bobbing fitfully, now sinking slightly, now floating free. Finally, tonight, I have touched bottom, cultural zero. This is the point from which all my future progress at understanding must be measured.

I do not know how Mohedja and the spirit are experiencing our interaction here. Certainly, being ignorant of my culture, they can have no full idea of the meeting's significance to me. And yet the spirit is trying to impress me, trying to make me feel something. Now it leers up at me and says it will visit me again, later tonight, in my own house. I am not certain if the spirit means it will appear in the flesh or in my dreams. It asks me whether I will be scared. Determined to steer a course between foolhardiness and total loss of face, I reply "maybe." The spirit laughs and instructs me to be sure and tell Mohedja the next morning whether I have seen and talked to it again during the night. The spirit refers to Tumbu in an offhand way, as if he were a third party, of no great interest to us here.

The spirit then prepares to take its leave. Mohedja, ever mindful of my role as student, asks me whether I don't have any more questions. I gather my wits a little and discover that it is a *patros* spirit, that its home is in the sea, that it is decidedly not the spirit of a dead person, that it visits several other individuals besides Tumbu. Just now, these matters seem quite beside the point.

The spirit stops talking. For a few moments it sways its head and upper body as if in a dance, then begins to rub and scratch as at the onset of the trance. The figure scratches its head and neck vigorously and rubs its arms and legs, perhaps in exaggerated reaction to the cold. The spirit lies back on the pillow. There is a momentary pause, and when he sits up again he begins to rub his stomach. In a tone of wifely concern, Mohedja asks her husband if he has a stomachache. It is her tone of voice that tells me Tumbu is out of trance. The spirit has gone and the man returned. Tumbu appears extremely tired, as indeed we all are, and lies back on the bed. Without further ado, I bid them good-night and retire to my own little house of wattle and daub across the village.

I do not know whether further communication ensues between Mohedja and Tumbu, but for me the event is not yet quite over. Later that night, about four in the morning, I am dreaming that the spirit is on its way to visit me. It has the appearance of Tumbu. Suddenly, I am awake in the darkness and there is a loud knocking at the door. Surely not Tumbu in trance . . . ? Nervously I ask who's there. It is only my neighbors, wishing to borrow my flashlight so that they can get an early start on the trail for a distant festivity. A coincidence; but if I am so impressionable, how much more convincing must the spirits appear to the local people? The neighbors make fun of the way I started, and I reply testily that in my country it is not the custom to go banging on other people's doors in the middle of the night. The neighbors go off with the flashlight, and the next time something interesting happens during the night, no one comes to wake me because they have learned that I don't like to be disturbed.

In the morning, Tumbu does not mention the previous night's activities at all. Mohedja enlightens me considerably on the "business" transacted during the session that, because of my lack of fluency in the language and ignorance of spirit affairs, I failed to pick up. The spirit said it was very happy with the new cloth and as a result would stop bothering Tumbu. Apparently, when its original demands for a cloth had been ignored, the spirit had made Tumbu ill. All week long he had been taking medicine for a disorder in the belly. I remark on the contrast between the import of this circumstance and the spirit's assurances to me that it is perfectly friendly and well meaning. In fact, the villagers never know what to expect from the spirits. At one moment Tumbu's spirit asserts that it is unwilling to harm humans; at another, it announces that it will make Tumbu sick until its demands for gifts are met. Somehow, spirits always manage to disconcert.

Acknowledgments

This work is a revised and shortened version of my doctoral dissertation, submitted to the University of Michigan in 1978. Research was generously supported by a doctoral fellowship awarded by the Canada Council (now Social Sciences and Humanities Research Council). Travel to Mayotte and some additional expenses were born by the National Science Foundation (Grant #GS–42337X). Portions of Chapter 5 appeared in my article "Spirits and Spouses: Possession as a System of Communication among the Malagasy Speakers of Mayotte," *American Ethnologist* 7(2):318–31 (May 1980).

At Michigan I am greatly indebted to Alton Becker, Vern Carroll, Ray Kelly, Conrad Kottak, Roy Rappaport, Henry Wright, and Aram Yengoyan for their intellectual inspiration and practical support. In particular, Aram Yengoyan's counsel and friendship have been invaluable at all stages of this project. The process of revision was greatly assisted by the generous support and advice of Clifford Geertz, the rigorous editing and numerous suggestions of my colleague Laurie Arnold, and the comments of Bernie Lambek and two anonymous reviewers. The cost of revision was partially offset by a faculty grant from the University of Toronto, which likewise supported a return visit to the field in the summer of 1980.

I benefited greatly from the courtesy, advice, and enthusiasm of a number of leading scholarly specialists in countries bordering the western Indian Ocean, in particular, Geneviève and Georges Boulinier, Georges Condominas, Paul Ottino, Jean-Aimé Rakotoarisoa, and Pierre Vérin. Without their assistance, fieldwork in Mayotte would have been unthinkable; indeed, it was Pierre Vérin who first suggested it. My colleague Jon Breslar, who has been pursuing ethnographic research in Mayotte independent from, but concurrent with, my own, responded with characteristic generosity to my frequent visits and suffered my endless stream of impressions and half-baked ideas.

I thank also the officials of the Comoro government and of the French administration in Mayotte during 1975–6 for their courtesy and support. Everywhere in Mayotte I was received with kindness. In Mamutzu I am most grateful to Hassanat Bakar and the members of her *mraba,* especially "Shehu." Although I wish to protect their privacy here, my teachers, friends, and neighbors in "Lombeni" know how much I owe them and how much I enjoyed living among them. In particular, I must thank the curers, the clients, their families – and, of course, the spirits – who so patiently tolerated my intrusion into their affairs.

Through their boundless intellectual enthusiasm, tolerance, and generosity, my parents established the conditions for the enterprise. Many other friends and colleagues have provided support, suggestions, and encouragement during the course of fieldwork and in the subsequent long periods of writing. The book is dedicated to the memory of Jane Sallade, an anthropologist of extraordinary talent, integrity, and style, who gave me unstinting support and whose work continues to set the standards.

Stylistic conventions

My orthography is rather idiosyncratic. Because Malagasy, Swahili, Arabic, and French systems do not always coincide with one another, nor yet with Mayotte pronunciation, I have tried to borrow from each of them whatever seems easiest for English readers. The main differences from standard Malagasy transcription are distinctions between *o* and *u* and between *s* and *sh*. Malagasy does not normally include markers for the plural, and I have adhered to this where possible. Whether the sense of a Malagasy word is singular or plural must be gained from the English verb. Final *e* is always pronounced *é*. I have found no completely satisfactory way in which to refer to the spirits in the third person. Although spirits have gender, I refer to them in the neuter in order to clearly distinguish them from their hosts. Because most hosts are women, I refer to hosts using feminine pronouns unless referring specifically to male hosts. This should not be taken to indicate that possession is restricted to women.

Zanzibar

*Dar es
Salaam*

Mafia

SEYCHELLES

TANZANIA

Grande-
Comore

300 K

Anjouan

Mohéli

Mayotte

Nosy-Bé

ÎLES COMORES

MOZAMBIQUE

SAKALAVA

Majunga

Tananarive

N

MADAGASCAR

The Comoro Islands

Introduction

This work is a cultural account of trance as it occurs among the Malagasy speakers of Mayotte. It presents a detailed description, analysis, and interpretation of trance behavior, elaborating the cultural system of "spirit possession" by which such behavior is organized.

Fieldwork in Mayotte

Mayotte, or *Tany Maore*, as it is known in the local Malagasy dialect, is the southernmost island of the Comoro archipelago, lying in the Mozambique Channel between the coast of East Africa and Madagascar. Mayotte is approximately 250 kilometers from the northwest coast of Madagascar and twice that distance from the mainland. Some 375 square kilometers in area, with fertile volcanic soil and a surrounding reef, Mayotte appears to the outsider as something of a tropical paradise. On the west coast the villages lie along sandy beaches, dwarfed by the peaks and ridges that rise behind to a maximum of 660 meters. The gentler east coast faces the rocky outcrop of Dzaoudzi, the base, since the end of the eighteenth century, for successive groups who have claimed dominion over the whole island.

The history of the western Indian Ocean is complex and as yet poorly understood. For nearly two millennia the area has been the scene of extensive trade, population movement, and the emergence of stratified societies. With population, cultural, and linguistic influence from three major original sources – sub-Saharan Africa, the Muslim Middle East, and insular Southeast Asia – a basic matrix has formed from which new institutions and societies have regularly emerged (cf. Ottino 1974). In contemporary Mayotte it is relatively easy to divide the population of approximately forty thousand into two cultural and linguistic groups: speakers of Comoran, a Bantu language closely akin to Swahili, who comprise approximately two-thirds of the inhabitants, and speakers of Malagasy, an Austronesian language. Only the

1

An audience of women and children.

speakers of Shimaore, a dialect of Comoran, claim and are recognized to be the original inhabitants of the island. But not only do these categories incorporate much cultural and dialectical variation, they have relatively little historical depth as discrete units. Malagasy culture itself has a strong African component (Kent 1970), and what we perceive today is merely a moment in a long process of cultural fusion, fission, and refusion along new lines. Furthermore, the ethnic and linguistic labels have relatively little immediate sociological significance. Intermarriage and bilingualism are common, and group membership in Mayotte is defined according to principles of residence, ownership, and participation in ceremonial exchange networks rather than more abstract ascriptive criteria. Mayotte is an open society; despite the great cultural heterogeneity there is a vigorously affirmed social unity, based on Islam and a common loyalty to the island as an indivisible whole.[1]

The claim, therefore, of this monograph to be a study of "the Malagasy speakers of Mayotte" is something of a convenient fiction. In fact, fieldwork was carried out concurrently in a pair of adjacent villages of Malagasy speakers and was conducted entirely in the local dialect.[2] Although many of the village members trace their ancestry to Madagascar, a significant proportion are the descendants of East Africans brought to Mayotte as indentured laborers or of Comoran speakers. Even though the majority of cultural features are held in common, there is much internal variation within these villages and presumably between them and the villages of other Malagasy speakers. I cannot claim either that the facts described here are common to all the Malagasy speakers of Mayotte or that they are unique to them; I do suggest, however, that they emerge from a common underlying matrix. I assert that the institution of spirit possession as described here is *intelligible* to all members of Mayotte society.

This book is the product of fourteen months' (May 1975–June 1976) ethnographic fieldwork in Mayotte.[3] I did not go to Mayotte in order to study trance; the research focus emerged gradually, during the course of more general investigations of social and cultural life. Trance is most evident in the riotous public spirit dances. These celebrations, characterized by an enthusiasm, an energetic and total involvement of the sort that Lewis (1971) has called "ecstatic religion," were hard to study. Never quite as captivating to me as to the central participants, at the beginning they were reduced by their volume and energy to a noisy blur. In the absence of movie camera and adequate sound and lighting equipment, they were also impossible to record with any precision. I was fortunate, then, to discover calmer and less public contexts in which possession could be observed and in which its principles could be learned and discussed. I have tried to convey something of the nature and style of this activity in the Preface.

In particular, it should be clear that my interaction with hosts and spirits was one of participation as much as observation. This was so despite never entering trance myself. There were two main aspects to this participation. In the first place, I was engaged in active communication with the spirits. More precisely, the spirits engaged me in communication. In the incident recorded in the Preface, I could not have sat quietly, pen in hand, trying not to affect the situation. Spirits rise precisely in order to interact with people. Upon arrival, they always shake hands and engage in formalities with everyone present. Having asked to be present, I was committed to establishing a relationship with the spirit. Over time, I increased my ties of friendship with this and other spirits, as we engaged in conversation and asked and received favors from one another. Much of my understanding of the spirits has been achieved through reflection on my own position. In particular, such reflection assisted the development of the view of possession as a system of communication to be presented in Chapter 5.

Tumbu's spirit was eager not only to talk to me but to create a particular kind of impression, to mold an experience. My experience during the first encounter is in itself a valuable source of information, perhaps not too dissimilar from the experience of the villagers themselves. My reactions stemmed primarily from the uncertainty of knowing neither what to expect nor what was expected of me. Struck by the contrast between particular cultures (mine and theirs), I was brought to a state of emotional suggestibility and to a consideration of culture in the abstract. The villagers who observe spirits are brought to a similar condition (presumably with somewhat different results) by the contrast of their culture with that of the spirits.

I am acutely conscious that the people of Mayotte, influenced, perhaps, by the dominant ideology of Islam or by the attitudes of European observers, are not particularly proud of their interaction with spirits. I may, therefore, owe them an apology and an explanation for having chosen to write on this aspect of their life first. Most important, I wish to offset the impression I fear this work will give the reader that the people of Mayotte are solely, or even predominantly, concerned with spirits. This is by no means the case, and this work makes no claims to "open up" Mayotte culture in its entirety through the analysis of a single institution.

Like other members of their society, Tumbu and Mohedja claim to view possession not as a vocation but as an affliction that they wish would go away. Yet they are also aware of the subtlety and complexity of possession. Through their generous tutelage I learned much about the symbolic richness, the humor and compassion, skill and sensitivity that spirit mastery entails. However, despite their frequent appearance in these pages, I did not rely entirely on Tumbu and Mohedja. My research on possession was at all times grounded in the daily particulars of village life and I interacted regularly with the vast majority of the inhabitants. I observed several spirit curers at work and discussed possession with large numbers of individuals, both hosts and nonhosts, curers and laity.

The cultural basis of trance

The narrative that follows is about spirit possession in Mayotte; more precisely, it is concerned with what possession is about. It thus falls into the broad category of recent anthropological work whose central concern is with meaning and whose primary goal is interpretation or explication. The activity of the anthropologist here, like that of the philologist, is one of "contextualizing conceptually distant texts" (Becker 1979). More simply put, the goal is to reduce the strangeness of other people's symbolic constructions without thereby sacrificing their richness and complexity. This aim is more ambitious than is often realized, and its success can only be a matter of degree.

At the same time, this approach contrasts with most previous studies of possession. In general, and with some notable exceptions (e.g., Crapanzano 1977, Obeyesekere 1970, Métraux 1955), the literature on trance and possession has focused on explanation (in terms of function or cause) to the neglect of meaning. That is, it has tended to ignore the fact that the elements of possession may form part of a coherent symbolic system that, in turn, may be of deep significance for the generation, ordering, and interpretation of experience by the members of a society. Important previous studies have been concerned primarily with epidemiological matters, with the incidence of trance in particular societies (e.g., Bourguignon 1973) and in particular individuals and classes of individuals within these societies (e.g., Lewis 1971). Among the questions that commonly appear to guide such investigations are the following: Why do acts of trance and beliefs in spirit possession occur and co-occur in particular societies? Why do certain individuals enter trance and why do they belong predominantly to particular status groups within the societies in question? What are the positive effects of such behavior? These approaches tend to ignore the fact that behavior is mediated by thought structures, guided and constrained by cultural models.

This relationship between trance behavior and cultural models is worthy of further consideration. Trance itself may be viewed as one kind of "altered state of consciousness," a phrase referring to a family of rather ill-defined conditions such as sleepwalking, hysterical fugue, hypnosis, psychomotor epilepsy, various drug-induced states, and so on (Ludwig 1968; cf. Zaretsky and Shambaugh 1978, Bourguignon 1976). For our purposes the following facts are relevant. First, although individuals are not all equally susceptible to particular trance-inducing stimuli, the potential for trance appears to be universal. In a recent cross-cultural survey of 488 societies, "90% are reported to have one or more institutionalized, culturally patterned forms of altered states of consciousness" (Bourguignon 1973:11). Thus, the potential for trance, which, in any case, includes a broad and ill-defined range of behavioral changes, may safely be said to be biologically inherent, or "natural," in humans. One may reasonably suspect, then, that the presence of trance is not necessarily a sign or consequence of psychological or social pathology.[4] Second, despite this universal potential, the incidence and frequency of trance vary widely cross-culturally. Third, the forms that trance behavior takes, although obviously constrained by biological factors as well, vary cross-culturally yet are standardized within cultures. Fourth, although specific states of trance may erupt "spontaneously," stimulated by the trancer's immediate psychological and physiological condition (involving such factors as excitement, stress, hypoglycemia, and hyperventilation), trance usually follows certain cues in the outer environment. In fact, trance appears to be learned behavior. The original incidence of trance in an individual is usually induced with the aid of deliberately applied techniques, most frequently including drumming, dance, and hypnosis.

Taken together, these facts suggest that whereas the potential for trance is normal in humans, the appropriateness of its manifestation is frequently a matter of cultural definition. Furthermore, spirit possession is not a naive folk theory developed ex post facto to explain or rationalize the incidence of peculiar behavior. Rather, the symbolic structure is necessary to form and generate the behavior in the first place. As Walker concludes in a recent survey of the subject:

> It is ultimately the belief system and values of the society which determine the existence, nature, and psychosocial function of the complex altered state of consciousness known in folk theory as possession. It is the cultural beliefs which make possession a positive phenomenon in the societies in question [Walker 1972:150].

In other words, the potential for trance has to be activated through specific cultural means, given specific cultural form and substance.

Geertz has argued cogently that "there is no such thing as a human nature independent of culture" (1966a). Humankind and, in particular, the processes we call the human mind evolved together with culture and are literally unthinkable without it. Following Geertz, "symbols are thus not mere expressions, instrumentalities, or correlates of our biological, psychological, and social existence; they are prerequisites of it" (1966a). A human being without culture would be an "unworkable monstrosity." Now, if this is true for humans in an ordinary state of consciousness, then it must also be true for those in a state of trance. To the extent that trance blocks off memory and, therefore, culture, it must replace this with a special "trance culture." The nature of such trance cultures can vary widely, just as do the particular cultures of which the trance cultures form a part. It is precisely Mayotte trance culture we are after here.

This view suggests that we must be wary of possible biases introduced by our own cultural models of trance. In point of fact, trance holds a particular and extreme position in contemporary mainstream Western culture. With the significant exception of certain subcultures (or "peripheral cults"), the West of the present day is quite unusual by world standards in radically devaluing the trance state, providing few, if any, control mechanisms, positive models, or integrated symbolic structures with which to organize it. As a result, trance is peculiarly empty, a virtually cultureless state to which no one but the insane could have consistent recourse.[5] In Western culture, the individual in a deep trance may become, in a very real sense, Geertz's cultureless "unworkable monstrosity." If not that, he will develop a private, idiosyncratic mode of behavior. Such behavior reinforces the extremely negative cultural models of trance as insanity or possession by the devil. Because there is no positive cultural model for trance behavior, it must be abnormal. And because it is relatively undirected, trance can be a terrifying experience for a Westerner, a "bad trip" (cf. Wallace 1959).

The trance state is thus often frightening and extremely perplexing to members of mainstream Western society, appearing to run counter to basic assumptions concerning the nature of human experience. The occurrence of trance in other societies is considered exotic, crying out for "rational explanation." Many investigators, fascinated by the "noise" of possession and armed with a number of psychological hypotheses to explain it, never even considered the possibility of patterns and context behind the noise. Métraux lamented of this approach, "must we attach the label 'hysteric anesthesia' to the impressive spectacle of men or women inhabited by Gods . . . ?" (1955:30). In many societies possession is largely a matter for women (Lewis 1971), and there has probably also been a bias against according women's activities the status of cultural performances with import for the entire society. But in point of fact, the unusual society in this case is the West. Most societies do provide models for trance behavior (Bourguignon 1973:11), albeit of varying degrees of specificity, elaboration, and integration with the wider symbolic system. These symbolic structures are logically prior to behavior. In the case of Mayotte we will see how trance behavior is symbolically organized and governed by a collective system of constraints and rules. Trance, in this sense, is merely an aspect of "spirit possession" (as it is defined in the culture), not vice versa. The question for the West becomes one of understanding why trance has been so rigidly excluded or ignored. Why have we forbidden or lost the cultural forms that could shape and control it?[6] But for Mayotte, the focus must be on understanding the structure and meaning of possession as a whole.

The model of the text

If we are to understand trance behavior, then we must start with trance culture, that is, spirit possession. The organizing model or metaphor here will be to consider culture as a "text" or series of texts (Geertz

1972). The theoretical basis for such a position has been established by Ricoeur as part of his project to reconnect explanation and understanding in a dialectical theory of "interpretation" (1978, 1976). In brief, Ricoeur argues that just as the fixation or inscription of discourse in a written text preserves or extends meaning while also separating it from the subjectivity of the speakers, so too can the objectification of action preserve meaning while separating it from the event. A dialectic between a work or act and its interpretations is set up such that, whereas "the meaning of an important event exceeds, overcomes, transcends the social conditions of its production and may be reenacted in new social contexts," such reenaction inevitably " 'opens up' new references and receives fresh relevance from them" (1971:543–4). In consequence, human action, as observed in ethnographic context or, more precisely, as inscribed by the ethnographer, can be interpreted, or "read," like texts, without immediate recourse to either socioeconomic infrastructures or the subjectivity of actors or authors. In sum, as Geertz has said, "culture is public because meaning is" (1973a:12).

This approach is at once broader in scope and more precise than traditional forms of anthropological inquiry. For example, in his study of the aesthetics of Javanese shadow-puppetry "texts," Becker (1979) suggests a minimum of four kinds of contextual relations that have to be described – the constraints upon coherence, invention, intentionality, and reference. These refer, respectively, to the relations of units within a text, the relations of a text to other texts, particularly those in the same genre, to the creators and audience of the text, and to nonliterary events outside the text. Although Becker meant his ideas merely as a solution to the particular rhetorical problem of organizing his understanding of the Javanese material, it is possible that all texts conform to similar sets of constraints.

The scope of relations proposed by Becker as necessary for an adequate description of the Javanese texts contrasts with the narrower concerns engendered by defining the object of study in more substantive terms. Where the object of study is defined as a specific category of activity, such as "art," "ritual," or "poetry," the basic cultural assumptions by which these categories are rendered natural are taken for granted and therefore concealed. Whereas this merely restricts the depth of analysis when the analytic categories are indigenous, it fatally biases the interpretation when the categories are transposed from another culture. In other words, we cannot assume that our analytic constructs correspond to natural classes of activity, whether in our own or in another culture; in consequence, the constructs must be relational rather than substantive. One could, for example, derive definitions of "art" in different cultures in terms of particular intersections of

Becker's four kinds of contextual relations;[7] in contemporary North American culture, the category of "art" tends to exclude those activities where the intent is pragmatic and the constraints on invention severe.

How then to describe the interaction of human beings and spirits in Mayotte? If we were to focus, as American culture tends generally to do, on the aspect of intentionality, we could label the activity "curing." Were we to focus on the formal order, we could label it "ritual." An emphasis on the inventive aspect suggests "drama," and on the referential, "symbolic activity" or perhaps "myth." The point is, of course, that possession juxtaposes a number of different contextual relations and therefore corresponds to no one of these categories in particular.[8] However, the notion of text subsumes them all, furnishing the possibility for a flexible, yet well-rounded, understanding of the observed behavior. To speak of possession as text is to avoid the biases and constraints imposed by a narrower approach.

In spirit possession as it is practiced in Mayotte, the intentional, or curing, aspect of the activity is the most explicit. The larger feasts and ceremonies are held with the express intent of effecting cures in individuals afflicted by spirits. Possession cures belong to a large class of activities and performances labeled *asa*. This includes individual life-crisis rites, ritual feasting, and all intravillage and intervillage religious and political gatherings of a special nature. *Asa* is derived from the verb *miasa* 'to work' and also means 'work,' 'occupation,' 'doings,' 'workmanship,' and the like.[9] *Asa* contrasts with both *service*, meaning 'chores' or 'odd jobs,' and *soma*, meaning 'play,' 'amusement,' 'entertainment,' 'celebration.'[10] *Asa* conveys a sense of seriousness and responsibility, an activity carried out in the context of long-range goals and of a moral system. The spirit cure is *asa* in that it is serious business and entails intensive preparation and eventual participation by a group of individuals larger than the nuclear family household.

This local view of things is powerful but insufficient. That possession is culturally placed in a "medical" domain tells us nothing about its material or formal nature. Possession has a precise internal structure or coherence independent of the biological and psychological dynamics of human disease. Indeed, as I will argue later, were it not for possession, the individual might never feel sick in the first place. Furthermore, there is scope for invention and elaboration in possession. Spirit representations incorporate elements from the periphery of the culture, from the past, and from neighboring and intrusive cultures, combined in the intriguing and sometimes surprising manner that Lévi-Strauss (1966) has labeled "bricolage." Collectively, possession transforms details of an otherwise not wholly comprehended history into atemporal structures.

Although historical change may be brought about by political, economic, and demographic forces largely beyond the immediate control of the islanders themselves, the surface details of the structures change according to a local aesthetics working through the historical material. Yet the conflicts of history are fought, as it were, in the bodies of individuals. These individuals may also be able to reorganize or refocus details from their respective pasts and personalities (Lévi-Strauss 1966). At the same time, the creativity of the individual is a factor in the pursuit of private ends through the public medium of possession.

Trance is symbolically ordered, and the spirits who constitute the trance world are not outside culture, yet, as we shall see, they are viewed as being outside the particular culture that constitutes ordinary life in Mayotte. We can recognize a degree of the fear and astonishment with which we ourselves view trance. However, in Mayotte this juxtaposition of human culture and spirit culture, and the possibility of movement between them is essentially constructive, providing a fertile field for the generation of novel intellectual and emotional experience. In this way possession may be considered a system for thought and expression.

If possession can be viewed in this general manner, what are the procedures by which particular instances of trance should be analyzed? The text model suggests turning to literary criticism, as Geertz suggested some time ago (1964). The field of structuralist poetics seems an appropriate place to start, because it asserts, for heuristic purposes, the autonomy of the text and shares with much of anthropology a theoretical grounding in linguistics. The movement, then, is from language to action by way of literature. A key insight of structuralist poetics is its focus on the activity of reading (Culler 1975). The aim is not to ascribe a particular meaning to a work but to account for the work's intelligibility, that is, to discover the system of conventions it allows the reader to apply in order to produce meaning from it. In Culler's words, "the semiological approach suggests . . . that the work be thought of as an utterance that has meaning only with respect to a system of conventions which the reader has assimilated. If other conventions were operative its range of potential meanings would be different" (1975:116). Thus, "the task of a structuralist poetics, as Barthes [1966] defines it, would be to make explicit the underlying system which makes literary effects possible" (Culler 1975:118). In sum, Culler speaks of a theory of "literary competence."

I will follow this general approach in Parts II and III, introducing my methodological concepts as I apply them. For the moment, the Preface presents an example of this problematic in the field of action, demonstrating the incompetence of someone confronted for the first time with a new kind of "text." The way to render such a text intelligible is precisely to learn the system of conventions by which its actors render it so. In this way it can be shown that a trance sequence contains a number of conventions that permit the participants to interpret it as an episode of possession. Following Jakobson's (1960) elaboration of the constitutive factors in any speech event (code, context, addresser, addressee, contact, message), the following can be listed for Mayotte possession:

a.   The distinction between humankind and spiritkind is signaled primarily by codes of food and gesture.

b.   The primary referent (context, in Jakobson's terms) is illness.

c.   Host and spirit are distinguished as separate persons; the spirit dominates the conversation, making demands and dispensing or withholding information.

d.   Contact between human and spirit is established first by means of incense and then through the neurophysiological state of trance and, in the "absence" of the host, through third parties.

e.   The message contains the contradiction between the explicit benevolence and implicit malevolence of the spirit.

These sets of conventions, to be explored in detail throughout the book, serve to guide or constrain the participants in the interpretation of the event. They do not, however, either singly or in concord, assign to it any particular meaning. Rather, they define the space or world in which such meaning can be constructed by the individual participants. Our task will be to locate this world.

The text of the model

In a study of this sort there can be no sharp breaks between the descriptive material, the analysis, and the interpretations; to a large degree, the order of presentation itself suggests the interpretation. The form that emerges here is meant to correspond in a general way to Ricoeur's "interpretive arc which goes from naive understanding through explanation to knowledgeable understanding" (1978:154).

Part I is concerned with situating possession in Mayotte culture and society generally. Chapter 1 introduces Mayotte society. Chapter 2 distinguishes possession from the practice of Islam. Chapter 3 outlines the main aspects of possession and attempts to locate it in terms of indigenous medical theory. Chapter 4 evaluates possible explanations for the incidence of possession, notably higher among women than among men in Mayotte. It is argued that not only are the spirit hosts psychologically normal, but possession itself is an integral aspect of social life. Possession is a relatively autonomous cultural form, distinct from the subjective states and immediate social conditions of the hosts. Chapter 5 extends this theme, demonstrating the usefulness of considering possession as a system of communication.

In Parts II and III the text model becomes more explicit. Part II, alternating between descriptive case-study material and passages of analysis, attempts to clarify the "syntagmatic" aspects of possession. That is, the sequential coherence of the course of events is demonstrated. We see how the individual case of possession is naturalized, rendered intelligible, acceptable, and real for the participants. The primary tool here is current theory of ritual. Part III has been labeled "paradigmatic" because it analyzes the steady, basic relations or oppositions from which possession is constructed and to which it refers, primarily the metaphor between the human and the spirit worlds.

Toward the end of Part III, I depart from the strict structuralist program and, following Ricoeur, attempt to apply the results of the structuralist analysis to a "depth interpretation" of the text. Although this last segment of the hermeneutical arc may be the most problematic, it is not based on claims to an unachievable subjective *verstehen* or a nonexistent key to, or dictionary of, symbols. Validation of the interpretation comes from the analytic process that precedes it. Understanding, in this view, means "to grasp the world-propositions opened up by the references of the text . . . . to follow its [the text's] movement from what it says, to what it talks about" (Ricoeur 1971:558).

The core of anthropological theory lies in the dialectic between human cultural unity and diversity. There has been a tendency in recent symbolic analyses to emphasize the latter at the expense of the former. The thrust of the present study is to bring the two together. After an excursion through the particularities of an exotic culture, of a genre, texts, and style foreign to our own, we discover a "deep semantic" that is, I think, more familiar to us. The world that possession points to, or "opens up," is not so different from the world we know. Were this correct and generalizable, it would support Lévi-Strauss's vision (1955) and his general methods (1963) but place the universal at a lower level of abstraction. Yet neither would it deny the insight of Geertz (1966a), who argues that what is universal to humankind is our radical investment in the particular. The depth interpretation of a foreign text (culture) is only reached through the mediation of a structural (cultural) analysis. A common view is revealed, to invert the metaphor, only from the very tops of different mountains.

Part I

Spirits and hosts in Mayotte

Rarely has man been depicted as more completely and inextricably anchored in this world, more obsessively earthbound . . . Man does not, for instance, ascend to heaven to have intercourse with the gods; the gods descend to earth.

Paul Radin, Introduction to *African Folktales*

1. An overview of Mayotte society

History

This chapter presents a brief exposition of the social context in which the possession phenomena to be described occur.[1] To begin, a glance at the recent history of Mayotte will help to clarify the contemporary situation. For centuries, the Comoros have maintained trading ports inhabited or dominated by Muslim populations who traced their roots to the Middle East. During the early nineteenth century the islands experienced a period of decline, characterized by internal fighting and the encroachment of the Western imperial powers. The Comoros were subject to annual raids from the expanding chiefdoms and states of northern Madagascar, and Mayotte in particular seems to have suffered. It is unclear how many Malagasy speakers were present at this time, but toward the middle of the century the northern Sakalava ruler Andriantsuly took refuge in Mayotte from his wars with the Merina, bringing with him a sizable number of followers seeking more settled conditions. The descendants of Andriantsuly's followers presumably form the backbone of the contemporary population of Malagasy speakers in Mayotte.

In 1841, some nine years after his arrival, Andriantsuly ceded Mayotte to France. Early colonial policy was governed by two aims, the abolition of indigenous slavery and the creation of a supply of cheap labor for the newly established sugarcane plantations (Martin 1976). Regulations were created requiring a period of service on the plantations from all sectors of the indigenous population, and there was an extensive importation of manpower, especially from Africa and the other islands in the archipelago. Despite the fact that by 1905 sugar profits had declined and the refineries and most of the plantations had been abandoned (Faurec and Manicacci, n.d.), the early French policies had far-reaching effects on the local social structure. Part of the land originally alienated from the population was put on sale to the old and new inhabitants, thus weakening the traditional system of stratifi-

15

cation. The initial aim of this procedure seems to have been the consolidation of the population (many of whom were in the habit of fleeing the plantations) in known localities where they could be more easily controlled and called upon when their labor was desired. Many of the contemporary villages, including those in which I worked, trace their origins to this period in the late nineteenth century when individuals or small "corporations" (*société*) purchased tracts of land and attracted landless followers. In this manner, the number of French settlers declined, and the non-French population grew and became more cohesive. The African and Malagasy immigrants became Muslims if they had not been so before, and African identity and customs were largely dropped.

With the decline in the sugar economy, French policy became one of relatively benign neglect. The French retired within the fortress they had set up on Dzaoudzi and administered the Comoros as a single whole, eventually moving the capital to Moroni, on Grande Comore. Most of the Muslim population of Mayotte continued to live in the villages, pursuing subsistence horticulture along with some additional wage labor on the remaining plantations. The modernizing sector was given limited opportunity to expand, and most of the bureaucrats and administrators emerged from the other islands.

Subsistence in Mayotte is based on dry rice, manioc, bananas grown on shifting plots, and fish taken from the extensive lagoon. Other crops include coconuts, maize, and sugarcane; small numbers of cattle, goats, sheep, and poultry are raised. The diet is supplemented with shellfish, legumes, taro, sesame, and various other fruits and vegetables. Most subsistence farmers today cultivate cash crops as well, notably ylang-ylang, whose flowers are distilled for perfume oil, and some vanilla, coffee, and copra. Money is also earned within the village through such part-time activities as fishing, carpentry, tailoring, house building, curing, and petty shopkeeping.

Although in the past many inhabitants of Mayotte did not own land, usufruct rights were easy to establish. Population growth has led to the gradual insufficiency of productive land on the original village tracts, and individuals and groups have purchased land outside the village of residence, occasionally leading to the formation of new villages but more frequently to a pattern of seasonal dispersal. In recent years the land shortage has become more significant as there is less free land available to buy and the rights of usufruct are becoming gradually curtailed. Fallowing cycles have been shortened, with a resulting decline in rice yields; much of the original village land is now useless for rice. The land shortage is exacerbated by the greater attention paid to cash crops, which remove land from the subsistence cycle. Many of those without sufficient land for rice must rent plots on an annual basis. Usufruct or rental rights are rarely granted for cash crops, and those without productive land are cut off from a major source of income. Thus new class differences are emerging gradually at the local level; in Lombeni in 1975 some individuals were periodically hired for a wage within the village.

Although these economic problems are not yet severe on a large scale, they presumably lie behind the drive on the part of the majority of the population to sever relations with the other islands in the Comoro archipelago (which became an independent republic in 1976) in favor of closer ties with France. The other islands, with their denser populations, poorer resource bases, and more stratified societies, are conceived as a threat to the established small freehold basis of production in Mayotte. Other political issues and the particular interests of the leaders of the pro-French (Soldat) movement aside, the option has been seen by the rural cultivators in stark economic terms – between an almost certain curtailment of landholdings and individual productivity, on the one hand, and a possible expanding economy, on the other. The political conflict between the pro-French and pro-Comoran parties split Mayotte deeply for more than a decade. By 1976 the struggle appeared to have been won by the pro-French forces; fines were levied on outstanding members of the opposing party and formal reconciliations were held. France has responded by rapidly intensifying its presence.

The village order

The named nucleated villages form the most significant units of Mayotte society. The census of 1974 lists seventy such settlements, ranging in size from 25 to 2,250 inhabitants. Mayotte villages are generally neatly patterned, with the houses oriented in roughly parallel rows along the contours and a mosque in the center. Most of the villages inhabited today lie along the coasts. Of the two villages in which I concentrated my research, Lombeni Be sits adjacent to a sandy beach, whence the single outrigger fishing canoes depart, and Lombeni Kely is just over the first hill inland.

Villages are landholding, ceremonial, and jural corporations. The degree of individual incorporation into the village is based on rights of inheritance, place of residence during maturation, immediate residence, and participation in the ceremonial cycles of exchange. The residents of a village may be divided into three classes according to their rights of ownership: owners (*tompin*), affiliates, and strangers (*mugyen*). Full owners comprise the purchasers of the property on which the village is constructed and their descendants. Descent and inheritance are bilateral, and anyone, male or female, whose claims to such descent are accepted has the right to build a home in the village and participate in its affairs. Ownership status refers primarily to civic matters; it no longer provides the individual with sufficient farmland.

Events in the past also validate the position of the affiliates, who are descendants of people who were given the right to settle in the village by the *tompin* and who were born or brought up there and consider it home. In day-to-day affairs such people are not distinguished from *tompin*, and they are usually tied to them through kinship. However, their position is characterized, both in their own words and those of others, by its insecurity. Although extremely unlikely, they could always be ejected from the village or asked to abandon a particular house plot. Their authority can be challenged by the remark "*Anao bok' ayya?*" equivalent to the English "Who do you think you are?" but meaning literally "Where do you come from?"[2]

The position of people who have married into the village from the outside depends on how long they have been present, whether or not they have kin, especially *tompin* descendants, in the village, and the degree to which they choose to participate in village activity. Generally, the shorter the length of time they have been present, the less happy their position. Both sexes are sensitive to slight, may suspect villagers of initiating affairs with their spouses, and may feel themselves to be the objects of sorcery. Such people are referred to as *mugyen* 'strangers' or 'outsiders,' and this epithet remains applicable, at least in theory, forever.

The distribution of wealth, power, authority, and decision-making roles and the nature of factionalism and the political process vary from village to village. In general, villages rely on a fairly large number of elected or acclaimed officials, supervised by respected elders, to maintain internal order, lead worship in the mosque, plan ceremonies and organize the redistribution of food that these entail, adjudicate disputes, and act as buffers between the villagers and the state apparatus. The main difference between the *tompin* and the other inhabitants of the village is that the *tompin* have the final say on all matters concerning the village as a whole. Non-*tompin* elders may participate in deliberations, but they do not normally officiate or pronounce judgment, although they may be given the prerogative to do so. The actual power wielded by the *tompin* depends in good part upon the social composition of the particular village. In some villages, such as Lombeni Be, the majority of the inhabitants may be *tompin*, whereas in others, they may form a relatively small proportion of the population. All the *tompin* may or may not be related to one another, and they may or may not be related to the bulk of the non-*tompin*. The land that the village of Lombeni Kely now occupies was originally bought by one of the husbands of a woman from whom the largest proportion of the present inhabitants are descended. There is only one remaining son of this man and he is the chief figure of authority in the village and has the final say in such matters as the acceptance of new residents or the ejection of old ones. He is treated with respect. However, he spends most of his time living elsewhere, in the village of a wife, and is not the elder to whom quarrels are taken regularly for mediation nor the person responsible for organizing village feasts or dealing with the island administration. The title to the land is kept by one of his full sisters, also a *tompin*. As mother's brother to most of the village, *tompin* and non-*tompin* alike, the authority figure has significant kinship obligations that temper his position as owner.

Although villages may be internally sectioned by interest groups of closely related kin (*mraba*), the members of a village are linked up into a single exchange system such that each has rights and obligations to every other based on their common membership in the village. In particular, each member has the right and duty to participate in rituals planned by the village as a whole and performed for the common good. Likewise, each member can expect assistance at the performance of his own major family rituals and the invitation to participate in those of others. This system of ritual exchange, complex in detail, is based on the mediation by the village in certain major exchanges among its members. This is expressed in the institution of the *shuŋgu*. The *shuŋgu* is a formal debt or obligation that every member of a designated group must perform for all the other members of the group. *Shuŋgu* groups may form for the express purpose of reciprocal feast giving. Most of the age groups into which a village is divided will also have their own *shuŋgu*. That is, each member of the age group (*shikao*) must provide a feast of rigidly specified proportions for the other members. In most male *shikao* each member has the obligation to pay the *shuŋgu* on the occasion of his wedding to a virgin and may not pay on any other occasion.[3] In addition, the village itself forms a single *shuŋgu* group with a series of obligations that it expects every member, owner or not, to perform during his or her lifetime for the village as a whole. The precise requirements of the *shuŋgu* vary from village to village, but in general terms they are very high, demanding that every adult produce a certain amount of food (so many kilos of rice, so many cows, so many cakes) to feed the entire village a specified number of times. The village *shuŋgu* are normally carried out in the context of feasts associated with life-crisis rites, primarily at a daughter's first wedding, a son's circumcision, or a commemoration for deceased kinsmen. The entire village participates, organized by age group. Not all members of a village are able to meet their obligations, but they must in order to maintain self-respect and earn the full respect of their fellows. Certain individuals may prefer to opt out of the system as a whole, staying away from the festivities of others in order to avoid obligations of their own.

Family and kinship

Kinship ties are recognized bilaterally, and an individual's kin network is likely to spread across several villages. Nuclear families form the primary units of production and consumption, but they may also cooperate with the siblings or parents of either partner in economic ventures such as the purchase of land or the production of cash crops. Fluid and overlapping groups or clusters of kin who share common economic, ceremonial, and political interests on a regular basis are known as *mraba* and may be identified by an apical ancestor or prominent contemporary. Ties of affinity and fictive kinship are in practice significant in *mraba* maintenance as well.

Each nuclear family household is responsible for its own production of subsistence crops. Husband and wife generally share the labor involved. Rice yields are stored in the household granary and consumed and distributed during the year as the couple sees fit. Although husband and wife share in subsistence activities, it is expected that the husband also supply the minimum amount of cash necessary for the purchase of household staples such as kerosene, salt, cloth or clothing, soap, and occasional purchases of meat or fish, sugar, flour, and so on. Additional cash is needed on ceremonial occasions, to ride the cross-island taxis, to buy or repair tools, to pay diviners and curers, and, if at all possible, to purchase land. In recent years cash has also become necessary to supplement the rice harvest with imported rice. A man not only needs cash in order to get married, but a steady (if small) supply in order to stay in the state; no woman will put up for long with a man who cannot provide the minimal necessities. Unlike men, women are not expected to support themselves or others through money and may do whatever they like with any money they earn (assuming they have a man supporting them at the time). Most women own their own houses and household furnishings, which they receive from their parents upon marriage.

Husband and wife may own or have shares in separate pieces of land and they may also purchase land jointly. Cultivation is carried out on the land of either or both, and it is not uncommon for a couple to maintain separate subsistence plots in any given year. Corporate land-holdings (*shirika*) are generally controlled by sibling groups and are said to have continuity beyond the death or quarreling of any members of the corporation. Although each sibling (together with his or her spouse) may cultivate a private plot annually, the property as a whole belongs to all. *Shirika* usually last at least until the third generation, at which point they may be subdivided into new *shirika,* one for each subset of siblings. *Shirika* may also remain intact much longer, until they are owned by so many people as to make equitable division unrealistic. The property on which a village is located may be a *shirika* of this sort.

Inheritance and division of land is said to follow Islamic law so that every brother receives an equal share and every sister half as much. In practice the proportions vary, but the central point is that each sibling is supposed to look out for the welfare of the others. This is sometimes expressed concretely by a change in kin terminology, whereby on the death of a parent one or more of the children of that sex take on the parental role toward the rest of the siblings. Thus, a man or woman may address or refer to a (generally older) sister as "mother" and likewise call a brother "father." The use of these terms is optional and far from universal, but it expresses the underlying ideal of siblings as kin (*havaŋa*) of the closest degree, a denial of segmentation. Married siblings maintain separate households from one another but are the ones to turn to in need. Some males are readier to build houses for their sisters than their wives, because, they reason, the sibling relationship is one whose endurance is assured.

The significance of the sibling bond is continued in the subsequent generation, so that a child calls his mother's sisters by the same term he calls his mother and his father's brothers by the same term he calls his father. None of the parents' siblings have particular rights or duties greater than, or distinct from, those of the centrally recognized pair. Siblings frequently rear one another's children. The mother's brother and father's sister fulfill similar functions, but they are called by special terms and may also engage in joking relations (*obishy*) with the children (if they themselves are not rearing them). The marked quality of this relationship is explained by informants as a result of the cross-sex distinction, the anomaly of a "female father" and "male mother."

Marriage and divorce

There is no consensus in Mayotte on correct patterns of marriage. Although certain families, notably those Comoran speakers claiming descent in the Prophet's line (*Sharifu*), practice parallel-cousin marriage, most people proscribe it. This is particularly true of the Malagasy speakers, many of whom also feel uneasy about marrying close cross-cousins (cf. Baré 1974, Ottino 1964). Although cross-cousin marriage does occur and is sometimes arranged deliberately, it is not prescribed. The general opinion states that cross-cousin marriage is dangerous because marital conflict can quickly spread tension within the *mraba*, particularly between the siblings of the ascending generation, that is, between the parents of the bride and groom. In other words, it threatens sibling solidarity. Whereas village endogamy is in itself neither prescribed nor preferred, 38 percent of marriages in Lombeni Be and Kely combined (*N*=139) occurred between partners reared in the same village. Both men and women prefer to reside within their own villages for the social and economic advantages such residence offers. In general, because women receive houses from their fathers, a couple's initial place of residence is likely to be the village of the wife's father or the village in which she was reared. In village exogamous marriages, this pattern is likely to interfere with the husband's access to his own land. A number of couples reside duolocally, particularly the men engaged in polygynous marriages (which, in any case, are infrequent and tend to be unstable).

The wedding of a virgin bride is the longest, most expensive, and most complex kinship ritual found in Mayotte. It entails a week of feasting, organized around the establishment of the bride and groom in the former's new house. However, the major exchanges are carried out not so much between the affinal parties as through them. Such a marriage is the occasion for the fulfillment of the *shuŋgu* obligations of the bride's parents to the village and the groom's *shuŋgu* obligations to his age group, and thus his age group's obligations to the village. The transformation of the bride into womanhood in a socially legitimate manner signals the completion of the parents' successful rearing of their daughter and the public recognition of her own respect for her parents. Through his payment, the groom also achieves adult status in a legitimate manner. The groom gives the bride's parents a large sum of money, which they then use to carry out the requirements of the groom's *shuŋgu*, that is, they take over responsibility for feasting his age group. In other words, the exchange between the groom and the bride's parents is one in which each side is dependent upon the other to fulfill its exchange requirements to a third party, which is ultimately the entire moral community. Each party is the vehicle for the social achievement of the other. The exchange is completed and the material consumed during the course of the wedding; the increase in prestige that each party receives is irrevocable.

For the bride's part, in return for her own role and contribution – the preservation of her virginity until marriage and the submission to defloration by the groom – she is supplied with a house and furnishings by her family and with a suitcase full of clothing, jewelry, and other gifts by the groom. No further return is expected on her part for these gifts; they should stay in her possession whatever the outcome of the marriage.

Given this picture of marital exchange and the fact that women own the houses and that both women and men have separate means of access to land and may have conflicting interests over choice of village of residence, it is not surprising that the divorce rate is high[4] nor that separation is frequently initiated by women. In the absence of contest, a marriage is terminated with little formality, mere physical separation and the discontinuation of support. Remarriage is also a relatively simple affair. A man is expected to marry only a single virgin in his lifetime. The marriage of a non-virgin entails no large-scale exchange, no house, furnishings, clothing or jewelry, no public festivities, no fulfillment of *shuŋgu* obligations or gain in prestige on anyone's part.

Affinal ties are maintained after divorce, especially if the marriage has produced children. In fact, alliance relationships are maintained less by the permanent or successive exchange of wives than by the sharing and exchange of the products of marriage, that is, the children. Divorce or no, children may be transferred in more or less permanent relationships of fosterage; in the subsequent generation, children may return in the opposite direction.

The position of women

The preceding discussion allows us some insight into the relative position of women in Mayotte. Women gain autonomy through their status as village owners, their rights to productive land, ownership of houses and household goods, and equal control with their husbands over subsistence crops. In marriage, and in return for sexual favors, they expect to receive cash and material goods (cf. Benedict 1967, Ottino 1964). A woman should remain a virgin until her first marriage, and indeed it is in her best interests to do so, but from this point she has as much control over her sexuality as a man has over his. The wedding is a celebration of the bride's emergence into womanhood as much as it is anything else, and ease of divorce means that women are not pawns in an exchange controlled by men but can act as independent agents on their own behalf. Likewise, adult women participate in, and gain prestige through, *shuŋgu* exchanges. By means of judicious marriages and child fosterage over time a woman can develop a coterie of followers;

A young pupil studies a passage from the Koran while his teacher weaves a
mat.

she can also establish "friendship" (or "fictive kinship") relationships
with other women and with men. A few women also maintain their
own regular sources of cash income independent of men. In addition,
women are politically organized among themselves, have certain rights
and responsibilities in village affairs, and select their own leaders. The
Soldat women's movement is generally recognized, by women and men
alike, as having been the driving force behind the original vision and
eventual victory of the pro-French forces on the island. With victory,
the women are said to have "handed over control" to the men, but the
women's organization is still tightly controlled and its power feared.

Nevertheless, despite such autonomy, women have less authority
than men. Men usually exercise close control over the household bud-
get and need not account for their income or expenditures. Politeness
requires public deference to men. As village leaders, the roles of
women are secondary to those of the men. A woman will usually ask a
man to represent her in legal matters. The public position of women is
particularly weakened by Islam, which segregates the sexes to a degree
and restricts and discourages female access to the sources of sacred
authority. Male ideology also states, albeit somewhat equivocally (see

Chapter 4 under "Sex role and cultural constraints"), that women are men's moral and jural inferiors.

In sum, as in most societies, relations between the sexes are not without their contradictions and their inequality. Mayotte women are strong and forceful in certain public, as well as private, spheres and partially mystified by male ideology, but also resentful of male privilege.

This chapter has been a brief examination of certain features of Mayotte social organization at the village level.[5] Mayotte is a dynamic society, well accustomed to change. The principles of corporate territorial ownership and collective residence and management form the basis for the major social groupings: the nuclear family household, the village, and the island viewed as a whole. Bilateral descent and complex marriage rules permit a great deal of flexibility in social relations, and siblingship forms an ideal model for solidarity. In a context of increasingly limited and asymmetrical access to, and greater demand for, the basic resources, the individual strategy is to maintain and intensify particular relationships at the expense of others. This creates a certain tension within the moral order of the village.

2. Who the spirits are not: possession and Islam

The place of spirits in Mayotte cosmology

In order to understand the spirits it is necessary to see them in the context of the wider system of belief in Mayotte. The dominant component of this system is provided by Sunni Islam (of the Shaf'i branch). According to Mayotte cosmology, the universe is composed of two realms, *dunyan* and *kiyama* 'this world' and 'the other world' or *etu* and *aiɲ* 'here' and 'way-over-there.' *Dunyan* is the world that we experience, interact in, and learn about through our senses. *Kiyama* cannot be experienced by the living and it cannot be described or located. It is known, through the sacred scriptures, to be divided into *pevony* and *mahamay* 'heaven' and 'hellfire.' Apart from their association with good or evil, reward or punishment, respectively, these places are not described according to a consistent pattern. Any concrete features have been gleaned from Islamic sources and are meant, I believe, metaphorically. The other world is so alien that it simply does not make sense to ask questions about it in terms that are relevant to this world. To ask where it is located in terms of the spatial dimensions of this world is illogical. Thus, people are incredulous at the simplistic Christian view of heaven above and hell below. Even more emphatically, it does not make sense – and indeed it borders on the sacrilegious, as well – to consider the physical attributes and whereabouts of God. We know God through his recorded laws and messengers (prophets and angels); any other approach is illogical and incorrect.[1]

The spirits are not located vaguely in between these poles; they are decidedly phenomena of this world. Like humans, they are created by God. They exist in space and they have physical characteristics that can be apprehended by human perception and described by the categories of human cognition. Although it is true that some of the attributes and abilities of spirits are different from those of humans, these attributes and abilities are governed by the same set of laws as those of humans. Humans cannot do everything that spirits do, but they can

26

comprehend the actions of spirits and, if conditions are right, perceive them through the use of the senses. Unlike humans, spirits are normally invisible. But the notion of invisibility implies its opposite, and there are times when they do become visible to humans. On the other hand, the entire distinction visible/invisible has no meaning when applied to God.

There exist numerous kinds of spirits and numerous terms with which to label them. However, my attempts at eliciting the dimensions of semantic contrast of these terms failed; the terminology does not provide an unambiguous system for ordering the spirit world. Instead, the choice of term employed in any given context appears to be dependent upon features of the particular speech event.[2] That is, although there is no clear-cut means of distinguishing and interrelating the spirit classes in the abstract, in practice there do appear to be differences in the ways in which the terms are used. Thus, although there is no regular distinction expressed between the terms *shetwan* and *lulu*, both of which translate as 'spirit,' *shetwan* appears to be used in situations where the reference is more abstract or impersonal. For example, when someone who should know better is being criticized for a fault, the cause of the error will be laid, if the speaker wishes his criticism to be indirect, to the interference of *shetwan*. In this context, where the term *lulu* is less appropriate, *shetwan* functions as a euphemism. It would be pointless (and embarrassing) to inquire what form these *shetwan* have or how they are related to other kinds of spirits or spirit activities.

We may postulate, then, the existence of an axis along which references to the spirits become more concrete and the immediacy of the spirit presence more significant. A spirit that scares you on the path at night will be "just a spirit, that's all." It will provide a tale to tell the next morning and may provoke a change in your habits of nighttime ambulation, but it is of no more concern than that. If, however, a spirit is making you sick, then it becomes important to start defining it more precisely. In fact, the treatment of spirit possession entails the process of definition, beginning with the identification of the species and climaxing in the revelation of the spirit's individual identity. The most vividly experienced spirits and those that are of most concern to people are thus also those that are most elaborated conceptually. They are generally referred to as *lulu* or *djin* or, in the appropriate contexts, by their specific names: *patros, trumba, mugala, kakanoru,* and others.

These classes of *lulu* share many physical and behavioral characteristics with humans. They are social beings, live in villages, have families, and are concerned with economic matters. Like humans, they have an emotional and an intellectual side. They have desires, they calculate, they may study and be learned. They believe in God but may practice a religion that departs from Islam. They lead lives parallel, but usually invisible, to humans.

Spirits are empirically observable, and belief in their existence is validated, when they are observed in possession of humans, when they rise up into the heads (*manuŋga an'luha*) of their victims and take over control of their bodies. When a person is actually in the throes of possession (*menziky lulu*), she is absent from her own body, no one know or asks where. It is the spirit who talks, eats, drinks, dances, or thrashes about, who laughs or cries, cooperates or quarrels, argues volubly, sparkles with wit, or remains sullen and morose.

Spirits are governed by the natural laws of space and time. For instance, there is much play on the idea that, although spirits travel extremely quickly, a given spirit cannot be at two places at once. If several people, all of whom receive the same spirit, are participating together in a ceremony, they cannot all be possessed by this spirit simultaneously. As the spirit jumps back and forth among them, the individuals concerned go in and out of trance or switch rapidly among the different spirits that can possess them. Tumbu's spirit, who likes to appear in several individuals in Lombeni, demanded the shawl from Mohedja in order to indicate his movements more clearly. During *patros* ceremonies the shawl is passed back and forth among the participants, serving to indicate in whose body the spirit resides at any given moment. However, the signals that allow individuals to synchronize their movements in and out of trance are more subtle than the shawl. In fact, the shawl itself is only transferred after the spirit has made its move.

Spirits are not in any way worshipped in Mayotte. Rather, people interact with them on a social level. Their ontological status is more similar to humans than to God or the angels. The contrast between God and the spirits is twofold. God is extremely well defined, his existence absolute and beyond question. At the same time, God is empirically unobservable. He is known and approached indirectly, through his written laws and prayers. The existence of God is an "ultimate sacred proposition" (Rappaport 1974), enunciated in the *Shahāda*, the credo of all Muslims. Spirits, on the other hand, are empirically real. Belief in spirits and in individual manifestations of spirits is based upon sensory experience and the empirical validation of certain propositions concerning their natures. However, in the abstract, the nature of the body of spirits as a whole, or "spiritness," is rather unclear and ill defined. The elaboration of an explicit understanding of spirits is primarily a matter of pragmatics.

In summary, spirits obey natural, although at times nonhuman, laws.

Spirits are described in terms of the similarities and differences of their lives and habits to those of humans. Spirit society, although it does not mirror human society, is a transformation of it. It thus makes no sense to call spirits supernatural phenomena. Rather, they are extracultural,[3] that is, beyond the bounds of human culture as the people of Mayotte conceive it. It is the extracultural aspect of spirits, rather than their precise place in nature, that is of concern.

Boundaries of possession and Islam

The notion of possessing spirits may be further clarified if we continue to pursue the matter of what, in terms of Mayotte culture, they are *not*. The spirits we are concerned with are not, for the most part, the spirits of the dead, the ubiquitous "ancestor spirits" of the African literature. A brief explanation of what happens after death will establish this fact. Each person has a *rohu* (Arabic *rūḥ*), a kind of 'life force' or 'essence' that expresses his existence and that, while he is alive, is referred to as the seat of deep feelings. Thus, a person may say, "*Rohu nakahy kutruliya*," "my 'soul' is untroubled," or, in certain contexts "I have a clear conscience." Likewise, it may be said of someone that he has a *ratsy rohu* a 'wicked disposition.' When speaking of his *rohu* a person may point to the soft spot just above the center of the breastbone at the base of the neck. The *rohu* is breathed into the embryo by God during the third month of pregnancy; it is at this moment that the mother first feels the baby move within her. The *rohu* leaves the body at death. Toward the end of a funeral, water is poured over the newly filled grave. The water is said to trickle rapidly through the soil until it touches the corpse. At this moment, the *rohu* returns to the body and the deceased revives to face temptation by the envoys of the Devil (*Ibilisa*, a poorly developed concept in Mayotte) and questioning by the angels concerning his faith and his conduct in life. After three days of questioning, the *rohu* again leaves the body and goes to some unknowable place beyond *dunyan* in order to await the end of the world and the eventual reunification with the flesh.

The *rohu* is not the same thing as the spirit (*lulu*) of the deceased. According to one informant, the *lulu* only comes into existence upon the death of the individual and will cease to exist upon the future reconstitution of body and soul. The *lulu* stays in this world, and it is the *lulu* that we see in dreams when our own *rohu* misses the deceased individual and seeks him out. The *lulu* is good or bad, following the character held by the deceased in real life. It is only bad *lulu* who will harm people, and this only at the bidding of a sorcerer.

Such sorcery (cf. Chapter 3) is extreme in its method and is a particularly difficult kind to cure. Its practice involves raising the corpse from the grave in order to acquire portions of the hair or wrappings. Interference with the proper burial of a dead person is the most outrageous and disgusting form of behavior that people can conceive of, the most extreme expression of the antisocial. The subject remains more in the realm of the collective imagination than in the real world of diagnosis and accusation. Actual cases in Lombeni occurred only in the past and happen today only in distant villages where morality and attention to the teachings of Islam are known to be lax.

The people of Lombeni normally are not troubled by the spirits of the dead and do not concern themselves with them. Such speculation as there is focuses upon the grotesque actions of the sorcerer and image of the raised corpse rather than on the malevolence of the particular deceased. Spirits of the dead do not interfere with the normal concerns of health and illness. Most spirits that enter people and speak and act through them are of different species from humans and are not dead. In fact, they are considered to be immortal, continuing to live until the resurrection.

There is one exception to this generalization. Received wisdom has it that the *trumba,* spirits from Madagascar that sometimes possess people, are, in fact, spirits of the dead.[4] This association is a source of embarrassment to those involved in *trumba* activities. Some participants deny that the *trumba* are deceased humans, and others claim that they can have no certain knowledge of the matter one way or the other. Once these individuals are in a state of possession, however, the actual *trumba* are not evasive in admitting their origins. Despite this clash of beliefs, the fact remains that the deceased represented in the *trumba* are from long ago and far away; none of them are remembered from life and none of them have any direct genealogical ties to the village.[5]

The *trumba* case illustrates the complexity of belief in a society that has gained its traditions from many sources. The issue in Mayotte is less that of choosing between Islam and spirit possession than that of ensuring that a confrontation of doctrines does not take place by restricting the domains of each so that they do not conflict with one another. Death is a primary concern of Islam and is thus an area from which considerations of spirit possession are excluded. More generally, the scheduling of possession activities must be managed so that they do not interfere with those of Islam. The former are separated in both space and time from the latter and must give precedence to them. Spirit ceremonies are held outdoors or, if indoors, only in the women's room of the house. Spirit ceremonies are preferably held at night, starting after the last prayers. Should a ceremony last through morning, drumming and dancing stop while the dawn prayer is recited at the mosque. No spirit medicine is provided on Fridays before the noon mosque service, nor to anyone in the village in the interval between a death and burial. No public possession ceremonies may take place during the entire month of Ramadan. Some people call up their spirits annually, just before Ramadan, to warn them that they will have to terminate all interaction during the month. Others say that it is all right to speak with one's spirits privately, as long as it is done during the period after sunset and before sunrise, that is, that period when Islamic law permits indulgence in such other profane activities as eating, drinking, and sexual intercourse.

Following the establishment of a Friday mosque, which occurred while I was a resident in Lombeni, the villagers became rather self-conscious about their religious habits and concerned with the maintenance of certain standards. They established a new law that barred the performance of possession ceremonies for the night preceding the Friday service. This ruling was accepted by all the villagers. However, when one overzealous soul, eager to demonstrate the degree of his knowledge of, and commitment to, Islam, attempted to say a prayer in the mosque that would send punishment to anyone ever again holding a possession ceremony in the village, the results were other than he had intended. The reactions to an incident of this kind bring to the surface some of the underlying assumptions and beliefs of the participants. In this case, they ranged from amused disapproval to outrage, to a quick dismissal of the prayer and the continuation of an imminent ceremony as originally planned. The basic opinion was that this individual was interfering with the rights of other individuals to attempt to cure their illnesses. As one of the spirit curers forcefully said, it is God who brings sickness and God who expects the sick to endeavor to cure themselves. When people are sick on account of the spirits, then they must treat themselves with the appropriate means. Should the man who called for the termination of the ceremonies ever become sick with spirits, he, the curer, certainly would not agree to treat them. And, he hinted darkly, the man was showing signs of latent possession already.

The Imam and leading Koranic scholar of the village held a more temperate view. God has his own medicines, recorded in books, which are different from the possession ceremonies. As a consequence, God does not really approve of the latter. Although the scholar himself does not participate, even as a spectator, in possession activities, and has expressed disapproval of his sisters' participation, he advocates tolerance of such activity. He argues that if people believe in a cure, then it will work, and therefore should not be interfered with. Both the Koranic scholar and the spirit curer pointed out that such tolerance is demonstrated in all the villages with Friday mosque service throughout the island.[6] In sum, what is challenged is never the existence of spirits, but the respectability of possession activities. Considerations of health and efficacy take precedence over the latter.

There is one form of spirit possession that is recognized as occurring legitimately in a specifically Islamic context. A number of Sufic rituals have an important place in Islamic practice in Mayotte. Although much of the ideology of mysticism (and of sectarianism) apparently has been lost, participants in these rituals do tend to work themselves up to states of excitement that could be labeled "altered states of consciousness." Particularly sensitive individuals are sometimes said to be possessed by a special kind of spirit known as a *jathiba*. In Lombeni this was true of a single individual, an elderly man married late in life into the village from one of the centers of Islamic learning on the island. Under the influence of the *jathiba*, this individual would pierce himself in the flesh above the shoulder blades with special sharp iron instruments during the performance of one kind of Sufic dance (the *Mulidi*). The *jathiba* also had the tendency to rise in the old man whenever he felt particularly moved by the quality of a particular piece of Koranic recitation. Unfortunately, the *jathiba* liked to indicate its arrival by giving a high shriek that was singularly out of place in the solemn atmosphere of the recitation of sacred liturgy, particularly of the Friday reading of the *hutuba* 'sermon,' when a rule of absolute silence is enjoined upon the congregation and self-consciously maintained. The reaction of the congregation to the arrival of the spirit was not, as one might imagine it would be, one of awe, nor respect, nor fear, nor even censure for breaking the rule of silence, but rather a kind of titillated, amused embarrassment. Inside the mosque people elbowed one another and attempted to suppress giggles. Numerous worshippers broke their train of thought to turn around and see how the anthropologist was responding to the event. The spirit itself was quite ignored.

The reaction of amusement rather than of awe or outright disapproval suggests the basic incongruity of the event. Spirits and sacred services simply should not mix. Although according to their knowledge of Islamic tradition it was not wrong or sacrilegious for this kind of spirit to appear, nevertheless, it did not seem quite right either. Again, what is being expressed is not a denial of the existence of spirits nor of the necessity for some people to sometimes interact with them, but the idea that such activity must be kept separate from, and at times give precedence to, other forms of activity, especially the recitation of the liturgy. Where the two overlap, there is conceptual confusion, providing humor at the mosque and obscenity at the graveyard. In the normal course of events, however, the rules of "pollution" keep the two activities apart or, rather, keep Islamic sacred, or "marked," activities free from secular references to spirits. Spirit cures, on the other hand, do generally make use of the basic Islamic invocations, especially of the *fātiḥa*, which is used to initiate all forms of activity. Curing is essentially a pragmatic and experimental enterprise, which juxtaposes any techniques that are thought to have a chance of working. Furthermore, as a general endeavor, curing is considered to be sanctioned by Islam and to be operating within its norms.

Why must spirits be kept away from Islamic ritual? The most important reason is probably that possession is disruptive to ritual order, with its demands for bodily and mental control. But beyond this, as we shall see, spirits are in some sense challenging to the fundamental sociopolitical assumptions and implications of Islamic ideology. If Islam suggests that power and justice somehow go hand in hand, if the most powerful and richest men in the village automatically sit in the front of the mosque and the meek toward the back, the spirits make a mockery of this. It is not so much that a weak person, helped by a spirit, can become suddenly powerful, but that the spirits, by their very natures, throw into question the whole moral basis of power. Spirits are potent yet parasitic, educated yet extortionist, self-seeking and self-motivated, vain, ungenerous, untrustworthy, querulous, and irresponsible. Treating with the spirits requires knowing when to be tactful and patient and when to put your foot down and be self-assertive in turn. Some people do become clients or allies of the spirits, but such ties are never developed without the endurance of physical suffering or material expense and are never undertaken without a certain apprehension for whatever may happen next.

3. The nature of spirits: first approximations

Having discriminated between the metaphysical conceptions and activities of spirit possession and those of Islam, we must now examine the distinctions between spirits and humans and locate possession in terms of secular life. The establishment and maintenance of contrast between spirits and humans is actually two problems: Spirits and humans must be distinguished from one another as general categories of thought, and particular manifestations of spirits must be separated from their individual human hosts. We will consider these problems separately, although the solution to each clearly reinforces the other. That is, the conception of spirits as other than human is supported by the recognition of individual cases of possession and vice versa. Any given act by an individual in trance indicates simultaneously the gulf between spiritkind and humankind, the distinction between the particular spirit and the human host it is inhabiting at the moment, and the current status of the relationship between spirit and host. These topics will be introduced in this chapter and elaborated further throughout the rest of the book.

How spiritkind contrasts with humankind

Although there is no single inclusive classificatory scheme for spirits, those that enter human beings or actively intervene in their affairs are grouped into a number of discrete, labeled classes. It is these classes that each contrast with humans. The members of a particular class are identified not on the basis of abstract principles according to conceptions of the spirits' differing natures but by concrete signs, by the peculiar customs and habits ascribed to the class. If we bracket from consideration the details of individual histories, indeed, if we set aside the very fact of trance itself, we can see that these characteristics of spirits are organized in a logical structure. Spirit classes are products of "the science of the concrete" (Lévi-Strauss 1966).

The diversity among spirits that possess humans is sometimes explicitly likened to the diversity among human groups, so that the classes of

34

spirits (*trumba, patros,* etc.) are referred to as *kabila* 'ethnic groups.' Although this social metaphor is used to clarify the spirit domain, the spirit classes can also be seen as a metaphoric representation of the prevailing ethnic variability. However, it may be more useful to consider the differences between the major classes of spirits on the order of species.[1] Certain kinds of spirits never directly interact or confront one another but appear to inhabit different worlds. For example, in Lombeni the most common spirits are the *trumba* and the *patros.* Spirits of both kinds enter individual humans, make them sick, rise in their heads, and demand ceremonies. Although the situations they create in and for their human hosts are very similar to one another, and although spirits of each kind can visit the same host, the contexts in which they are referred to or in which they appear are generally kept quite distinct from one another, separated initially by the kind of incense used to call each species. Thus, a *patros* spirit will never rise during a *trumba* ritual and vice versa.

The spirit classes are not stable, unchanging phenomena and should not be reified. The long history of spirit possession in the area and its wide spread over much of Africa and Madagascar provide evidence of much change. New classes of spirits appear, and old ones gradually vanish or merge.[2] Although the names of the spirit species and the details of their rituals change from place to place, basic structural similarities are readily apparent among particular examples ranging from Senegal and Egypt to Zimbabwe and Madagascar. These local manifestations appear to be particular expressions of an underlying structure or, to put it differently, transformations of neighboring expressions of that structure.[3]

All spirit classes contrast with humans and with one another. The contrasts are established by means of concrete signs "whose terms consist of odds and ends left over from psychological or historical processes and are, like these, devoid of necessity" (Lévi-Strauss 1966:35). The particular features of spirit life are significant less for their substance than for the system of oppositions they establish; what is meaningful about spirits is their contrast with humans. Here we will examine one class of spirits, the *patros,* selected because they were the most common form of possessing spirit present in Lombeni during the course of fieldwork.[4]

Patros

Patros spirits are native to Mayotte. Most *patros* are said to inhabit underwater villages adjacent to the coast, often at points where there are mud flats or mangrove swamps, that is, where the boundaries between land and water become ill defined. These are not locations that are favored as the sites of human villages today, although they may once have been in the past (Kus and Wright 1976). A few *patros* are also associated with inland bodies of water. The villages are named but little discussed, although two informants independently described visits to them during sleep. One informant says she was taken by taxi-brousse (bush taxi) and canoe in her sleep to the village of Pole, the home of one of her spirits. The village has so many spirits that were they all to decide to rise up in people, there would not be a single human inhabitant of Mayotte unaffected. Certain other villages are much smaller than Pole, in the range of small human villages. Both informants describe conditions of relative prosperity or westernization: meat, houses of stone or cement, animal pens, and the like.

When a *patros* spirit finally announces its name, it is always according to the standard formula:

   x offspring of *y, z*

where *x* is the name of the speaker, *y* is the name of his or her father, and *z* is the name of the home village. For example, Runany bun Jumna, M'Bombez. The names thus provide a series of truncated genealogies.[5] *Patros* maintain a family and village organization similar to that of humans, and, like humans, are vitally concerned with subsistence. *Patros* are said to be old and young, male and female, lighter skinned and darker skinned. However, the majority of *patros* that actually possess people are male, either mature adults or impetuous youths.[6] The older males are sometimes referred to as elders (*ulu be*). In *patros* society, like that of Lombeni itself, status is not ascribed but achieved; leadership is held by a well-qualified male of later middle-age.

Despite the similarities of social organization, *patros* contrast with human beings in many ways. Aside from their invisibility, their immortality, and their ability to possess humans, these contrasts are cultural. *Patros* have their own form of speech,[7] their own music and style of dancing. Food habits provide the most salient contrasts. *Patros* enjoy some substances that humans consider inedible or unworthy of eating, reject certain favorite human foods, and eat others out of context. The major elements of the *patros* diet are:

1. *Cologne.* Cologne is ingested by the *patros* both on private occasions and during public ceremonies, where it is a necessary ingredient. The cologne is drunk in small, rapidly swallowed mouthfuls, straight from the bottle. Its alcoholic content is recognized, but it is claimed that only the spirit feels the effects, never the human host.

In sharp contrast to the spirits, humans consider cologne undrinkable, both by definition and proscription (because of its alcohol content). Held something of a pleasant and simple luxury, cologne is a common household item. It is sprinkled on the clothing or head on festive occasions and is associated with joy and social fulfillment.[8]

2. *Blood.* Drinking blood is the food habit of the *patros* that humans find most disturbing; frequently it is indulged in circumstances designed to enhance the shock. Humans can only consume the flesh of animals slaughtered according to Islamic formula, which entails draining the blood. Blood is thus forbidden to humans and, in addition, is considered dangerous, causing illness or death. Their consumption of blood is thus strong evidence that the *patros* are nonhuman and that any given manifestation of a spirit is indeed what it claims to be. Drinking blood is considered extreme even by the *patros* themselves; it is only the youthful spirits who indulge. The habit is renounced, much as most human males renounce palm wine and game, as the spirits grow older. The elder spirits still consider the blood to be delicious, but it becomes an inappropriate indulgence.

Blood is normally consumed by the spirits only during the course of public spirit ceremonies. The blood from the goat or chickens that are slaughtered (according to Islamic formula, because humans will be sharing in the meal) is caught in bowls and put aside to congeal. The next morning the bowl is placed in the center of the dancing ground for the spirits to drink. The spirits may go to great lengths to demonstrate their tastes to the audience, falling over the bowl face-first and lapping up the blood in ecstasy or even drinking directly the blood flowing from the neck of a freshly slaughtered goat (Jon H. Breslar, personal communication), much to the horror or titillation of the crowd.

3. *Sugar. Patros* spirits like to eat handfuls of refined white sugar. Humans too are very fond of sugar but consider it a luxury. Although spirits eat it plain, humans add it, when they have the chance, to tea or cakes, which are shared.

4. *Eggs and chicken. Patros* spirits enjoy raw eggs, although some *patros* prefer them boiled. Humans only eat cooked eggs and then quite rarely. Many people, particularly women, observe dietary restrictions against both eggs and chicken. These avoidances, usually explained by the fact that chickens are "dirty," peck in refuse, and have indiscriminate eating habits of their own, are frequently conditions placed on women by their *trumba* spirits. Transgressors become physically ill, experiencing discomfort and sometimes acute pain and vomiting. It is only when these women are in the throes of possession by their *patros* spirits that they can and do eat chicken with enjoyment and no ill effects.

The chicken eaten by *patros* spirits is cooked for them by humans in

The food laid out for a *mugala* feast includes bottles of cologne and raw eggs set in piles of sugar, milk, and betel. (Photograph courtesy of Jon H. Breslar.)

a tasty but saltless sauce. *Patros* do not eat salt. Although humans consider chicken second-rate fare as opposed to beef, goat, or mutton, *patros,* by contrast, will not touch these latter meats. Nor will *patros* eat cooked rice, the preferred staple of humans and the essential ingredient in any "good" meal.[9]

   5. *Liver. Patros* do eat cooked liver. At the occasion of a *patros* feast important enough to include the slaughter of a goat, the liver is the exclusive property of the spirits, and the rest of the meat is shared among the human participants. At most human religious feasts that include an animal sacrifice, the liver is reserved for those individuals who participate in the recitation of the sacred liturgy; frequently it is served and consumed in the mosque itself. When a sacrifice is held in order to protect a given group of people, pieces of the cooked liver, however small, are distributed to each member of the group.

   6. *Cake.* Every *patros* feast requires *mukary juŋgu,* a starchy baked pudding of rice flour. This is one of a number of "cakes" that are also prepared on human festive occasions. Humans classify cakes as a sweet, eaten only on special occasions, whereas the spirits consider it a staple food (*haniŋ*).

   Viewed in its entirety, it is apparent that the *patros* diet exhibits strong contrasts with the human one. *Patros* consume certain substances raw – blood, eggs, and sugar – whereas all substantial human food is cooked. *Patros* ingest substances that humans consider nonfood, poisonous, or forbidden – cologne and blood. Furthermore, *patros* demand and treat as staples foods that humans judge luxuries – sugar, cake, and domestic animal protein – and reject the products that make up daily human fare – green vegetables, tubers, salt, and fish. Some of the foods that *patros* eat are reminiscent of human festivity, notably, cake, liver, and cologne. But again, *patros* reject the major elements of human feasts – rice and red meat. In sum, the spirits' self-indulgence, indiscrimination, and want of a sense of proportion form a central theme.

The cake and the cologne, as two elements essential to the *patros* ceremony, can also be seen as performing a mediative function or transfer point between the human and spirit systems, clarifying the significance of the occasion for both sides. In this way, the spirit's subsistence activity can be interpreted as a festive occasion. The mediation occurs at the concrete level as well. Cake is the one food that is shared among both the spirit and human participants. The cakes are carefully divided according to the curer's discretion and the accepted custom of the particular village in which the ceremony is taking place. Proper apportionment is one indication of a skillful curer. Pieces are set aside for the curer, the patient and her family, and any important visitors. The remaining pieces, cut small enough so as to go around, are first passed out among the spirits and then to each of the human spectators. The onlookers, in turn, may take their pieces home to redivide among members of their family, so that, in similar fashion to a human ceremony, a large proportion of the villagers receive a share.

Whereas the food habits just described are characteristic of the *patros* as a class, there are other tastes particular to individual *patros* spirits that serve to emphasize even more sharply the distinction between spirits and humans. The substances consumed are those that humans classify as inedible. They include unhusked rice, raw chicken intestines, and, in at least one case each, fire and snakes. To take just the latter, humans fear snakes and consider their ingestion revolting and probably deadly poison to humans. One informant recalls seeing a *patros* bite into a live raw snake. The spirit had drawn a large crowd of spectators, but my friend had to turn away to keep from vomiting at the sight. Such episodes, of course, tend to build up the reputation of the manifestation of a spirit in a particular host. In the case of the snake eater, my friend went on to recall how people had said he was "certainly a real spirit" (*lulu aŋkitiŋ*) because he didn't die or suffer any ill effects from eating something fatal to humans.

In addition to the nature of the specific substances in which they indulge, spirits have a number of strategies to emphasize their unusual habits or, as in the preceding case, to create shock deliberately. First, as I have already described, spirits tend to ingest their food in a public context; the stranger the food, the more public the situation. Similarly, the *patros* frequently make a point of offering blood or cologne (but not sugar or liver!) to the humans with whom they happen to be conversing. This forces the humans to decline, that is, to openly commit themselves to their human identity. I was once engaged in a private conversation with an elderly *patros* spirit when the host's three-year-old granddaughter happened to wander into the room with a minor cut on her finger. The spirit at once remarked how tasty the little girl's blood appeared. Spirits do not, of course, drink human blood, especially not that of the host's grandchildren. The remark was merely intended to draw attention to her spirit nature and, therefore, to the contrast between us.

Such gambits may lead to further discussion and speculation on the part of the human company that appear to underline at once both the conventional and predetermined nature of culture and the adherence of the speakers to a particular version of it. What is most significant about the spirit representations is not their substance, their individual properties, but the relationships of difference they set up with the established cultural norms.

How spirits are distinguished from their hosts

Spirits enter the bodies of human beings and rise to their heads, taking temporary control of all bodily and mental functions. In Western terms, we would focus on the continuity in the event, on the single individual whose body we recognize before us, and we would say that he or she has undergone a change of state, that she is now in trance. In Mayotte, however, the emphasis is on the *change* that has occurred. Despite the fact that the body remains the same, it is now occupied by a different person. A rigorous distinction is maintained between the identity of the individual who enters and leaves the trance state and the individual who is actually present during the former's "trance." The former is the human host, the latter a possessing spirit. During the trance, the human host is absent, no one can say where, and is temporarily replaced by the spirit. Spirit and host are two entirely different persons. If one of them has cause to speak about the other, it will always be in the third person. It is thus extremely important to keep in mind in all that follows when it is the spirit who is being referred to and when the host.

This opposition between two discrete identities, host and spirit, is the single most crucial element, the axiom, upon which the entire system of possession rests. If it is not maintained, the case is simply not possession. The distinction between host and spirit is explored, elaborated, and played upon in a number of ways. For example, it implies that the relationship between spirit and host does not have to be one to one: A given human individual can be host to more than one spirit, and similarly, a given spirit can visit more than one human host. One implication of the distinction that may prove somewhat confusing at first is the possibility of a switch in gender. The humans who receive spirits in Mayotte are most frequently women (Table 4.1); most of the visiting spirits, however, are male. Thus, male spirits are frequently observed in female bodies. The other permutations – male spirits in male hosts, female spirits in male or female hosts – are also possible, although less common. Shifts in age and personality also occur. There is no paradox here, because the body belongs to the host and is merely being temporarily inhabited by the spirit visitor.

Convention has it that during trance the host herself is absent from her own body. Thus she can have no memory of what took place while she was in trance.[10] The host can only learn what went on by asking someone else who was present. Likewise, the spirit's indulgence in pleasure has no effect on the host. A spirit may spend the night dancing and drinking; when it leaves, the host, in theory, feels neither inebriated, hung over, nor tired. A child *trumba* spirit stuffs itself with food; when it leaves, the host expresses hunger and immediately begins to prepare herself a meal. This behavior reinforces the message that spirit and host are different creatures.

Such are the conventions. However, it is recognized by the knowledgeable that some trances are less deep than others and that on certain occasions certain individuals will retain some memory of what happened while they were possessed. They will have felt that they were observers, not actors, in whatever happened; nevertheless, if they are working as curers or have some other interest in the maintenance of the dual identity, they will not speak about the experience. Thus the convention stands firm but is recognized for what it is.

This leads to the question that Westerners always ask: whether possession is or can be fabricated; that is, whether the person who claims to be in trance is consciously acting. The readiness with which this question comes to mind probably says more about the nature of trance in the West than it does about any inherent weakness in the Mayotte model. Pretense is possible but rarely occurs. For one thing, there is no need for it. Those who are adept at trance and who may be using it with certain conscious ends in mind (e.g., during the performance of a cure) are confident enough of the willingness and capacity of their spirits to do the job as well or better than they could manage themselves. For another, those who have no spirits can have little desire to imply that they do and little chance to cheat successfully. A spirit must work to impress its audience with its authenticity. People are wary of the possibility of cheating and consider each new manifestation of possession critically before validating it in the curing process.[11]

The integrity of spirit identities adds immensely to the richness of the possession sequences. Indeed, in Becker's terms, coherence of the plot is based largely on the conception of person. The following case (recounted to me by the principal) provides a striking example of the constraining effects of this notion of person:

> Musy Malandy was the first woman in Lombeni Kely to become possessed by a *patros* spirit. Preparations for the naming ceremony were arranged with the curer Siaka Salim. Several days before the ceremony, Musy went to Lombeni Be to invite those with *patros* spirits of their own to participate. But people laughed at her and said she didn't really have a *patros*. Musy became very depressed and thought to herself that maybe they were right; the expense would be for nothing and her illness would not be cured. On the day of the ceremony, very few people came from other villages. The people of Lombeni Kely attended, but only as spectators, because none of them had *patros* of their own. The participants sang and clapped and urged Musy's spirit to rise, but nothing happened. Musy kept thinking about what the Lombeni Be people had said. Finally, she overheard one visiting lady remark that the whole thing was a waste of time and that there was no *patros* spirit; she had never heard of a *patros* that requested a naming ceremony and then refused to rise to perform it. Musy felt very upset and embarrassed. People were getting tired of sitting and clapping and wanted to go off to sleep. All this time, her curer, Siaka Salim, had been in trance himself, chatting to Musy's husband and others. Now his spirit announced that it was leaving and everyone said that if it did so then that would be the end of the affair. But the moment Siaka went out of trance, Musy entered it. They gave her the medicine and everyone began dancing. At the appointed hour, Musy's spirit entered into their midst, climbed on a chair, and announced its name. It was the same as the spirit of Musy's curer, Siaka Salim! Then the others understood why her spirit hadn't risen earlier: it was already present in Siaka, and a spirit cannot be in two places at once. The reason no one had thought of it was that in those days (some twenty-five years ago) they were all still rather inexperienced at dealing with *patros*.

Classes of illness

Because possession is viewed as a form of illness and the process of accommodation to the entering spirits as a kind of therapy, a general overview of affliction and cure in Mayotte is in order. The medical system of Mayotte is complex, involving indigenous, Islamic, and Western traditions.[12] The islanders recognize three broad classes of illness: illness caused by God (*boka n'draŋahary*), illness caused by humans, and illness caused by spirits. The first of these classes corresponds to our category of "natural disease." As Janzen has said about an equivalent category of the Bakongo, "the notion 'of God' does not imply divine intervention or retribution but simply that the case is an affliction in the order of things, unrelated to human intentions" (1978:8). Appropriate responses to such illness range from preparing home remedies to visiting local curers or entering the Western hospital. The second category can be glossed as sorcery (*voriky*), and the third as spirit possession. These sorts of illnesses are treated by local curers, usually by spirit mediums. Western health personnel are inappropriate here. However, it is frequently the case that a patient suffers from natural disease, sorcery, and possession concurrently, in which case a number of different specialists are consulted. Sorcery and spirit possession are secondary to illness that comes from God. Neither can enter the body except when it is already vulnerable through natural illness, and neither can be the direct cause of death. Both the onset of illness and its termination in death are the sole prerogatives of God. The forces of sorcery and spirit possession remain in the body once the natural illness that was present at the time of their initial entry has been cured. In fact, sorcery and possession are frequently diagnosed from a lingering manifestation of symptoms after the natural disease has been treated. Sorcery and spirit possession thus capitalize upon and complicate natural illness. Rather than initiate the symptoms or conditions of illness, they prolong them and prevent their termination.

Sorcery refers to deliberate, secretive, and unjustly aggressive acts committed by one person against another by means of the application of esoteric knowledge. Sorcery is not considered a discipline of its own; rather, the potential for committing sorcery is inherent in the attainment of any body of powerful esoteric knowledge. Anyone with the knowedge to cure, through whatever means, has also the knowledge to harm. Even Western doctors, by intentionally misapplying medicines or techniques, for example, by poisoning, can commit sorcery. However, the most common form of sorcery (i.e., that which is most frequently diagnosed) entails hiring spirits to infect people and cause them harm. The sorcerer rarely deals with spirits risen in human hosts; rather, he communicates with them indirectly, by means of written spells, incantations, and sacrifices. The bravest and most advanced sorcerers are also considered to be able to meet the spirits face to face in their natural and normally invisible condition, and the most depraved sorcerers are believed to make use of the spirits of the recently deceased. Whatever the means of negotiation, once a spirit has been hired to harm someone it follows that person about, waiting for a moment or state of vulnerability in which it will be able to lodge in the body. Occasionally it infects the wrong person; children in particular are vulnerable to such accident. The symptoms of sorcery vary: They may include lingering illness, discomfort, depression, or repeated recurrence of a particular symptom or set of symptoms. Sorcery may be associated with any natural disease, thus with any physical symptoms. Diagnosis is based on divination or on careful examination of the patient's "psychological" state. Tumbu, who is a master curer of sorcery, uses such techniques as looking in the patient's eyes, observing nervous reactions, and feeling the pulse. He also bases his judgment on his general impressions of the patient's condition, including whether he thinks the patient believes himself or herself to be a victim of sorcery.

The most common cure for sorcery, and the one Tumbu uses, involves locating and extracting a small, rotting cloth packet filled with dirt, nail clippings, hair, broken glass, and the like from either the body of the patient, his house floor, or the ground of his compound or fields. This packet of dirt is the physical representation of the harm caused by the spirit itself. The extraction of the packet is a formal activity that may be considered ritual. It is carried out with the recital of Koranic verses and requests for God's help, with a certain number of gestures, and with lighted incense. The curer touches the patient's body, frequently squeezing the afflicted portion so hard as to bring the patient to tears or yelps of pain. At the right moment, the curer wordlessly tosses down the packet and cuts it open. The patient and any relatives who may have been observing examine and exclaim over the packet's contents and are instructed to throw them out. Then, upon the payment of the appropriate fee, generally a small fowl, the patient's symptoms should, and frequently do, disappear. If they do not, there are a number of explanations open to both curer and patient, such as re-attack by the sorcerer, astrological incompatibility between the curer and the particular case, and so on.

It should also be pointed out that whereas the diagnosis of sorcery is a common occurrence, viewed more with outrage, annoyance, or bewilderment than with horror, public accusations of sorcery are rare. The aim is to keep conflict, including retaliation, at a minimum. Curers are strongly discouraged from revealing the names of the perpetrators to their victims and, in fact, have to go through a search that is not part of the regular process of the cure to gain the knowledge themselves. Curers sometimes do tell their patients but generally only when they consider them to be capable of receiving the information in a mature fashion. One extractor who revealed the names of sorcerers indiscriminately was considered a mischief maker and untrustworthy. An important consequence of this situation is that the frequent occurrence of sorcery does not cause social ruptures and realignments of the sort, and to the degree, described for other African societies.[13] Rather, the experience of sorcery leads to a painful awareness of the discrepancy between public norms and private sentiments. Indeed, another reason frequently given for not identifying publicly the names of sorcerers is that such identification would incriminate a large proportion of the population. It will be argued later that this sort of experience is a major theme of possession.

Although everyone believes in the possibility of sorcery and the existence of sorcerers, the attitudes toward the process of extraction just described vary from belief to skepticism. A minority of individuals in Lombeni claim that the procedure is a fraud, perpetrated by the curers for their own financial ends. The curers maintain, however, that they are performing a significant service. They point out that an individual who believes himself to be suffering from sorcery will get well if, and only if, he perceives the sorcery to be removed. Extraction of the packet, as an effective representation of such removal, generates within the patient the conditions for cure.

An extractor must have received long training in his art from another curer; in addition, the extractor should have a *patros* spirit of his own.[14] Through dreams, the *patros* spirit serves as a guide and adviser to the host; it may also sometimes rise in the host to perform the extraction itself, though it need not.[15] In addition, the *patros* protects the extractor from the wrath of the spirits he has removed from the bodies, houses, or land of his clients. These spirits come to attack the extractor on the night following the operation and wage battle with the *patros* spirit during the curer's sleep. The curer spends a very troubled night. Thus, in addition to being able to rely on the assistance of a spirit, the curer must himself be of a strong disposition (*ɲora mahery*) in order to withstand the attacking spirits.[16]

The third class of affliction is spirit possession. Although sorcery is frequently conceived to involve the presence of a spirit within the body of the patient, possession is quite different. In possession, the spirit does not merely enter the body (*miditry an'neɲin*), but climbs to the head (*manuŋga an'luha*). Furthermore, possession cannot be stopped by simple extraction of the sort previously described. In possession, the relationship of the spirit to the host is much more complex; instead of curing the patient, extraction of the spirit by force would leave her harmed for life. The initiation of a relationship between a spirit and a human host is entirely the responsibility of the spirit. The spirit may have originally entered the patient at the bidding of a sorcerer, but the decision to remain and to intensify the relationship is always that of the spirit alone. If the spirit has entered as the result of sorcery, the packet must be extracted, regardless of what the spirit does next. Extraction terminates the conditions of sorcery and leaves the way free for a possession cure if it is necessary. Some of the symptoms of possession are similar to those of sorcery: lingering, recurrent, or severe illness that does not respond to other forms of treatment. Other symptoms include strange dreams, particular reactions to diagnostic medicines applied by spirit curers, and spontaneous sequences of trance.

The relationship between spirit and host

Spirits are not an intrinsic part of the wider system of morality; the presence of a spirit is regarded as a sign neither of punishment nor of grace. A spirit decides to establish a relationship with a human because it has a special liking for the host or out of simple greed, perversity, or simply because the opportunity presents itself. From the point of view of the host, the situation is an embarrassing, expensive, and painful nuisance. An individual informed of the presence of a spirit may accept the diagnosis with great reluctance.

Following the initial decision on the part of the spirit, three broad stages in the development of the relationship between the spirit and host may be distinguished. The first stage lasts until the host takes positive action. The host may be unaware of the spirit's presence, may not have accepted the presence, or may not be suffering enough to desire a cure. In some cases, the relationship never develops beyond this stage. Despite diagnosis, a spirit never rises at all, rises only once, or on rare occasions in order to amuse itself at the ceremonies of others.

Once a spirit has made its presence felt, it is then up to the host to respond. This is done by means of an intermediary, the curer, who requests the spirit to rise, that is, puts the patient into trance. The spirit is asked to state its conditions for releasing the patient from her suffering. The spirit makes a list of excessive, if predictable, demands, and there ensues a process of bargaining and exchange, which stabilizes the relationship between spirit and host. The intent is not to exorcise the spirit but to come to an understanding with it, to negotiate the removal of the unpleasant symptoms rather than the spirit itself.

The essence of the conditions put forward by the spirit is that the afflicted individual (i.e., the host), or whoever wishes to do so on her behalf, provide the means for the spirit to entertain its fellow spirits at a sequence of two public feasts. If this is done to its satisfaction, the spirit will then reveal its name and thereafter desist from harming the host. In the Mayotte view, then, the spirit preys as a parasite upon humans, demanding their assistance in the fulfillment of its social obligations to its fellow spirits.[17]

This period, from the first attempts to convince the spirit to state its demands through the performance of the public ceremonies that inevitably form the core of these demands, makes up the second, and most dynamic, stage in the relationship between host and spirit. During this period, the spirit is treated with medicines and the host becomes cured of her ailments. With each step that the host takes toward meeting the spirit's demands, for example, with each purchase that the host makes toward the feast, the spirit lessens the suffering it is causing. However, should the return to health cause the host to drop her obligations to the spirit, the latter may again provide affliction as a reminder that it is growing impatient. There is an underlying tension here between the best interests of the host and those of the spirit. The reappearance of illness functions as a control mechanism, turning the host back to a consideration of the spirit's demands.

The second stage can be passed through in the span of a couple of years or it can take much longer. In some cases it is never completed, either because the illness disappears and the spirit loses interest in seeing its demands met or because the host simply cannot afford to carry them out. In those cases where a single host has, over a period of time, become possessed by more than one spirit of a single species, the later arrivals may be satisfied with only one small ceremony or with sharing a ceremony with another spirit. This does not hold true for spirits of different species, because the ceremonies required for each of them differ.

The third stage begins at the end of the second feast, when the spirit has successfully announced its name and perhaps also certain restrictions, mostly dietary, which it is placing henceforth on the host. The relationship between spirit and host matures. The spirit is only likely to make the host sick again if the latter ignores the restrictions, and the problem can usually be remedied fairly rapidly. The spirit can also make additional demands from time to time, for example, the request for a shawl by Tumbu's spirit. Mostly, however, the spirit remains cooperative and may, indeed, render positive assistance should it choose to manifest itself as a curer.

This stage frequently terminates only with the death of the host. The spirit may initiate a new relationship with a younger relative of an aging host. It may then continue to rise in both hosts or terminate its visits to the elder. In one case of my acquaintance, the same spirit visited both mother and daughter and had finished its ceremonies and become a curer in each of them successively. When the old woman began to find possession too exhausting, the spirit rose in her and announced to all supplicants that in the future they should seek it in the daughter. In another case, the relatives of a male elder found his not infrequent possession becoming an embarrassment and so called up his spirit in order to politely request that it discontinue its visits in the old man. The spirit never returned but was later recognized in the man's classificatory granddaughter. Spirits do tend to reappear within particular families, though they also appear among otherwise unrelated individuals.

The process of accommodation will be examined in much greater detail in the following chapters. As a final point here, it should be emphasized that the long duration of the relationship between an individual host and spirit is quite another matter from the actual manifestations of the spirit in the host (i.e., the periods of trance). The latter are intermittent and vary widely in frequency, both among individuals and within the same individual from year to year over the life-span. Frequency of trance also varies with the season, being significantly higher in the drier and post-harvest months. Spirits have their own homes and are also said to travel widely and to visit more than one host. Spirits do not normally rise up in their hosts except when they are specifically called over incense or tempted by the music and foods of a spirit feast. And there are times when, even when they are particularly appealed to, they show their obstinacy by choosing not to rise.

4. The incidence of trance

This chapter considers the relative incidence of trance among specific individuals and classes of individuals in Mayotte. Who is possessed and why? A major concern is to investigate why possession is so much more common among women than men. Throughout the chapter the view is maintained that trance need not be considered abnormal behavior. I try to show that explanations based on specific characteristics or motivations of individuals are relatively weak. This is not to say that spirits do not have psychological repercussions on their hosts, only that such effects cannot provide the impetus for possession and that they are neither uniform nor necessary. To attempt to explain possession in this manner is to mistake effect for cause. The question of incidence of trance cannot be approached from a priori functionalist assumptions, whether psychological or social, but must be grounded in the context of the particular symbolic forms that trance takes in the culture concerned. That is to say, cultural features play a primary role in constraining the incidence of trance.

The idiom of illness

What can we say of someone who is possessed? Are the possessed really ill? Although spirit possession, like perhaps all ritual, may serve the general psychological function of summarizing and digitalizing internal, individual processes (Rappaport 1974:19–23) and making these processes meaningful by interpreting them through a collective symbolic system, not everyone becomes possessed. The sorts of individuals within any particular culture who will be attracted to possession vary according to the manner with which possession is integrated with the wider symbolic system. Most psychological correlates of possession are thus culturally specific. In cultures, such as the modern mainstream West, that do not provide a positive model for trance behavior, trance may be engaged in only by severely disturbed individuals and is merely a symptom of such disturbance. In cultures such as Dahomey, where the model for trance behavior is elaborate and highly specific (Verger 1969), only someone highly capable in daily life will also be capable of performing in trance. In the latter sort of case, it is precisely not the very ill who participate in trance activity. In neither of these two contexts does trance appear to serve the troubled individual directly.

Intermediate between these extremes are cultures in which spirit possession trance is "a culturally constituted public idiom for the expression of psychological illness" (Obeyesekere 1970:105). Obeyesekere has presented a convincing analysis of spirit possession in Sinhalese culture, where individuals on the verge of psychotic breakdown revert to the cultural fantasy in order to stave off the idiosyncratic one. In this way they maintain contact with the culturally defined reality, attempt to communicate their problems and feelings, manage to express primary process material in a controlled context, and are able to gain confidence through the experience (1970:104–8). In Mayotte, although possession seems at first glance to be similar to the Sinhalese case, I will argue that it is closer to that of Dahomey in terms of being rigidly bound by convention.

Trance is not viewed as inevitable or typical behavior in Mayotte, but neither is it considered abnormal and frightening as in Ceylon. Spirits regularly interfere in the ordinary course of human life; spirits are viewed as predators, and possession is considered an extremely common, but relatively minor, local health problem. Everyone knows and interacts with people suffering from possession.

However, whereas possession forms a class of affliction in the Mayotte view, it corresponds to no Western category. It seems probable that what is represented by the symptoms of sorcery includes the "psychosomatic" aspects of disease. It is also possible that the experience of undergoing treatment for sorcery or possession harnesses or stimulates the body's reserves of strength to combat somatic or psychological illness. For example, the onset of possession sometimes marks the beginning of the end of what appears to be severe postpartum psychosis or exhaustion. But possession itself represents neither the physical nor the psychosomatic aspects of disease. It most certainly does not correspond to Western medical categories of psychopathology, epilepsy, or brain damage. This is clear because in Mayotte madness, epilepsy, and impaired mental functioning are classed quite separately from possession. In other words, and despite the way people talk about it, possession may not be the manifestation of an independently derived pathology at all.[1]

It may help matters to consider the constraints on the expression of primary process material during trance. First of all, in Mayotte, trance behavior is organized into particular role types, such as carousing youth or dignified elder, and each spirit is given a specific identity within the class. If the individual's psyche contains opposing tendencies, it is possible that she may show them by adopting, consecutively, but not simultaneously, two different identities; opposing tendencies can only be mixed in the same figure for as long as they continue to make cultural sense. Second, not only does the identity assumed by a possessed individual have to be internally coherent, it must also belong to the corpus of identities that the culture presents to her. This corpus, although perhaps somewhat flexible and relatively open to new members, maintains an internal coherence of its own. Third, there are numerous constraints on individual action in trance. The appearance of spirits is bounded in time and space. A spirit can be called up and it can be asked to leave again. It may stay in an individual any length of time, from a split second to as long as overnight but very rarely for longer periods. And although a spirit has relative freedom of movement, it would not, for example, enter a mosque. It does move beyond human cultural norms but only in certain well-defined domains, such as food preference and the open expression of greed. In other respects, for example in matters pertaining to overt physical aggression (as opposed to sorcery), to sexuality, and to bodily modesty, spirits stay well within the prevailing cultural norms.

If a spirit does begin to move beyond these norms, it is quickly stopped by the curer, other spirits, or onlookers. For example, on the rare occasions when there is danger of bodily exposure, someone will immediately step forward to hold the offending skirts down. Why the exposure of an emotion such as greed is tolerated, whereas physical exposure is not, obviously hits deep at the underlying cultural notions of order and restraint.[2] However, it must be remembered that from the local perspective the exposed emotion belongs to the spirit and is thus not revealing of the host, whereas the exposed body is clearly that of the host. Some people do notice correlations between the expressed concerns of particular spirits and the private imperfections of their hosts, although this feature is not part of the system. But physical exposure is carried out "behind the host's back" as it were. The manifest aim of the curing process is to ensure that the spirit does not abuse the body it has entered; physical exposure, just as much as the creation of pain and illness, is an abuse of the body.

A fourth and related set of constraints refers to the interaction among the spirits. A possessed individual, although she may switch identities, must stick to the rules of the game here. These include considerations of rank and deference among the spirits (Chapter 10) as well as the basic principles of the entire system, such as the fact that two individuals may not be possessed simultaneously by the same spirit or that an individual has long-term relationships with particular spirits' and cannot simply be possessed by a new one every time she enters trance.

Finally, a fifth set of constraints on the expression of the unconscious are those that pertain to the curing process itself, the process of mutual accommodation between spirits and humans. This accommodation proceeds in certain predictable ways. A spirit can be expected to modify its behavior accordingly, to gradually act with more consideration toward the body and person of its host and her sponsors. As we shall see, the spirit changes its behavior in two complementary ways: It becomes increasingly articulate and increasingly cooperative, that is, it is socialized. Although this may be partly a matter of the individual learning to control her behavior in trance, it is of great significance that the spirit itself generally anticipates such changes. The spirit waits to be initiated and then sets the cues itself, occasionally with some hesitation or backsliding but generally with the entire game plan well in mind. Thus, if the spirit expresses the unconscious, it also engages actively in the process of again repressing that unconscious, and it does so in an orderly, culturally established way, each stage in the curing process following necessarily from the one before it.

It is evident, then, that possession activities are predicated upon an intricate structure and governed by some extremely narrow constraints. Successful participation requires the engagement of a self-control that may be greater than severely disturbed individuals can manage. Thus, not all people with psychological problems become possessed or even exhibit signs of possession, nor are the claims of those who do necessarily believed. As with any other illness, cases of possession that do not follow a regular progression toward resolution upon the application of the appropriate therapy are likely to be rediagnosed. Such cases are those in which the patient does not operate within the constraints for regular movement in and out of trance and for behavior within trance. Here, in the face of what Western medicine would consider psychosis, two diagnoses are possible. Either the patient herself is said to be fantasizing and it is claimed that she is mad (*adala*), or the spirit is accused of dissimulation. In the latter case, the patient is possessed, not by a *trumba* or *patros* as the spirit itself claims, but by an ill-defined category of evil spirit (*lulu ratsy*), which must be exorcized, that is, entirely removed from the body of the patient.[3] Possession by the named categories of spirits is itself not equipped to deal with severe psychological illness, although it could be argued that in some cases perhaps it serves to stave such illness off.

Possession does frequently demonstrate great success with minor ailments – "psychosomatic" problems, mild postpartum psychoses, depressions and anxieties that have their source in the immediate social situations of the patients. But it would be difficult to account for the presence of possession in terms of such success. By no means do all the people suffering from such complaints become possessed. Nor does every host complain of illness. Among those who do, it might be that the original symptoms are merely a product of the patient's desire to be diagnosed as possessed in the first place. Many of the individuals who undergo possession, including the curers, appear to be mentally healthy.

In sum, the illness caused by the spirit is not necessarily considered to be of a mental or emotional nature in Mayotte, nor are the people who become possessed suffering, in Western terms, from severe emotional or personality disturbance. Possession is not necessarily preceded by an independent form of illness, which it overcomes; and, once under way, possession entails its own symptoms and pains. Rather than possession being a descriptive label or theory applied to a certain set of physical or mental symptoms or pathologies, in Mayotte illness is a label and theory for defining possession. Possession is necessarily neither a strategy for handling nor a symptom or expression of an underlying psychological or organic problem. That is to say, possession is less a metaphor for illness than illness is a metaphor for possession. Possession does not reflect illness so much as it establishes its presence performatively.

The onset of possession in the individual

Possession does bring real affliction. Possession is expensive, time-consuming, embarrassing, and physically painful.[4] Furthermore, because the association of spirit and host is quasi-permanent, and the spirit touchy and possibly dishonorable, the host is always vulnerable to a recurrence of unpleasant symptoms. Thus, whereas the very ill are incapable of becoming possessed or of sustaining credibility when they do so, the relatively healthy claim to be indisposed toward it. Contrary to providing us with an explanation of why people become possessed, the Mayotte view of possession as an unpleasant illness ought to constrain them from doing so.

Possession is, therefore, only likely to take place in circumstances in which this disinclination (which, in any case, may be relatively superficial) is somehow weakened. Two aspects of susceptibility appear to be: (a) neurophysiological – for example, the closeness of personal brain-wave frequency to the rhythm of the drums, and (b) sociopsychological – the degree of openness or defensiveness toward trance. Openness itself may have several components. Among these are: (a) flexibility of ego boundary, (b) depth of feeling concerning the propriety of possession, (c) practice at dissociation; and (d) degree of internalization of the model of behavior expected once the transition is made. This latter is a crucial point – without knowing *how* to behave in a strange environment, the thought of entering into that environment becomes all the more frightening. Only the guidance and comfort of a figure of authority, the curer, can lessen the fear.

It should be remembered that when a spirit first enters a host it does not necessarily rise to her head immediately but may lie dormant for any length of time, indicating its presence, if at all, by indirect signs, such as a mild illness that drags on, strange dreams, or attacks of illness after eating certain foods. If we consider when individuals first become aware that they are possessed, as opposed to when they first enter trance, we may reach a clearer understanding of the factors involved in possession. Three contexts of first awareness can be distinguished, each of them with a different combination of factors at work.

1. The patient has dreams that indicate to her that a spirit has entered and is demanding to be called up, that is, is demanding that the patient arrange with a curer to set up the conditions under which trance can be induced. There appear to be certain dreams or dream images that are recognized as indications of possession. For example, seeing a Westerner in a dream may indicate the presence of a *trumba* spirit, being chased by a donkey indicates a *patros*. Many individuals claim not to understand the significance of their dreams; should they find them troubling, they take them to a curer for diagnostic interpretation. If the dream images are those mentioned above, the curer is likely to diagnose possession, thus lending support to what may have been an original unconscious wish or decision on the part of the patient. However, I suspect that many such dreams occur only after an original suggestion on the part of the curer (see the following discussion) and thus represent attempts by the patient to come to terms with the diagnosis.

2. With no previous symptoms or warning, the patient suddenly dissociates and gives unmistakable physical indications of the presence of a spirit. These range from relatively uncontrollable movements and speech, which may be extremely frightening to the unprepared individual, to displays so coordinated as to indicate to a knowledgeable spectator the exact identity of the possessing spirit. In this situation, the first awareness of the spirit's presence, of the "latency" state, coincides with its actual manifestation. The trance may occur in a number of different contexts, for example:

   a. In the heady atmosphere of the private or public possession ceremonies of another host. The drumming and clapping, the observation of other spirits, the incense, and the support presented by the presence of curers and sympathetic participants all foster the transition.

   b. In an emotionally exciting atmosphere, such as the women's celebrations at a wedding or at a moment of crisis.

   c. Privately, at home, under no apparent immediate inducement.

In each of these three contexts, and presumably increasing in inverse proportion to the degree of immediate environmental stimulation, possession appears to be the expression of a hitherto unconscious desire on the part of the host. In the first context, it may be possible that the environmental stimuli are themselves sufficient to create the transition in susceptible individuals.

3. The original indication of latent possession may stem neither from an awareness on the part of the host nor from an action on her part that is publicly recognizable as manifest possession, but rather from diagnosis on the part of the specialist. Although the curer suggests and attempts to confirm, the patient herself may remain unconvinced; the process of acceptance may thus last for months or years until either the latent becomes manifest or the subject is dropped entirely. It is my impression that the majority of cases of possession by a first spirit originate in this way. This is not a matter than can be easily decided because it is possible that the curers are responding to very subtle cues indicating that the patients have already come to internal decisions of their own. In any case, the curers certainly take into consideration what I have above called the susceptibility of their patients and are usually the ones to bring forth and act on their decisions.

During my stay I witnessed several occasions at which possession was suggested by a curer. Sometimes the diagnosis was reached in the curer's own dreams. The subjects of these cases varied greatly from one another. One woman was deeply depressed over marital problems. Other individuals suffered severe or lingering illnesses or their children were continually ill. In several cases, the patients allowed the curers to incite their spirit to rise to no avail. The curer attempted to call the spirit (i.e., put the patient into trance) for a couple of nights in succession and then waited for a few weeks or months before trying again.

These are not cases of pretense or incapacity on the part of the curers. To take this view, which is certainly contrary to how the majority in Mayotte conceive of things, is to misunderstand the nature of the therapeutic process. The entry into trance, just as much as the subsequent behavior, must be learned, and this process takes more or less time in different individuals. In Mayotte, the length and difficulty of the learning period is publicly related to the recalcitrance of the particular possessing spirit, but in fact the curers are also well aware that it is a matter of individual capacity and habitude. Not only does the patient have to feel relatively comfortable with the idea of entering trance, she may also have to learn how to enter it.

Although, as remarked earlier, the curers may be responding to cues in the patient's behavior that indicate latent possession, it appears likely that in many cases they fit the diagnosis to the patient's external condition rather than to her internal one. Or perhaps the curer hypothesizes the internal condition on the basis of external factors, the patient's social position, immediate relationships, and so on. Thus, considerations of social control do become relevant. This is of crucial significance to the question of why particular individuals do or do not become possessed. In Mayotte, the germ of the process is frequently to be found not in the host's psyche but in the curer's perception of the situation. The reason why the majority of individuals remain unpossessed is that no authority ever suggested to them otherwise.

Possession and sex of host

If we can point to no immediate or precipitating causes of possession, we can speak about the presence or absence of constraints, discouragement or encouragement. The relevant factors must be social in origin and will help to explain the relative incidence of possession among different categories of individuals. In Mayotte, as in many other cultures with spirit possession, the majority of hosts are women (Lewis 1971). Although the precise figures should be accepted with some caution, more than one-third of the adult female population are possessed, as compared to about 10 percent of the males (Table 4.1). It is also interesting to note that despite this disparity, the ratio of women to men possessed by *trumba* spirits is very similar to the ratio for *patros* (Table 4.2).

Not only are more women than men possessed by spirits, but a higher proportion of nonpossessed women assist in the curing process and participate as spectators in the public ceremonies. Furthermore, the possessed women generally participate more frequently in spirit activities and over longer spans of time than the men. Relative involvement in possession can be roughly gauged according to the "stage" in the following scale at which the possessed individual remains. The scale is my own construction, and therefore artificial, but it does serve to clarify what is meant we talk about "possessed" individuals.

Table 4.1. *Possession and sex of host in Lombeni*

| | Hosts | |
	Women	Men
Only *patros* present	31	7
Only *trumba* present[a]	13	3
Both *patros* and *trumba* present[a]	15	1
Total with spirits present	59	11
Spirits possibly present[b]	4	2
Spirits absent	73	124
Incomplete information[c]	17	–
Total adult population[d]	153	137

Note: The figures in this and subsequent tables should be regarded as highly tentative and as representing the *least* possible number of people with spirits. They represent those individuals I actually observed as possessed or those I was informed about by reliable sources. This category includes individuals who were once observed in trance but who perhaps no longer participate in spirit activities. I was not able to systematically canvass individuals on their own histories of possession because all of them, including otherwise excellent informants, invariably denied being possessed themselves and were hesitant to report on others. The figures do, however, represent a greater number than the individuals who *regularly* go into possession or the individuals possessed at any single ceremony.
[a]The figures for the *trumba* spirits are probably even less accurate than those of the *patros* because I was able to observe only one public *trumba* ceremony in Lombeni itself and that was at a time when I was not yet able to identify most of the population by name.
[b]This figure includes both individuals diagnosed as possessed who had not yet entered trance and people whose claims to possession were regarded somewhat skeptically by the majority of the population. The latter category is made up of two women.
[c]I have not included any males in this category. Nevertheless, it should be noted that because men are possibly even more anxious than women to conceal an association with spirits and because men with spirits exhibit their possession far less frequently than do women, it is likely that a higher proportion of the males recorded as being without spirits were in fact once involved with them than is true among their female counterparts.
[d]"Adult" indicates all those individuals who are, or have ever been, married, plus one elderly male who never married (and who is not possessed). Because women tend to marry earlier than men, there are a greater number of young women than young men in the sample. Stratified by age, the proportion of women to men possessed would be even more striking. No unmarried men, indeed no men under thirty, are possessed, and only one unmarried girl, and she has reached the age of marriage. Unlike some societies (e.g., Bali), in Mayotte trance is restricted to adults.

Table 4.2. *Number of people possessed by trumba and by patros in Lombeni*

	Hosts		
	Women	Men	Total
Trumba	28	4	32
Patros	46	8	54

1. Possession is diagnosed but no spirit manifests itself.
2. Evident trancelike behavior with no follow up; single appearance of spirit.
3. Occasional appearances of spirit at public ceremonies, but no interest expressed in revealing identity or proceeding with cure; does not make the host ill.
4. Frequent appearances, anxious for a cure; host is periodically ill but either not strongly motivated or not able to hold ceremony.
5. Cure is held and the spirit never, or rarely, reappears thereafter.
6. Cure is held and the spirit continues to make frequent appearances.
7. Cure is held and the host subsequently becomes possessed by new spirits; cycle begins again.
8. Cure is held and the spirit subsequently assists the host in becoming active as a curer.

In Lombeni there are possessed women at each of these stages. However, among the men classed as having spirits, I have only observed three in actual states of trance and each of them was a curer (Stage 8). Three other males with spirits were over sixty years of age and, therefore, too old to participate. One of these had formerly been a curer; the other two apparently had enjoyed occasional appearances (Stage 6). Of the remainder, one had so far exhibited trancelike behavior on only a single occasion and in the privacy of his house (Stage 2). I learned of it the next morning from the curer he had secretly sent for in his fright. Another claimed to have passed on his spirit to his daughter, and the ceremony was held for her rather than for him.[5] Two others had reached Stage 5; their possessions were never referred to. The one male I did observe undergoing cure (not a resident of Lombeni and, therefore, not a part of the sample) appeared extremely withdrawn and embarrassed throughout the proceedings. He submitted to the medicine but refused, despite the coaxing of the curer (a woman), to dance in public. It is significant that there are no men at Stages 3, 4, or 7, and only two, both elderly, at Stage 6. That is, rather than remaining at stages where the spirits simply recur, men progress

toward a terminal point where the pattern can be broken and possession activities stopped.

The three male curers (Stage 8) are exceptions; they gain a certain
status and employment from their activity. They are both feared and
respected because of their knowledge and powers. Their occupation
makes them indispensable to the community because their practice has
a wider scope than that of the female curers. Male curers are more
mobile; they can combine indigenous herbal remedies with the recitation of sacred scripture and the writing of amulets, and, most important, they are strong (*mahery*) enough to cure sorcery, a task that they
are frequently called upon to complete.

Thus, although possession is rarely diagnosed in men to begin with,
once a man publicly exhibits signs of possession he progresses rapidly
to a stage at which he may terminate his activities or begin practice as
a curer. Should he prosper as a curer, he may continue to practice for
the rest of his life, although his activities will decline with age. Some
women also follow this pattern of rapid progression (e.g., Habiba Hussein, Chapter 6), but the majority progress more slowly. Some of them
do not even demand cures but are content to remain at Stage 3. Others
achieve their cures and are content to stay at Stage 6 or 7 rather than
dropping out (Stage 5) or becoming curers (Stage 8). Sometimes a new
spirit is acquired before the cure of the previous one is finished.

The roles of men in possession thus appear to be more narrowly
constrained than those of women, oriented to more immediate goals
and to goals that lie outside the possession experience itself. This
conclusion is supported by examining the conditions under which men
first realize their possession. Although my data on this subject are
weak, men appear less susceptible to the suggestions of the curers in
this regard than do women. Diagnosis only follows upon evident pos-
sessionlike behavior. In the one case I know in which the curer diagnosed possession prior to such behavior, he kept the information to
himself because he felt the patient was not ready to accept it. By
contrast, I have observed on numerous occasions curers attempting to
raise spirits in doubtful women.

If women are more frequently possessed than men, they also become
possessed in a wider number of contexts and with less direct aims in
mind. We may, therefore, speak of possession as more *generalized*
among women than among men.

Sex role and cultural constraints

Why are more women possessed than men? Lewis (1971) has recently
attempted to provide a functional, cross-culturally valid explanation

for the attraction that possession holds for women. According to Lewis, in societies in which the "possession cults" are "peripheral" to the central morality system,[6] participants too will be drawn from the ranks of the peripheral, that is, from among the members of the oppressed and marginal classes. Participation in possession activities serves to counter feelings and experiences of deprivation. Because in most, if not all, societies women are deprived relative to men, women are more frequently possessed.

This is a powerful argument as far as it goes. However, it is questionable whether possession should be treated as an epiphenomenon. Rather than viewing relative deprivation as a prime mover and explanation of women's possession, that is, possession as a "counterculture," I argue that it has to be situated within the wider system of meaning, at least initially. Symbolic attributes assigned men and women contribute to their constructions of the self and suggest appropriate roles for them in all areas of social life. That women become possessed is complementary to the fact that most men do not. An explanation of women's possession must consider its absence among men. If trance has positive features, as Lewis suggests, why shouldn't everyone, men and women alike, become possessed?

The point is that behavior and structure have to be kept analytically separate. Lewis tends to see possession in terms of calculations of individual advantage. This suggests that the structure of possession is merely an explanatory or rationalizing device developed to interpret trance behavior, which is what is really at issue in this kind of theory. I regard the structure of possession as relatively autonomous. We have seen how the structure constrains behavior at the psychological level, and we can examine constraints at the social level as well. And yet, it should be kept in mind that although the structure constrains behavior, it does not determine it. Behavior has its own roots. Not everyone behaves according to the ideal models, and the models themselves leave room for a range of behavior. Individual hosts can use possession to their own advantage, as Lewis points out and as we will see in subsequent chapters. But this says nothing about the nature of possession or about its appropriateness in women or men.

The discussion in the literature of "rituals of rebellion" is relevant here. Rigby's analysis (1968) of Gogo purification rituals demonstrated that sexual role reversal has to be explained in terms of its place in the overall symbolic structure. Its function for the society (Gluckman 1954) or for the individual (Lewis 1971) is secondary to the coherence of the symbolic structure. However, in contrast to the situation analyzed among the Gogo, performance in the role-reversal rituals in Mayotte is neither prescribed to women nor prohibited to men. Furthermore, the scheduling of such performances is not determined by specific outside events of high collective significance (such as cattle disease or the birth of twins among the Gogo), but, within certain calendrical constraints, is a matter of personal convenience and calculation. Performance of possession is thus not as constrained by the symbolic system in Mayotte as the rituals of reversal are in certain other societies. In Lévi-Strauss's terms (1963), we may say that performance of possession has strong elements of a "statistical" as well as a "mechanical" nature.

Nevertheless, although it does not determine participation by women, the symbolic structure of possession in Mayotte does favor it. The transsexualism is significant less for what it says about male/female relationships per se than in its support for the basic thesis of the whole business: that the host and the spirit are two separate individuals. The authenticity of a particular incarnation and the disparity between the human and spirit worlds in general are heightened by contrasting the sexual identity of host and spirit. The event becomes more theatrical, more piquant; reversal claims the attention of observers and clarifies the action.

Because men are the main actors in public life the majority of characters required are male. Male roles are performed to best effect when the actors, the hosts, are female. For example, a central theme of possession concerns notions of power and responsibility. These are explicit aspects of male performance in everyday life. When the roles are played by *women*, the particular abstract qualities portrayed – power, energy, authority, and so on – can be more readily grasped by onlookers. The anomalous element – the female individual visible behind the role, the wife and mother whom everyone recognizes – serves to separate features that are usually automatically associated and thus provokes an analytic and thoughtful attitude on the part of the observer. What was once an indissoluble behavioral whole is shown to be an arbitrary association of disparate conceptual elements. Were men to play these parts, the process of abstraction and reflection could not be carried so far (cf. Turner 1967:103–6).

I am arguing here that the considerations of the drama suggest and support participation by women. Yet this aesthetic argument clearly cannot fully account for the high proportion of female participants. It must be acknowledged that the choice of a play to be produced is constrained not only by its appropriateness and aesthetic qualities but also by the availability of suitable actors. Recognizing this interdependency, we must ask what the cultural factors are that constrain the participation of men.

In brief, possession behavior is viewed as contrary and detrimental to a man's self and public image. This perspective stems from particular conceptions of maleness and the male role in society and in Islam. Possession, with its ambiguity and apparent loss of physical and moral control, threatens the image of men as self-controlled and as upholding public morality. Possession among men is perhaps too dangerous for society and for the host's ego.[7] Women do not participate in this image. For example, a myth recounted among some of the men (but ignored by the majority of women) accounts for the male prerogative in leading prayers:

> Long ago, Biby Fatimah complained to her father the Prophet that there were no women Imams (prayer leaders). Why couldn't a woman be an Imam? The Prophet determined to show her why. He told her to go to the men and tell them that if they killed their wives they would go straight to heaven. She did so, and the men were tempted. But as each man looked at his wife he couldn't bring himself to do the deed. The Prophet then told Biby Fatimah to take the same proposition to the wives. The wives proceeded to kill their husbands, and the Prophet turned to his daughter and said, "You see, women have no faith.[8] Therefore, I will not make them Imams."

Ideally, men deliberate slowly and cautiously over political, judicial, and administrative matters and are reluctant to legislate the behavior of their fellows. Impetuosity, disorderly conduct, irresponsibility, and the expression of self-interest in public life are scorned. Yet, it is recognized and accepted that in their private affairs men do operate on the basis of self-interest. A wise man is thus one who is circumspect about private matters and deliberate about public ones. Men should also be *tsantsaŋa* 'forthright,' 'alert,' and 'active.' Possession, especially in its early stages, runs counter to all these qualities. Spirits appear undignified, often frantic, sullen, selfish, and all too willing to expose their inner desires. Irresponsible, they are unconcerned with public or family welfare. And although most spirits are male, structurally they take on roles that have certain strong similarities to those of women. Just as wives demand and expect gifts, so too do spirits. It is a man's responsibility to earn a living in order to support his wife and children. The kerosene to light the lamp, the salt needed for cooking, all household items are felt to be the demands of women; yet they must be provided by men. Men are producers, women and children consumers. When a man becomes possessed, he too becomes a consumer, another demanding mouth to feed. He, therefore, takes on an unmanly relationship with the person who is supporting the spirit (unless, in return, he turns his possession into a source of income by operating as a curer).

A major factor constraining the participation of men in possession activity is their adherence to Islam, which views possession with dis-

A man dressed for the mosque.

dain. The maintenance of male status and the achievements of public position depend on the observance of Islam. Indulgence in possession activity weakens a man's claims to precedence relative to other men. Thus, in addition to viewing participation in possession activities by women as a product of deprivation or ill feeling resulting from exclusion from Islam, we may consider the absence of possession among men as a deprivation resulting from their inclusion in Islam.

Although this view is ostensibly quite similar to that of Lewis, its implications are very different. Spirit possession is not abnormal behavior or a "counter-culture" resorted to by women in desperation but an integral part of the whole culture, access to which is restricted for men to the degree that their status is dependent upon participation in Islam.[9] The view that Islam and possession are conflicting systems is a male perspective. In Mayotte participation in possession activities by women is not so much an expression of opposition toward Islam as freedom from it.

Relative status among women

The deprivation and "compensation/retaliation" arguments are further weakened by the evidence furnished by female possession itself. First of all, because the spirits themselves form a status hierarchy (Chapter 10), it cannot be the case that all women become possessed simply to get "on top." Among the possessed, some play senior spirits and some play junior ones. A woman with a spirit of each class may alternate between them. Possession is thus not a matter of outright competition among women (Wilson 1967) but a context in which to express the status quo and alternatives to it and to document changes and growth in the life of the host. Generally speaking, the greater the seniority of the host in daily life, the greater the seniority of her most important spirit. This is not, however, to argue that possession is to be explained as a mere reflection of the social structure.

It may not be too farfetched to compare possession behavior among women in this regard to male behavior at the mosque. The Friday-noon mosque service is an important community affair. Men begin to arrive shortly after the first call to prayer at around 11 A.M., and the mosque gradually fills up until the arrival of the *hutuba* 'preacher' (Arabic *khuṭba*) at 12:30 signifies the beginning of the service. During this interval the members of the congregation have ample time to displace themselves within the room. The space in the mosque becomes more sacred and, therefore, more desirable for prayer as one approaches the end facing toward Mecca (*ḳibla*), which the congregation faces in prayer. If there are present only as many worshippers as the width of the room permits to stand abreast, then a single line will be formed as close to the front as possible. On Fridays, the size of the crowd necessitates several rows, each row located at successively less sanctified distances. An individual's choice of row is based not upon a rule of first come first served, nor upon any other single objective criterion, but according to how far forward, relative to the other worshippers present, he feels comfortable in resting. Criteria of residence, citizenship, age, worldly success, and degree of scholarly learning are all taken into account. During the period in which I made my observations, the same group of appointed and self-styled community leaders sat in the front row week after week and the same group of youths, of men who had only recently married into the village, and of those who couldn't afford proper dress for the mosque in the back. Particularly modest but deserving individuals were urged forward, whereas those who wished to be considered modest made a show of relinquishing their places to men of greater stature who had remained behind. Over the course of the year, many of the regular participants attempted to move their positions gradually forward.

The point is that there are no hard and fast rules by which relative status is measured and displayed in public. The process is one of delicate juggling, designed to appear on the surface quite spontaneous and uncalculated and played out in an arena in which, officially, all men are judged equals. Now, just as a man is fitted with a place in the mosque, so is a woman matched with a spirit of particular stature. The element of choice may be less conscious on the part of the woman, but the process and results are approximately the same: Individuals acquire the seats or spirits that are as important relative to others as they wish, or feel they may dare, publicly to aspire to. Choice of seat or spirit is intended as a "model for" social position as much as being a "model of" (Geertz 1966b).

There are also, of course, differences between these domains. A man moves forward gradually and sheds his past as he does so. But spirits are discrete entities, and so a woman advances in evident spurts, possibly accumulating a stable of spirits. Furthermore, whereas the woman may claim modesty, her spirits will advertise their position to all who care to listen. And whereas a man wears his status heavily, a woman does so more lightly, alternating among her several spirits with an agility both unseemly and unseen in the mosque. Men who reach the front of the mosque tend to stay there; women who acquire senior spirits will temporarily abandon them for the pleasures of the young and lowly whenever they feel inclined. Possession, then, is a domain in which women can express concerns of relative status and the conflicting ideals of getting ahead and giving others their due consideration.

The problem can be further investigated by comparing the rates of possession among women of various categories. According to Lewis's hypothesis, possession should be higher among women faced with polygyny or barrenness, both of which are viewed as unfortunate conditions by Mayotte women. If all women are deprived relative to men, polygynous and barren wives are in greater competition for the appreciation of their menfolk and may feel inadequate compared to other women. Yet the data show the proportion of possessed women in these

Table 4.3. *Possession among co-wives and barren women*

	Spirits	No spirits	Spirit developing
Co-wife	7	10	1
Barren	4	8	—
Total female population	59	73	2

Table 4.4. *Possession among pairs of mothers and daughters*

	Mother possessed	Mother not possessed	Incomplete information
Daughter possessed	19	1	6
Adult daughter not possessed	17	13	9

categories to be no higher than among the female population at large (Table 4.3).[10]

Although there is no correlation between these forms of "deprivation" and possession, it is the case that three of the four barren women with spirits are curers or are possessed by spirits of high status who wish to become curers. It thus appears that possession may be a strategy employed by women in particular positions, but it is by no means a necessary one. Our conclusion here must be identical to that reached earlier in this chapter under "Possession and sex of host": Possession among women is highly general. We cannot define possession in terms of particular social attributes or motives of the hosts.

Who is possessed?

Whether or not possession is linked to conditions women find unhappy, why are some women not possessed, and how can we predict who will become possessed? There is evidence that susceptibility to possession is greater among women who have had a correspondingly greater association with possession behavior in others. Table 4.4 compares the incidence of possession in mothers and daughters for all cases in Lombeni in which both mother and daughter are still living. In nineteen out of twenty cases in which the daughter is possessed, so is

Table 4.5. *Possession among pairs of sisters*

	Older sister possessed	Older sister not possessed	Incomplete information
Younger sister possessed	17	4	4
Younger sister not possessed	10	17	9

the mother.[11] In the single remaining case, the girl's father is possessed and his older brother, who died leaving no direct descendants, had been a spirit curer of some renown.

The pattern among pairs of adult sisters (Table 4.5) also supports the general hypothesis.

The little information that is available concerning the families of possessed males does not suggest a similar pattern. In the one case where the mother was still alive, she was not possessed. In the six cases where I have information on the possessed individual's sister or sisters, two sets are possessed, two unpossessed, and two contain both sisters who are and who are not possessed. Along with the fact that men generally tend to become possessed later in life than women,[12] this suggests that participation in possession activity by men is less a product of their general background than is participation by women. Men tend to become possessed during or because of crises or in order to establish themselves in a career. The possession histories of some women follow similar patterns, but in general women's possession appears to be a part of their life cycle (or, perhaps, of the cycle of the nuclear family household) because it takes place soon after marriage.

Just as defenses against possession are acquired by growing up male in Mayotte, so susceptibility is acquired in the process of growing up female in a domestic environment in which possession among other members of the family is not uncommon. In part, surely, the expectation of possession is self-fulfilling. People create the world according to the image they have of it. The experience of one generation is repeated in the next. In terms of the components of sociopsychological susceptibility listed earlier, this might account for a relatively shallow concern with the propriety of possession and a relatively complete internalization of the model for trance behavior. However, the process of growing up female, including the regular observation of trance, may also have a more direct impact on susceptibility.

An important aspect of possession is the hypnoticlike state of the host (Walker 1972:26–51). Induction is brought about by the curer, by the context, or eventually, perhaps, by the host herself. Despite much effort, researchers have not had much success in correlating suscepti- bility to hypnosis with personality traits (Hilgard 1967). Nevertheless, by taking a communicational approach, that is, by focusing on the relationship between hypnotist and subject, rather than simply on qualities particular to the subject herself, some light may be shed on the question of relative susceptibility. Haley (1963) has argued that the hypnotist imposes paradoxical (incongruous or contradictory) demands upon the subject.[13] The subject can continue to cooperate with the hypnotist and follow his commands, but only by claiming that it is not she herself who is carrying out the behavior. However, to do so (i.e., to enter a hypnotic trance) is to accept the interpersonal implications generated by such action, namely, to leave all control of the continuing definition of the relationship up to the hypnotist. Haley hypothesizes that such a response to paradox may have been learned in past rela- tionships, particularly those within the family (1963:39).

Although I do not have detailed evidence to support this contention, it is my impression that in Mayotte girls are more exposed to paradoxi- cal commands than are boys and are more accustomed to dealing with them in a manner that predisposes them toward a hypnotic response. Young girls, from about the ages of five to twelve, are frequently the workhorses of the Mayotte household. Burdened with heavy de facto responsibilities in cooking and child care, they are nevertheless not judged to be fully responsible. An anxious housewife will often shout orders to her daughter from the sidelines, berating her impatiently and treating her now like a servant, now as a young child. Older sisters and other relatives may do likewise, and at times the specific commands as well as the definitions of the relationships they presuppose may appear contradictory. Sleeping in her mother's house, a young girl cannot easily make her escape. Nor is she frequently given the opportunity to reply with requests for clarification or assertions of her own. Her only recourse at times may well be to avoid trying to define the relationship at all.

Boys of this age, by contrast, lead somewhat easier lives. They begin to build and inhabit their own small houses and they eat the evening meal at different households on different evenings. Thus they do not come into as frequent contact with their parents as do girls and are not as dependent upon a single set of relationships. The moments when they are directly subjected to the authority of their elders may be more sharply defined than are those of girls and the consequences of disobe- dience less ambiguous. Thus it may be the case that boys are less frequently faced with paradoxical commands or situations than are their sisters, and that when they are so faced they may more readily escape from the situation. They have less opportunity to learn to respond to paradox by "blanking out" or by role playing than girls do, and they are, therefore, not as prepared to enter trance.[14]

One possible source of paradox is the experience of a parent in a state of possession. Being faced with someone who is at once mother and not mother must create confusion in a child.[15] One means of handling the problem of relating to people in trance may well be to approach the trance state oneself. In this way, the children of possessed individuals have not only a role model and a greater acquaintance with the model for trance behavior but also a significant head start in learning to enter trance. They are readier to accept both the diagnosis of possession and entry in trance.

Our findings may be summarized as follows. Affliction is an idiom of personal transformation, not necessarily a prime mover.[16] Possession is much more common among women than men and less restricted among women to specific social positions, occasions, symptoms, or motives. A number of cultural factors have to be taken into consideration to account for this situation. Whereas considerations of status constrain participation by men, aesthetic factors suggest the suitability of possession for women. Women may be "preselected" for trance by their particular experiences in growing up and by the position of females in the society as a whole, but these factors do not prove determinative. Possession is not restricted to the performance of specific functions and cannot be explained simply in terms of its functions.

Possession is an autonomous, culturally constituted system. It is not the product of a few deviant individuals, nor necessarily the symptom of a deeply divided society. Virtually every member of Mayotte society comes into contact regularly with spirits, either by direct possession or by interaction with the spirits when they possess friends, neighbors, curers, or kin. The relationships formed by an individual in trance have a social reality; they mesh with the ties of kinship, alliance, and locality to form a single whole. From this perspective, men also participate in possession, but simply in different roles from the women. Possession is thus a basic aspect of the social structure, not a by-product of it. It is to the social nature of possession that we turn in the next chapter.

5. Possession as a system of communication

Although possession is a collective phenomenon, it entails changes of state in particular individuals. A dialectic operates between the culture and the individual. Trance presupposes a meaningful structure. At the same time, this structure is reproduced through the particular trance states and therapeutic histories of individuals; the structure is not merely acted out on a stage but *lived* out in trance. In order to approach the social basis of possession, it is helpful to view it as a system of communication. By this I mean simply that possession operates to transmit messages (verbal, material, etc.) between senders and receivers along particular channels. Senders and receivers can be individual or collective, and thus possession is creative and expressive at both levels. Here we will pursue the system of communication at the interpersonal level. I first describe the basic system and then demonstrate some of the ways it functions in interpersonal relationships. My examples involve three sorts of relationships: between spirits and their hosts' curers, spirits and their hosts' spouses, and spirits and their hosts' patients.

The communication triad

The notion of possession as communication is not original. Balandier remarked some time ago that "sacred possession, . . . tool of so-called archaic societies, undoubtedly characterizes a certain era of intellectual communication" (1966:50). More recently, Baré (1973a) has examined the role of *trumba* mediums in factional conflicts of the Sakalava monarchy in this light. However, whereas most students of trance and possession phenomena have concentrated their efforts on the well-defined contexts of public ceremonies or curing rituals, possession sequences can also appear in the course of domestic life. It was during encounters such as the following that my own conception of possession as communication emerged.

70

Lombeni, January 27

I visited Mohedja this morning, only to find her in intimate conversation with her adult daughter Nuriaty. Mohedja seemed very reserved, and I soon realized that she was possessed, and verified that I was speaking to her *patros*, Mze Bunu. Nuriaty was asking the spirit for advice about her baby, whom she found too thin. Mze Bunu told Nuriaty to bring over the baby, and then held it up, felt it carefully, and announced it was suffering from worms. The spirit told Nuriaty to feed the baby (Western) worm medicine. Nuriaty departed, and I expected that Mohedja would come out of trance. But Mze Bunu announced that it felt like staying awhile. The spirit said that Nuriaty had not specially called it up for a consultation; rather, it had risen of its own accord to warn the family that illness was approaching and to tell them to hold a *shidjabu* 'Islamic blessing ritual' in order to ward off the worst effects. Mze Bunu spoke to Nuriaty because Tumbu had already left for the fields. The spirit instructed Nuriaty to pass the message on to her father.

Mze Bunu added that it had been rising for years to warn the people in Mohedja's *mraba* 'extended family' of impending events. The spirit supposed that there were no other spirits in either Lombeni Kely or Lombeni Be who so consistently performed this service for the people of the host's *mraba*. Although all spirits can see into the future and know God's plans, most refrain from helping people out.

Mze Bunu stressed that it was particularly good friends with Tumbu. Tumbu had given the spirit many gifts over the years, and, in return, the spirit liked to help him out whenever it could. Mze Bunu said it also got along with Mze Jabiry, Tumbu's own *patros* spirit, but less well. Mze Jabiry was too quick to anger and repeatedly made Tumbu sick.

Mze Bunu went on to talk about Mohedja. It said that Mohedja often did not listen to the advice it tried to give her directly (i.e., through her dreams). Therefore, the spirit frequently chose to communicate with her through third parties. Mohedja always complained that she didn't like being possessed by spirits and that they were bad things to have, yet Mze Bunu had never once caused her any trouble since the original illness when it first entered her (some twenty years ago). Mze Bunu added that Mohedja was a very knowledgeable spirit curer in her own right but did not like to practice. When Kasimu Juma (another host to Mze Bunu, a well-known spirit curer, and the person in charge of Mohedja's own cure) was still alive, he wanted to make Mohedja his apprentice. He took her to observe his cases and taught her a lot. In fact, Mohedja knew a great deal, and in earlier years Mze Bunu used to extract sorcery packets (Chapter 3) when it rose in Mohedja. Later Tumbu went to Kasimu Juma on his own initiative and began to learn from him, but Mohedja still knew more than Tumbu and was able to advise him occasionally. Mohedja would perform cures when clients came to her in Lombeni, but she was embarrassed to practice outside the village.

Mze Bunu rose and went to fetch a bottle of cologne from which it began to take swigs. It tried to tempt a couple of Mohedja's small grandchildren who were playing in a corner of the room to try some, but they refused. Turning its attention back to me, the spirit asked if I would pass on a message to Mohedja. It said that Mohedja wouldn't listen if it told her directly, and it didn't want to communicate through the usual channel, namely Tumbu, because what it had to say would undoubtedly make him angry and would lead to fighting. Mze Bunu asked me to tell Mohedja not to be so fearless and sure of herself. Somewhat taken aback at the message, I asked the spirit what it meant and pressed for an example. The spirit replied that two days earlier, when most of the villagers had been attending a major political meeting in a nearby settlement, Mohedja had gone alone to the fields and had been accosted there by a man who wanted to sleep with her. Mohedja turned him down flatly and was prepared to fight him off. Mze Bunu said to tell Mohedja not to be so sure of her strength, that she was no longer as young as she had been. The spirit said Mohedja should have turned down the man in an indirect manner, thus saving him embarrassment and minimizing the possibility of his anger. She should have said something like, "I'm not feeling well, perhaps another day." But instead, Mohedja took pleasure in annoying such men and refusing them outright. Mze Bunu concluded with the warning that if Tumbu heard about the incident he would press Mohedja for the identity of the interloper and would begin to fight with him, which would be a bad thing.

After a little more chitchat while I pondered the story, Mze Bunu finally left, saying it was afraid that if it stayed, it would polish off the entire bottle of cologne. The spirit suggested in parting that perhaps I would soon be giving it a gift of another bottle.

A few moments later, Mohedja regained consciousness, and I passed on Mze Bunu's message. Mohedja appeared surprised, but listened with grave interest. When I had finished, she recounted the original incident in the fields to me in great detail, telling me how bluntly she had refused the man, how insistent he was, although he did back off in the end, and how frightened she had been. She then went on to tell me about a few other times in her life when she had been in similar situations. Altogether, she talked for well over an hour. Mohedja was usually quite laconic and must have been feeling a strong urge to talk over the matter with someone. Although she did not say outright that Mze Bunu's advice was correct, she did concede that she was not as physically capable of defending herself as she once had been. She seemed, as indeed the message from her spirit would imply, to be in some uncertainty over how to handle such unpleasant situations.

Discussion. Let us start by laying out the act of communication that occurs in the latter portion of the text. This can be stated briefly as follows: *A* (the spirit, Mze Bunu) wishes to send a message to *B* (the host, Mohedja). Instead of doing so directly, *A* passes the message to *C* (in this case, the anthropologist) who in turn passes it on to *B*. Thus, instead of *A→B*, we have *A→C→B*. What is remarkable about this from the point of view of a Westerner is that *A* and *B* are actually the same "person." Thus, the process we observe is actually one of "autocommunication," and the transmission by way of *C* seems entirely unnecessary. But in the Mayotte view, of course, *A* and *B* are separate individuals. In such a case, transmission via *C* appears reasonable, even if not, at first sight, most efficient. Mze Bunu, moreover, asserts that indirect communication *is* more efficient, because Mohedja is not likely to listen (i.e., to receive the message) if approached directly. What I wish to suggest is that the triad is the irreducible minimal structure of possession. That is to say, communication entails a minimum of three figures – sender, receiver, and intermediary or, in other terms, the host (the subject out of trance), the spirit (the subject in trance), and the person or persons with whom the spirit converses.

One of the criteria used by Western scientists to define the trance state (Prince 1968), which is also an established convention regarding possession in Mayotte, is that an individual has no, or very little, recollection of what transpires during trance. If a host is to know what happened while she was in trance, she must have a trustworthy intermediary present who can report back. People recognize that the actual degree of recall varies according to a number of factors, but the norm is considered to be no recall. This rule, that the states of trance and of ordinary consciousness are discontinuous in a single individual, is the major condition of the system of communication. It is this fact that makes possession a social activity.

It is true that the spirit can communicate directly with the host in dreams and that the host can communicate with the spirit by speaking over lighted incense. However, these pathways do not generate or underlie the possession complex. It is perfectly conceivable that there exist cultures in which tutelary spirits are addressed and received through such channels without anything like the Mayotte possession complex being present as well. Possession in Mayotte presupposes the minimal triad. A spirit that rises in a host always does so in order to make its presence known to a third party, that is, in order to speak *to* someone. Most frequently, spirits are called up by intermediaries to begin with, but even when no intermediaries are present (as is sometimes the case in "autohypnosis"), as soon as a spirit rises, it rushes off to talk to someone.[1]

The questions that a psychologist might wish to ask of this material would include: What is the nature of the relationship between *A* (spirit) and *B* (host), and what are the consequences for that relationship of the fact that messages between *A* and *B* are passed through a third party (*C*)? The sociological question concerns the consequence for relationship *B———C*. An anthropological approach, however,

must also examine relationship A————C and must consider as a whole
the structure

As well as sustaining an exchange relationship with an outside intermediary, another important aspect of the communication triad is that it
maintains the separation between host and spirit. Were host and spirit
to communicate regularly between each other directly, their distinc-
tiveness would be broken down. In passing its messages to a third
party, the spirit attempts to shield the host from being implicated as an
accessory to the generation of the spirit's messages. To the degree that
such separation between host and spirit is maintained, the spirit can
say and do things that would be impossible or unthinkable for the host
(and also say things *to* the host), such as to make unilateral demands
or to publicly challenge or scorn the host's spouse, relatives, or curer.
Such freedom of expression is further enhanced by the fact that host
and spirit are frequently of opposite sex from one another. A male
spirit in a female host, by far the most frequent combination, speaks
with the authority and prerogatives of a male in contexts in which it
might be inappropriate for women to speak or act and in which their
male listeners might otherwise lose face.

Possession thus allows for the coexistence of mutually incompatible
ideologies, for example, concerning the status of women, without
thereby overtly violating either one.[2] A good example of this sort of
incompatibility is provided in our text by the statement of Mze Bunu to
the effect that although Mohedja is a very competent curer, she does not
like to practice her art. It would seem that Tumbu constrains his wife's
activities, whereas Mze Bunu wishes she would be more active. The
disagreement expressed by Mze Bunu indicates that these tensions are
psychic as well as social, but it also suggests that Mohedja may be
working toward their resolution through the activities and speech of her
spirit and through the development of its male-to-male relationship with
Tumbu. In this context, it is not only a third party who mediates between Mohedja and her spirit, but Mohedja's spirit who mediates between her and her husband.

These points will become clearer with further examples. For the
moment, it should be apparent that, although virtually anyone can
take, or can be asked to accept, the role of C (as I did in the account
above), the most important intermediaries are the host's curer (and
frequently the curer's own spirit) and spouse or close relations. These
individuals generally enter into long-term exchange relationships with
the host and spirit during the curing process.

An example: Mwanesha's marital therapy

The relationships among the host's spirit, curer, and spouse are sometimes characterized by such an intensity, intimacy, and lack of inhibi-
tion during the first séances that one is reminded of Western family or
marital therapy. The following account illustrates how the communication system can be used pragmatically to suit particular problems.

The case to be described involves Mwanesha, classificatory older
sibling of Mohedja, aged about thirty-five and married to a Lombeni
man we will call Dauda. The couple lived across the island in Mwanesha's village but were spending a month in Lombeni for a family wedding. They had a single child, a son of about sixteen, who resided in
Lombeni with Dauda's mother. Mwanesha first married Dauda when
she was still an adolescent. The couple divorced and later remarried
each other after an interval of three years. Mwanesha had been suffering for many years from abnormally painful menstrual periods, with
lengthy and heavy bleeding. She had tried all sorts of cures and curers,
including Western doctors, but none were able to assist her. When her
period started during her stay in Lombeni, she decided to seek treatment from Tumbu and Mohedja. These two approached the case carefully, checking with an astrologer and administering diagnostic tests of
their own. They soon concluded that in addition to her physical problem, Mwanesha was suffering both from sorcery perpetrated by the
man she had been married to during the period between her marriages
to Dauda and from a *patros* spirit that wished to rise.

Mohedja and Tumbu tried a variety of treatments on their patient.
Here we need only be concerned with their attempts to call up the
patros spirit. These occurred as follows:

October 21

> The night after Habiba's *ishima* (Chapter 7), during which a fair
> amount of attention was paid to Mwanesha and her spirit was urged
> to rise to no avail, several people gathered in Mohedja's house in
> order to initiate communication with the spirit. Mwanesha, Mohedja,
> Tumbu, Mwanesha's mother-in-law, two other female neighbors with
> spirits, and I were present. Mwanesha's husband and son remained in
> the courtyard. Mohedja placed the lighted incense between herself
> and Mwanesha and began talking. In a low voice, she addressed the
> spirit, asking it to please come so that they could get to know one
> another and see what the matter was. She kept up a soft, repetitive,
> reassuring flow of words. After awhile, Tumbu took over. He talked
> on and on, never raising his voice, soft, smooth, convincing, and
> encouraging. The women sang and clapped. Finally Mwanesha

uttered loud, exaggerated crying noises and put her cloth up to her face. This was a sign that her spirit had risen. Mwanesha's husband and son were called in. The son entered and half reclined on the mat, putting his head on the spirit's knees and crying a little.

The women continued to sing and clap. Soon Mohedja entered trance and was replaced by Mze Bunu. Mze Bunu lifted Mwanesha's spirit onto the bed, stroking and hugging it and urging it to speak up and tell them what was wrong. Mwanesha's spirit kept its face hidden in its cloth. Mze Bunu called out for Dauda and, when he finally arrived, reprimanded him sharply for being absent. Mze Bunu seated Dauda at the feet of Mwanesha's spirit and then proceeded to tell the latter that everyone present was a friend, that we had all gathered to help. Mwanesha's spirit finally spoke, saying, "There's nothing the matter" (*tsisy kabar*). "Nothing the matter?" scoffed Mze Bunu. "Mwanesha is sick all the time and you claim nothing's the matter!" Everyone continued to urge the spirit to talk. Mze Bunu suggested that maybe the new spirit didn't like it and wanted it to go away. Mwanesha's spirit quickly denied this, affirming that Mohedja was its curer. The company kept badgering the spirit to speak. Finally the spirit requested more medicine and asked Dauda to buy a bottle of cologne to hang above the bed in which Mwanesha slept. It asked to be called up again before Mwanesha and Dauda left Lombeni and said it would have more to tell them at that time. The spirit then left, and Mwanesha lay back on the bed. Her husband and son, who had been sitting all the while silently, with their heads in their hands, exited together with the other women.

November 16

Mwanesha and Dauda came to call up Mohedja's *patros* spirit. Mohedja told me later that there was no need for this at all, that they should simply have called upon Mwanesha's *patros*, but she silently agreed to do what they asked. When Mze Bunu arrived, it was very angry. Dauda had been drinking and smelled of palm wine. The spirit told them it could not work under such conditions and they should come back the next day in order to call up Mwanesha's spirit. They wanted to be off for home, but the spirit ordered them to stay in Lombeni for another three or four days.

November 17

Mwanesha and Duada returned to Mohedja's this evening. Tumbu explained to me that Mwanesha was still unwell and he attributed it to the fact the Dauda had not done what he was told; he had not bought a bottle of cologne to put over his wife's bed. He claimed he had no money, and yet he seemed to find enough to buy palm wine.

Mohedja and Mwanesha sat down on the mat, and Tumbu, Dauda, and I remained nearby. Mohedja and Tumbu addressed Mwanesha's spirit over the incense. Finally it was Mohedja who entered trance. Mze Bunu then began coaxing in earnest, going over to Mwanesha and rubbing her back and shoulders and whispering for the spirit to rise. Mwanesha gave some dry sobs, indicating the onset of trance. The new spirit moved to the chair. Mze Bunu rose to the bed and ordered the other spirit to speak. Mwanesha's spirit complained that Dauda hadn't bought the cologne as promised. They turned to Dauda. He admitted it was true, explaining that he had no money in Lombeni. As soon as they reached their own village he would harvest and sell some of his cash crop and buy the cologne.

Mze Bunu asked if there were any further problems. The other spirit replied that when Mwanesha and Dauda were out in the fields, it wished they would wash their hands before preparing and eating food; furthermore, when they came home, they should wash before going to bed. "You mean you really don't wash before you go to bed!" exclaimed Mze Bunu incredulously. It turned to Dauda and asked him severely if he was listening. Mwanesha's spirit added that another thing it didn't appreciate was Dauda's drinking. "What about it?" Mze Bunu asked Dauda. Dauda looked abashed momentarily, but then said no, that frankly he was not prepared to stop drinking. His whole body ached after a day in the fields, and drinking stopped the pain. Palm wine was *his* medicine, and he requested his wife's spirit to leave him alone on this score. He said he would continue to drink "not too much, but enough." His wife's spirit did not respond to these remarks, and Mze Bunu asked if there was anything else. For a few moments there was silence, then Dauda spoke again. He said he was embarrassed when his wife shouted at him in public, for example, when he let the supply of firewood run out. He wanted her to speak to him in normal tones, to treat him not like a child, but as her husband. Both Tumbu and Mze Bunu agreed this was bad, especially to shame him where others could hear. They suspected that this was a matter he should take up with his wife rather than with her spirit, but Mze Bunu reprimanded Mwanesha's spirit anyway. Dauda then excused himself. Mwanesha came out of trance, and Mze Bunu, assisted by Tumbu, repeated to her the gist of the conversation, with the exception of the part about Dauda's drinking. She did not look very penitent at the mention of Dauda's complaint about her nagging.

Throughout the whole proceedings, Mze Bunu's tone was firm, self-assured, and forthright in exclaiming over what it found distasteful – quite unlike Mohedja's normal reserved demeanor. Mze Bunu was completely in control, comforting and concerned yet at the same time removed and disinterested; in sum, the spirit acted the part of an excellent therapist. Dauda, by contrast, sat in a corner with his head down, and Mwanesha's spirit, too, sat looking away from everyone, especially from Dauda. On both days I was not sure that Mwanesha ever really lost consciousness. She never exhibited any extreme loss of control, and she seemed embarrassed throughout the proceedings. However, Tumbu assured me that Mwanesha had been in trance on both occasions. He explained that when a spirit first starts to rise in someone, it does not always fill the body completely. In Mwanesha's case, her memory still came and went; she was often conscious but could not stop the spirit from speaking out. Tumbu said the spirit would enter more solidly later on, and Mwanesha would then no longer be embarrassed. Tumbu also predicted there would be more fighting between Mwanesha's spirit and her husband, Dauda. He noticed, as I did, that her spirit never responded to Dauda's request to continue drinking. Tumbu said Dauda's drinking habits were undoubtedly of concern to both his wife and her spirit.

Discussion. This case nicely illustrates some of the points made earlier. Mwanesha is replaced by her spirit in order that the latter may begin communicating with her curers and her husband, son, and mother-in-law. Mwanesha's kin demonstrate their concern for her welfare by their presence and their willingness to communicate with the spirit. In his grief over his mother's illness, Mwanesha's son even begins to cry. The spirit is urged repeatedly to say what is on its mind, and when it does so, its first major remark is to request a gift from Mwanesha's husband. This gift, which, significantly enough, is not given as promised, indicates the beginning of a (problematic) exchange relationship between Mwanesha's spirit and spouse, a relationship that may last the rest of their lives. The husband, Dauda, appears quite ambivalent about the whole business and is kept in line by the curer, in this case Mohedja's senior male *patros* spirit, Mze Bunu.

The therapy focuses less on Mwanesha's physical condition than on the quality of her relationship with her husband. In particular, Dauda's attachment to drink, considered a shameful sign of immaturity in a man of his age, is under attack. Here the spirits are able to tell Dauda to his face what his friends cannot. Dauda, in turn, is respectful enough of the spirits to ask their permission to continue drinking. Although this discussion is ostensibly about the relationship between Mwanesha's spirit and her spouse, it has clear implications for her own relationship with her husband. Dauda realizes the real nature of the occasion when he interjects what are, in theory, totally inappropriate remarks critical of his wife's behavior. In breaking the conventions of the system (i.e., in directing a comment to his wife in her absence), Dauda shows exactly how the system can be used. Just as his wife criticizes him without actually having to face him directly, so Dauda criticizes her during her alleged absence. The embarrassment of the main protagonists, a result of their inexperience with trance, indicates clearly that what they are saying would be inappropriate if communicated directly between husband and wife.

The curers not only act as intermediaries, they also direct the main speakers. Mze Bunu expertly draws out what Mwanesha's spirit has to say and makes sure Dauda listens to it. When Mwanesha is out of trance, it is Tumbu and Mze Bunu rather than Dauda who report to her what has gone on. The fact that Mohedja is in trance makes it easier for her to perform her role. As a spirit, a male, and an elder, Mze Bunu wields greater authority than Mohedja. Furthermore, Mohedja's relationships with Mwanesha and Dauda do not compromise, and remain uncompromised by, Mze Bunu's relationship. The therapist is, in effect, a stranger. Mze Bunu can readily say and do things that Mohedja cannot or does not say or do; for example, in the account above, it is only Mze Bunu who strokes the patient or who expresses impatience with Dauda. Mohedja herself can learn what goes on in the sessions from Tumbu, who stays out of trance.

How effective are these particular sessions as therapy? Tumbu, who is in a better position to judge than we, suspects that conjugal harmony is still a long way off. It is sufficient for our purposes to note that possession provides the context and channels through which problems can be aired.[3] The treatment of Mwanesha's physical illness is used as an occasion to discuss her family problems. At the same time, the possession context is narrowly enough defined so that the tensions raised during the séances do not spill out into her everyday affairs. In sum, it would seem that the potential for therapy is present, even if such therapy is not always effected. Nevertheless, not all communication with spirits is necessarily therapeutic in intent, and it would be a mistake to define possession in terms of a therapeutic function. To become possessed is to open new channels of communication; it is not necessarily to use them wisely or well.

Spirits and spouses

Relations between particular humans and spirits are not static. Like Dauda and his wife's spirit, spirit and spouse frequently are wary of one another initially. Relations may disintegrate to open disaccord and eventual rupture, or they may blossom into mutually positive alliance. The quality of the particular relationship is not determined by the nature of possession, although certain directions are suggested by the curing process.

Communication is a major theme of the curing process, of the development of a stable and mutually satisfactory relationship between host and spirit. In fact, an important aim of the cure is the development of the spirit's verbal coherence and articulateness. The spirit learns to listen to others and to speak its own thoughts so that others will understand in turn. Some spirits, such as Mze Bunu, eventually become so communicative that they rise on their own accord to dispense warnings and advice.

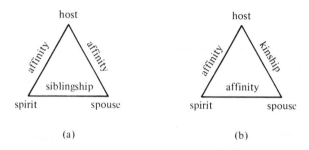

Figure 5.1. Relationships among host, spirit, and spouse.

Although the curing process is described as a matter of negotiating the relationship between spirit and host, in fact, the exchange is not so direct. The spirit must interact with the host's proxy or proxies, and it is with these individuals, as well as with the host herself, that relationships develop as the cure progresses. These proxies include, on the one hand, the curer or curers and, on the other, the host's sponsors, who keep a watch over the proceedings and who contribute on the host's behalf the material goods demanded by the spirit. The main sponsor is generally the host's spouse. In unusual circumstances, if the husband is too poor or too uninterested to give much help, the host's immediate family, her parents, siblings, or adult children, take on the major responsibility. The sponsors should be present when the spirit is called up, and they watch or assist as the curer attempts to convince the spirit to make its presence and its demands known. In this way a husband establishes the basis for a relationship with the spirit possessing his wife.

The relationship between a host's spirit and spouse depends upon the role of the spouse in the process of the cure and, in addition, is partially determined by the meaning of that process as it is construed in Mayotte. In brief, a spirit who initiates and develops a relationship with a host is entering the life of the host and her kin. In some sense, this is similar to what a man does when he marries. The spirit-host relationship is not viewed as one of actual marriage, but it is contractual in nature (cf. Lewis 1971:59), and it does entail the absorption of a stranger into the family unit.

The analogy drawn between spirit and affine (Chapter 9) suggests a comparison between the position of the spirit and that of the actual husband. As one man explained his friendship with his wife's spirit: "We are both married to the same woman." Spirit and spouse are not considered co-spouses so much as "siblings" in the general sense proposed by Kelly (1977). That is to say, the relationship of spirit to spouse is one of siblingship in that it is based on the symmetrical relationships of each party to a common third party, that is, to the host or wife. It is not the content of the relationships with the wife that are stressed but their symmetry (Figure 5.1a).

Alongside this equivalence, there is the matter of exchange. When the husband pays for the spirit's ceremony and arranges for the spirit's entry into the wife's family – a family with which the husband is already closely associated – he is entering into an exchange relationship with the spirit. The husband is performing a role equivalent to that of the bride's brother or father when he pays the groom's *shuŋgu* (Chapter 1), and his relationship with the spirit is affinal (Figure 5.1b).

As a result of these two aspects of their relationship, siblingship by a metaphoric association and affinity by exchange, spirit and spouse may become quite close. As a cure develops and a spirit becomes more communicative, it may decide to rise, or the spouse may decide to call it up, in the absence of the curer. Husband and spirit become male friends or male symmetric siblings (*rahalahy*) if the wife is possessed by a male spirit, or perhaps brother and sister (*anadahy/anabavy*) if she is possessed by a female one. Such a relationship is described by Mo-hedja's *patros* spirit, Mze Bunu, in the first section of this chapter. Tumbu had a similar relationship with Mohedja's child *trumba* (Chapter 12). However, these relationships take time to develop and their course does not always run smooth.

Spouse and spirit take on a set of culturally established rights and duties that are rather different from (but by no means the inverse of) those expected between husband and wife. The spirit depends on the spouse to listen to and carry out its requests; in return, it gives the spouse advice and companionship. The relationship changes, at least ideally, from extortion to balanced reciprocity. I once asked a man whether he would be angry with his wife if she slept with someone while she was in trance. The unexpected, but perfectly logical, reply was no, of course he wouldn't, but he certainly would be angry with the spirit. After all the gifts he had given it, using his wife's body in such a manner – what a way to betray his friendship!

One could not expect a clearer expression than this of the distinction between the two kinds of relationship, spirit-spouse and husband-wife. Yet despite the contrast, or perhaps because of it, the presence of a spirit also changes the conjugal relationship itself. In the first place, by his attitude and efforts during the original illness and cure, the husband demonstrates the degree of his concern for his wife and for fulfilling the obligations of his role as husband. A man's ties with his wife are affected by the ties he develops with the spirit who enters her body. The spirit treats him as an equal or as a slight inferior. Spouse and spirit address and refer to one another by their first names, something spouses never do between themselves. Alone together at night, one spouse may sit passively and enter trance when the spirit is called up by the other. Spirit and spouse can then discuss domestic matters in a context that encourages openness, careful reflection, and reasoned mutual compromise. These acts are all acts of intimacy; they cannot fail to change the quality of the conjugal relationship.

The tie between husband and wife may be further complicated if the wife has more than one spirit and if each of these spirits has its own particular relationship to the husband, or if the husband, in turn, has a spirit or spirits that interact with the wife. It is also possible for the spirits of both spouses to interact with one another, as do Mze Bunu and Mze Jabiry. The relationships build up, one on top of the other, bound together by the fact that they make use of the same pair of hosts. The tie that binds the hosts is no longer merely one of marriage between two socially identified persons but also one of various forms of siblingship and affinity between each of them and the spirit personae who at times inhabit the bodies of the other.

If any of the spirits demonstrates skill at curing, the husband or wife becomes a professional curer. The skills of the spirits and spouses at curing may complement and reinforce one another and the resulting division of labor overlap and strengthen that of the original marriage bond. Mohedja's spirit, Mze Bunu, enjoys particularly peaceful and mature relationships with both Mohedja and Tumbu. Both Mohedja and Tumbu are curers. They have learned their art from a combination of sources: from another human curer, from Mze Bunu arisen in that curer, and directly from their own spirits during sleep. Their spirits continue to share knowledge with them and to advise and fortify them on difficult cases. The hosts often refer to their spirits as their *fundi* 'teachers' or 'masters.' Hosts and spirits here work to the same ends. Thus, while it is Mohedja who is engaged to cure Mwanesha, in fact, she lets Mze Bunu do much of the work. The cure continues, whether she is in or out of trance. Tumbu assists Mohedja and Mze Bunu; on cases where he is the senior curer, they assist him and his spirits in turn.

Mohedja, Tumbu, and their spirits see their interests as being virtually identical. Mze Bunu considers itself the patron of Mohedja's family, and the family members, too, look to the spirit with trust and respect. Mze Bunu arrives to advise and to warn of impending illness, and Nuriaty brings the spirit Mohedja's grandchildren to cure. Sometimes Mze Bunu mediates family quarrels. However, Mze Bunu also points out that such a relationship between a spirit and its host's spouse or family is rare in Lombeni. Relations between spirits and spouses need not become or remain positive, nor does possession always support or strengthen the marriage bond. If the rights and duties of spirit and spouse suggested by the curing process are frequently observed, they can also be violated or never put into practice. Spirits and their hosts' spouses can be virtual strangers to one another or even foes.[4]

The new relationships do not so much strengthen the conjugal bond as, to borrow a metaphor from Geertz (1973a), they thicken it, they add on new layers of meaning. Any action between the partners in their identities at one layer shares in the meanings contributed at other layers; several things are going on at once. Possession does not turn the marriage relationship in any one particular way. It simply says something about it. It sets up the contrast between the conjugal bond and siblingship, the former very fragile in Mayotte and the later enduring, and leaves the conclusions to the participants. If they choose to take the hint, as Tumbu and Mohedja have done, they can develop relationships that partake of both.

We may suggest, then, that the possession complex is no less powerful, no less independent a social fact than the male-oriented jural rules of Islam or the local marriage customs. Possession is not simply to be considered when an individual is in trance; rather, the occasional occurrence of trance serves to create and to communicate new dimensions to relationships that are in effect all the time.

Part II
The syntagmatic dimension

Society dreads disorder but is forced to manipulate the categories and transcend the boundaries upon which its own order depends. In the continuance and development of social forms the consequent disorder is itself socialized in saturnalia, transvestism, and other chaotic or inverted modes of conduct. Any system of thought and action has to come to terms with disorder, and it is a radically interesting matter to see how it does this.

Rodney Needham, Review of Seth,
God of Confusion

Having established that possession is a system of communication, it remains to examine the content of the system, that is, the texts that are generated or transmitted through it. What is possession about, and how does it achieve what it is about? While each instance of possession is unique in that it involves particular actors, at particular moments in their lives, the host, the curer, the host's associates, and even the spirit all follow a general cultural model for establishing and responding to possession. The relationship of this underlying system or model to actual cases of possession may be considered analogous to that occurring between the grammar (*langue*) and speech (*parole*) of a language. In the remainder of this work the possession model will be elucidated. We will attempt to clarify the sequence of events that constitutes possession, to understand how possession is established, how it is treated, and how it is made intelligible to both the central participants and the disinterested members of society at large.

If possession be considered as text (Geertz 1972, Ricoeur 1971), it can be shown to consist of a juxtaposition of two sorts of statements. On the one hand, there is the emergence and separation of coherent spirit personae from their human hosts and the development of working relationships between them; on the other, the persistent representation of spirits as essentially different from human beings. These two kinds of statements can be considered the syntagmatic and the paradigmatic dimensions of the text respectively. The syntagmatic dimension is the diachronic, sequential, or linear aspect of the text, that which develops or unfolds over the course of an individual case of possession. The paradigmatic dimension is synchronic and nonlinear, the metaphors through which the text is constituted. It is the dialectic operant between these aspects, between what changes and what remains constant, that determines both the organization and the argument of the remainder of the book.

There is a continual tension between humans and spirits; both sides must compromise on specific issues, but neither concedes its identity.

The humans give the spirits to understand that they will not tolerate the abuse of the bodies of members of their kind, and the spirits maintain that they will not tolerate neglect. Resolutions are reached in the creation of alliances between particular spirits and humans in which reasoned communication between the two sides is made possible. Yet, even as each of these alliances is consummated, the spirits use the opportunity to display their "spiritness" to the utmost, indulging in the performance of activities quite foreign to humans. This tension between spirits and humans forms the central dynamic of possession, as I shall argue in Chapter 11, and a flux from which numerous ideas can emerge.[1]

In Part II we will be concerned with the syntagmatic dimension of possession. Using material from two case studies, we will follow the "plot" from the first onset of trance through the confrontation between spirits and humans to the apparent resolutions achieved in the curing process. The plot takes shape through the emergence of the possessing spirit as a coherent, autonomous persona, independent of the social persona of the host. This coherence is established and authenticated through the definition of the spirit's relationships with others, especially with the host and her party, but also with the general public, both spirit and human. Each case of possession must be made intelligible to the parties concerned and must be publicly accepted by them. In more abstract terms, what occurs is a process of naturalization, whereby the observed behavior is assimilated to what the members of the culture view as "natural." The behavior is assigned particular relations to the world, that is, the individual case is comprehended as "possession" to the degree to which it corresponds to previously established conventional sets of expectations concerning "possession."[2] The models of coherence of all parties must coincide if the experience is to be intelligible and acceptable to the community.

Acceptance is not a passive process. In discussing naturalization in terms of the writer and readers of literary texts, Culler (1975:192–202) speaks of a "narrative contract." The anthropological theory of ritual proves more powerful here than a purely linguistic or literary model. It will be demonstrated how, in ritual, the events of possession are rendered meaningful and are publicly accepted. The possession cure can be considered a rite of passage, both in the general, classical sense proposed by Van Gennep (1960) and recently elaborated by Turner (1969, 1967), and, more important, in the culturally specific sense in which other kinds of status changes are enacted in Mayotte. What occurs is a rite of passage from the point of view of both the patient, who wishes to get well, and the spirit, who wishes to elevate its status. The possession ritual develops the consciousness of significant status change in the participants by its metaphoric relationship to other rituals of status change. Possession shares a common symbolic idiom with these other rituals, so that the performance of one is illuminated and made more realistic by consideration of the others.[3]

The following chapters alternate among three sorts of rhetorical stance: description, commentary, and analysis. Extensive descriptive accounts, consisting of edited excerpts from my field notes, are presented for two cases of possession. These cases were selected because they are the ones for which I was able to observe the most episodes of the plot. Although both cases conform to the same underlying model of competence, they differ strikingly from one another in their surface features and will be used to illustrate different points. The cases are interspersed with short passages of commentary aiming to explicate the descriptive passages they immediately follow. Longer passages, the latter portions of Chapters 6 and 7 and Chapter 9 in its entirety, present a more comprehensive analysis of the syntagmatic chain. However, the interpretation is incomplete without consideration of the paradigmatic dimension to be discussed in Part III.

6. Negotiation and emergence: the case of Habiba

A *patros* cure normally entails two distinct public ceremonies with drumming, dancing, feasting, and trance on the part of a large number of the guests. The first of these ceremonies, the *ishima* 'courtesy,' typically lasts several hours, and the second, the *azulahy be* 'major drumming,' continues all night and often well into the next morning. The spirit normally announces its name toward the end of the *azulahy be.* The two ceremonies are similar in structure, but the *azulahy be* is larger, more important, and more expensive. It may take place only several years after the *ishima* or, should the host remain untroubled, not at all. Leading up to each of these ceremonies is a sequence of preparatory events, the subject of this chapter. These meetings between the spirit and the host's representatives serve to settle the spirit's requirements and to schedule the ceremony. Each of these events entails the gathering of the curer, the patient, and at least a few of the patient's immediate kin. Incense is lit, the curer and kin clap and sing, and the spirit is urged to rise in the patient and speak its mind in order that the arrangements can be agreed upon. These meetings may also provide the chance for preliminary treatment of the patient with herbal medicines.

Despite their semiprivate and relatively simple nature, these occasions are crucial for an understanding of possession as a whole. It is during the process of negotiation that the spirit persona begins to take shape and acquire coherence. This is also the time during which the host and her immediate kin come to accept the possession. The processes of naturalization and acceptance, which terminate only in the *azulahy be,* are evident in the creation and continuous testing of the communication network, in the generation and mobilization of emotion, and in the commitment of the concerned parties to dialogue and the purchase of the goods that the spirit requests. All of these developments can be seen in the case material that follows.

The sequence of events to be described concerns the *patros* spirit of

Habiba Hussein, a woman in her late twenties. The sequence will be followed from (1) the first appearance of the spirit (at which I was not present but received an account) through the following stages of negotiation:

2. Establishment of the spirit's demands for the *ishima* ceremony, early September 1975.
3. Clarification of the proceedings, October 8.
4. Introduction of Habiba's close relatives to the spirit, October 10.
5. Settlement of the date for the *ishima,* October 18.

The administration of the medicine at the *ishima* (October 20, 1975) will be described in the following chapter.

Any actual sequence of events in a spirit cure is determined both by the underlying cultural model of possession and by the particular circumstances of the patient and her family. The process of the cure may be considered the simultaneous unfolding of both a cultural drama and a social one. The cultural model is the ideal version. It is a drama because it has an unfolding aspect, a plot, a conflict to be resolved. It requires putting certain symbols into play in orderly, sequential fashion and, through them, saying something of general significance for all participants, whatever their capacity. But in order for this drama to be enacted, it must have individual participants, individuals who, like the patient, are present because this particular performance has a special significance for them. They bring their own particular hopes and desires, their own configurations of kin, allies, and resources to the general form that the model specifies. And through participation, they – and their hopes, their social relationships, and their resources – are changed. This is the social drama: because the cultural script is performed not on the stage, in a neatly demarcated space outside the ordinary course of life, but in that life and through the course of particular lives, changing them as it progresses.

Habiba Hussein was a bright, vivacious, childless woman, a classificatory sister's child (Figure 6.1) of the curer Tumbu. There was a strong affective bond between them. Habiba was a member of the branch of the family of Tumbu's father that lived in Changani, a large village about two hours' distance from Lombeni by foot. During the time these events took place, the population of Mayotte was polarized into two political camps, divided on the issue of whether to unite in an independent republic with the other three islands of the Comoro archipelago or to remain a dependency of France. Feeling ran extremely high over the issue, and normal social relations between kin and friends from the two parties were disrupted. In Lombeni, the entire village was unanimous in its support of one of the parties, whereas in Changani, the villagers were split on the issue. Habiba was the only

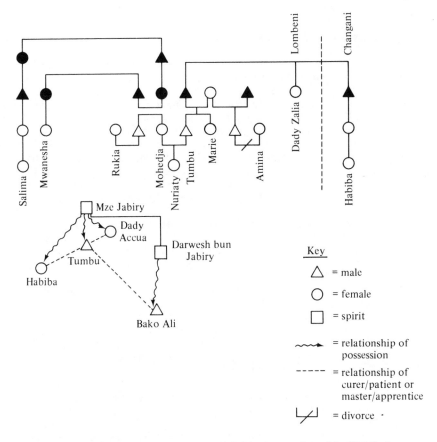

Figure 6.1. Relationships among the individuals mentioned in Habiba's cure. Black circles and triangles indicate deceased.

member of her family in Changani who at that time belonged to the same party as the inhabitants of Lombeni. She thus served as an important link between the two sets of kin.

Habiba's case is somewhat unusual because of the speed with which her *patros* spirit became a curer in its own right. Habiba's self-assurance, and the ease with which her cure was carried out, provide a striking contrast with the case of Rukia to be described in Chapter 8. The reader is reminded, however, of the argument presented in Chapter 4, that possession need not be an expression of actual illness. In Habiba's case, "illness" and "cure" are merely the idioms in which her transformation is expressed, the context in which it takes place.

The negotiations for Habiba's *ishima*

The first arrival of Habiba's patros

As Tumbu recounted the story, Habiba first became possessed a year
or two before the curing events took place. Tumbu had performed a
minor sorcery cure for a woman in Changani who did not have the
means to pay him immediately. The woman later gave CFA200
($1.00) to Habiba, asking her to pass it on to Tumbu, her mother's
brother. Instead of doing so, Habiba spent the money on herself.
Tumbu's *patros* spirit, Mze Jabiry (who was the one who had actually
treated the Changani patient), claimed to be angry that it had been
cheated of its cologne (i.e., cologne that Tumbu could have bought
for it with the money), and so it made Habiba ill. The first that
Tumbu knew of anything was when Habiba came and called up his
spirit to diagnose her case. The spirit told her that she had taken
something that didn't belong to her. Habiba couldn't think what it
might be. Finally Mze Jabiry mentioned the money. Habiba at once
remembered the incident, admitted her culpability, and said she
would return the money. Indeed, she paid Tumbu that very day and
returned home cured. That was the full extent of the physical distress
caused Habiba by the spirit. However, unknown to them both, the
spirit took the opportunity that day to move from Tumbu into Habiba
(so that henceforward it could rise in both of them).

Sometime later, a son of Habiba's sister was being circumcised in
Changani. When the boy was cut, the women began to cry. In their
midst, Habiba suddenly became possessed and started dancing like a
patros. Tumbu took one look and knew immediately by the spirit's
particular style of movement that it was his own Mze Jabiry, but he
kept silent. Everyone else was extremely surprised. Habiba already
had a *trumba* spirit – wasn't that enough?

Tumbu added one final point to his narrative. He explained that
Mze Jabiry liked Habiba very much and had been waiting long for the
chance to enter her. The spirit used the "theft" of the cologne
money, which was merely a sin of omission on Habiba's part and not
serious, as an excuse to do so.

Commentary. Why is Habiba possessed by Mze Jabiry? Tumbu remarks that his spirit has had its eye on Habiba for some time. When
Mze Jabiry rises in Tumbu, he operates as a curer. Mze Jabiry/Tumbu
is relied upon as a curer by the various members of Tumbu's family in
Changani. But Tumbu's reputation as a curer extends beyond his kin
and he receives numerous requests from other supplicants each time he
makes a trip to Changani. Although proud of his reputation, Tumbu
feels he receives little reimbursement for the time and trouble he takes
over cures and that he could spend this time more profitably by working on his cash crops. He often leaves Lombeni for his fields at the
crack of dawn in order to avoid supplicants. However, if Mze Jabiry

enters Habiba and if, to anticipate, the spirit also fuctions as a curer in her, Tumbu will be relieved of the responsibility of treating patients in Changani. At the same time, because he and Habiba are possessed by the same spirit, Tumbu will not be breaking his relationship with Changani. Because the spirit's manifestation in Tumbu will continue to be considered senior to that in Habiba, and because he and Habiba will develop a master-student relationship, Tumbu's influence over his Changani relatives will, if anything, be strengthened, whereas his responsibilities will decline. Furthermore, in this way Tumbu can avoid censure in Lombeni for associating with members of the opposite political party in Changani.

As compared with most patients at the onset of a *patros* cure, Habiba shows very little illness or physical discomfort. This is an indication of the affection with which the spirit holds her. It is also atypical that the first occurrence of trance be articulate enought to suggest immediately to a qualified observer the identity of the spirit. The spirit thereby presents itself as mature. Through her spirit's actions, Habiba is asserting her importance to her immediate kin in Changani and her independence from them. During her family's political isolation, she leaves them to hold her ceremonies in Lombeni; within a short time of her return, she is performing the functions of a curer.

Thus it appears that the spirit's arrival in Habiba, as well as its very rapid development into a curer, is unwelcome to neither Tumbu nor Habiba. The spirit's actions appear to be the result of mutual inclination and shared understandings.

Establishment of the spirit's demands, early September

> Impatient for her curing ceremony, Habiba Hussein came to Lombeni in order to have Tumbu call up her *patros* to discover what it required. After dinner, a small group gathered in the back room of Tumbu's house: Tumbu, Mohedja, Tumbu's father's sister Dady 'Grandmother' Zalia, his sister Marie, the wife of one of Mohedja's brothers, Habiba, and myself (Figure 6.1). We all sat on mats on the floor, rather than on the chairs or beds, in order to *maŋgataka*, to 'request,' 'make an appeal' or 'invocation.'
>
> Dady Zalia started some *uban* incense in a little clay brazier and pronounced the Islamic formula that begins all endeavors: "In the name of Allah, the compassionate, the merciful . . ." Dady Zalia addressed the spirit bothering Habiba, asking it not to refuse their appeal but to come speak with them. She urged it to arrive gently (*moramora*). Then Tumbu gave a long speech in an undertone over the incense, repeating the reasons for the invocation and the admonitions to come hastily but without furor. Habiba yawned, jerked a couple of times, and began to show signs of pain, shaking and crying

An elderly curer.

out, "*oy, oy, oy ye!*" Then she uttered a spurt of syllables: "*da-da-de-di-da-di* . . ." The others giggled or chatted softly with one another, generally ignoring the process of transition. Tumbu began to speak directly to the newly arrived spirit, asking it not to be uncooperative. Quite ignoring Tumbu, the spirit (i.e., Habiba in trance) sniffed loudly and commenced to sing, "*Galaweny mama, galaweny mama, galawe . . .*" The song, apparently a nonsense rhyme, interspersed the rest of the conversation and was to be repeated regularly over the next few months as a sort of theme, one that the young girls in the village took up as well.

First Mohedja and Tumbu and then the others began to hum along. The spirit broke into dry sobs and was gently admonished that that was enough. It sang another, more complex song, and then, despite its tears, shook hands with each of us. HABIBA[1] abruptly challenged: "Do you believe I am a spirit?" The others assured it they believed. More confident, HABIBA untied her hair, repeating, "I'm a spirit, Tumbu; I'm the offspring of a spirit" (*Zahu lulu, Tumbu; za' zanakan'ulu*). The spirit asked why we were gathered there. Tumbu replied, "to arrange your ceremony [*asa*]; to remove the illness that is bothering Habiba. She has been too sick."

The spirit responded aggressively, "You are appealing in a dirty condition! Why didn't you wash first?" (The spirit is here referring to Habiba herself, claiming she should have washed in medicated water.) Tumbu replied in calm but firm tones that he hadn't been aware that the spirit wanted the bathing; it is unusual. The spirit sulked, looked down and rubbed its leg. Then it complained that more people weren't told about the occasion. "Where is Bako Ali?" (Tumbu's former apprentice and current colleague). Tumbu tried to reason with the spirit. Suddenly it announced in a loud and firm voice: "I want my medicine! I want entirely new implements!" It laughed and began to sing, as the others hummed along:

> *Za 'ulu we-e*
> *zanakan 'ulu*
> *za'ulu fundi . . .*
>
> I am a spirit
> offspring of a spirit
> I am a curer spirit . . .

"I want – I want medicine!" the spirit asserted. It laughed and sang again. Then it said obscurely that it needed a woman, a girl child, some help. Mohedja admonished it not speak in riddles but to say straightforwardly what it wanted. She reminded it that Ramadan was imminent. The spirit replied that it wanted new cloths and new pots and bowls for the ceremony. It started singing again, then broke off suddenly to announce that Habiba would return to hold the ceremony in Lombeni (rather than in her home village of Changani). The inhalation of the medicine, the drumming and dancing, all were to take place in Lombeni. The spirit said it wanted everyone to see, wanted them all to stay straight through until morning. Although the spirit acted willful and hard to please, it assured us that Habiba would be cured. The others responded to the spirit firmly but patiently.

The spirit went on to say that Habiba should have washed out the pollution associated with her father's recent death. It issued a number of remarks in rapid succession: "I want some cologne; I am going now and will return later; Habiba will be made well; I want four meters of white cloth; seven pots full of medicine to inhale and medicine of ground twigs rubbed on the skin; I want three chickens, soft cakes, two new pots." The spirit sang a line in a Comoran dialect, said to mean something like: "I am not a child, why are you not talking straight to me?" It reminded the company that it wanted things to be very clean and then it said it was leaving. The others asked it to leave gently. HABIBA cried, "*o ye!*" and made other exclamations of discomfort, stretching, scratching, and rubbing her shoulder. In a rapid transition, she straightened up and immediately began to put her combs back into her hair.

The others suggested waiting until the next day to tell Habiba what the *patros* had said, but she asked to know immediately. Tumbu listed its requirements and they all laughed over them. Habiba seemed very tired.

Commentary. A cure cannot begin until a spirit states its demands. All spirits want more or less the same things, and the requests come as no particular surprise to the assembled company; nevertheless, they must be uttered by the spirit itself. In stating its demands, the spirit is indicating that it is willing to negotiate and that there is hope for a cure.

The session is characterized by the inequality between the spirit and the others and the difference in their respective attitudes. The humans are making an appeal, are pleading, first for the spirit to meet with them and then for it to tell them what it wants in order to make Habiba well again. The spirit is at pains to let the humans know that in responding to them at all it is doing them a large favor.

In this particular case, the negotiation is accomplished relatively easily. The spirit has not really been making Habiba very sick and it is quite ready to talk. It is able and willing to enunciate clearly and it does not claim to be at a loss for words. By comparison with other cases, it is almost as though the creation of difficulties is a mere formality the spirit goes through, a section of the plot that must be acted out. Nevertheless, the spirit does not come straight to the point but keeps the others waiting, singing to itself and making other nonspecific requests. The spirit knows well enough that it is not sufficient to say simply "I want medicine!" that it must be more precise about the details, particularly of quantity. Mohedja's remark that Ramadan is imminent is intended to speed the spirit up, because spirit business cannot be conducted during the Muslim holy month. The spirit also tries to throw in extraneous difficulties. Referring to her father's death, it complains that Habiba hasn't washed before the meeting. Although bodily cleanliness is frequently a concern of spirits, in fact, there is no cultural rule that suggests that Habiba ought to have washed first; the period of mourning for the death was over and there was no cause for complaint.

The spirit also asserts itself in more direct ways. It addresses individuals by their first names, a sign of seniority that Habiba herself could never use toward her mother's brother. Its assertions in speech and song that it is indeed a spirit, and a curer one at that, are produced, according to Tumbu, in order to show off its importance.

By making specific, concrete demands for a ceremony, Habiba is authenticating the spirit's presence. That is, by saying what spirits are expected to say, Habiba is not only reporting the needs of her spirit, she is also defining and establishing her state as possession and creating the identity of her spirit. The responses of the group do likewise. It is the entire process of negotiation, to be completed in the curing ceremony, that establishes the existence and validity of her possession, the "species" of her possessing spirit (whether *patros, trumba,* etc.), and, ultimately, its personal identity. Henceforward, Habiba's behavior will be judged according to the conventions established during this process (cf. Rappaport 1974). Not least important, this is a self-referential process: Reported back to her by others, the spirit's behavior helps to convince Habiba of her possession. In fact, Tumbu asserts that the spirit's first question, concerning belief in its identity, is directed toward Habiba herself.

The humans' response to the lack of courtesy and the unreasonableness of the spirit is courtesy, reason, and sympathy. The truculence of the individual spirit is contrasted with the solidarity and steadfastness of kin. In ordinary life, kin do not always act so patiently and gently with one another, but in front of the spirit they appear to go out of their way to do so. The humans take second place not out of fear, nor from acceptance of a position of inferiority, but from the decision that the improvement of Habiba's health should take precedence over matters of face. They watch over Habiba's condition and admonish the spirit to enter and leave her gently, causing her little pain or turmoil. They are not afraid of speaking their minds, but they will not be drawn into superfluous arguments.[2]

A final point to note about the affair is its privacy. With the exception of Mohedja's sister-in-law, all the individuals present are the close kin of Habiba, and all maintain the same mood of concern and seriousness. The meeting is arranged privately and is held in seclusion, indoors. Only adults are present. Dady Zalia, as the most senior relative of Habiba in Lombeni, chooses to start the proceedings, thereby demonstrating her particular concern.

Clarification of the proceedings, October 8

> Habiba Hussein returned to Lombeni to schedule the date of her *patros* ceremony. She said that Tumbu had appeared to her in her sleep the night before, telling her to come. Habiba briefly discussed the details of her cure with Tumbu and Mohedja. In order to save money, Habiba wanted to use a clay pot instead of the metal one the spirit had requested for the ceremony. The curers answered that the medicine would heat up too slowly. Habiba also wondered if a white plate would do instead of a bowl, and they replied that they supposed so, provided the spirit agreed. They waited for Dady Zalia to appear but soon just lit the incense and called up the spirit without her. As

Tumbu's daughter and niece watched from the doorway, the *patros* rose rapidly and greeted us one by one. Mohedja politely asked how its spouse and children were "over there," and it replied that they were fine. The spirit then asked why Dady Accua, an older woman and spirit curer from Lombeni, who also shared the same spirit with Tumbu, was not present. The spirit began to sing the same songs as on its last visit and seemed to be in better control of itself.

The spirit asked Tumbu to schedule and arrange the ceremony. It demanded a night with moonlight. Turning from the business at hand, the spirit insisted on seeing Dady Accua and inquired testily of Mohedja why she continued her sewing during the conversation. Wasn't Mohedja contented with the turn of affairs, wasn't she interested? Mohedja replied calmly that she would devote her full attention to the spirit on the day of the medicine; that today she hadn't come to sing but to finalize the arrangements. A child was sent to find Dady Accua. In the meantime, the spirit began to sing and Tumbu hummed along with it. Dady Zalia entered and then left again to attend to her cooking until Dady Accua should arrive. People talked to the spirit in response to comments addressed specifically to them. Otherwise they ignored it. The spirit mentioned a girl in the village by name and announced that it wished to enter her as well; it seemed she once laughed at Tumbu when he was possessed. The spirit then brought up a problem: It wished to put cologne on its head, but the *trumba* who also enters Habiba did not like the habit and had forbidden it to Habiba; the two spirits would have to come to an agreement. The conversation in the room shifted to the current prices of cash crops and the spirit announced that it would leave in the meantime. Tumbu told it to be patient. A few moments later, the message came that Dady Accua was not to be found. They finished the business without her, agreeing that the ceremony would be held the next week. The spirit clarified its demands. It consented to Habiba's used pot for cooking the medicine, but she would have to buy a new one for the second ceremony. It also asked that Habiba be given medicine in the meantime, before the ceremony, despite the fact that she had not been sick since her previous visit.

When Habiba came out of trance, she complained that her neck was sore. Tumbu told her what had been decided with the spirit, and she asked him to go to Changani within the next few days to explain things to her family there. Apparently, they weren't fully convinced of her possession. Once Tumbu went and called up the spirit in front of them, they would be prepared to help with the expenses.

Commentary. The month of Ramadan has passed since the first visit and Habiba has had the chance to begin her preparations. The meeting indicates the state of these preparations and moves closer toward setting the date of the feast. It keeps the parties in communication and continues the process of establishing the reality and nature of Habiba's possession.

It is important to note that there are two conversations going on here, one between Habiba and her relatives/curers and the other between the spirit and the curers and relatives. Thus, Habiba does not wish to buy a new pot and explains to Tumbu, who then arranges the matter with the spirit.

The atmosphere is more informal, and the spirit is in better control than during the last visit. Habiba moves in and out of trance more easily, with no exclamations of pain. The spirit continues to act self-important and demanding. It threatens another villager with possession, and it wants Mohedja to give it her full attention. It demands that Dady Accua be fetched from some distance away. Dady Accua has great practice at running spirit ceremonies. Although not related through kin ties, she shares the same spirit as Tumbu, and thus, although we don't officially know it yet, as Habiba herself. By calling for Dady Accua, the spirit is hinting at its identity. The humans do their best to advance the arrangements, but otherwise they do not flatter the spirit.

Introducing Habiba's close relatives to the spirit, October 10

Tumbu and I made the two-hour walk to Changani. There, a mat and a brazier with incense had been set out in the house of Habiba's younger sister. Habiba sat on the mat as Tumbu called the *patros* and explained that Habiba's relatives wanted to meet it. He told it not to fight but to arrive gently, then whispered to it, "Quickly, comrade!" Habiba's relatives entered the room slowly, looking disinterested. Habiba yawned, then sobbed. Her upper body shook and she uttered deep breaths and groans. She spluttered consonants for a moment and then settled into singing one of the songs I had heard before. Tumbu admonished the spirit to take it easy and sang along softly. The women now began to observe the proceedings carefully. The spirit shook hands with all of them, then Tumbu motioned it to sit up on the bed, next to Habiba's mother. Tumbu greeted the *patros*, explained that the family wanted to meet it, and suggested they all arrange the curing ceremony together. The spirit remarked that it wanted entirely new materials and in sufficient quantity. The mother said the problem lay with Habiba's husband, who had not yet been brought in on things. The spirit replied that it was up to them to help, they must not claim poverty. It assured them that they would be glad later. Tumbu interrupted to point out that this implied that Habiba would become a curer.

The spirit called for the cloth, which had already been bought. It examined the plain white sheet and then ordered it put away. It told Tumbu he must come back with an exact date for the ceremony. Habiba's mother asked whether the ceremony would be held in Changani or Lombeni. Tumbu explained that it had to be in Lombeni because Dady Accua couldn't travel far and the spirit wanted her present. The spirit asserted loudly that its affair was in Lombeni, not in Changani. Tumbu told the family to take up a collection until all the items were bought. The spirit repeated, "You are all going to be delighted here."

Tumbu and the spirit retired to the next room to talk in private. The discussion in the first room switched to the current price of plastic sandals. People began to get restless. Habiba's mother walked out. Habiba's brother promised the spirit the cologne it asked for and left too. HABIBA returned to detail again the requirements and to urge them not to be dismayed.

Tumbu's private conversation with the spirit covered a number of topics. The spirit told Tumbu its plans for the *azulahy be,* the second major ceremony. It would be held after rice harvest and the spirit would want either one large goat or two smaller ones slaughtered. Tumbu then put some questions to Habiba's spirit concerning a number of cures he was currently working on. The spirit diagnosed and prescribed for two of Tumbu's cases and admonished him not to be shy about demanding higher fees.

The spirit then said it wished to leave. Tumbu made sure Habiba's mother was called back first and explained to her how to administer to Habiba the medicine he had brought. The spirit yawned and stretched and left Habiba.

Commentary. Habiba's case is unusual in that her close kin did not participate in the first meetings with her spirit. Whereas the spirit is quite adamant in wanting its ceremony held in Lombeni, a village that Habiba's mother and siblings currently are not able to visit for political reasons, Habiba herself is anxious to involve her relatives. It is she, not the spirit, who calls for the Changani meeting in order to demonstrate her possession and engage her family's help in the cure. The white cloth is an indication that the family has already begun to help. In meeting and assisting the spirit, Habiba's family establish their acceptance of her possession.

Habiba's mother points to another unusual fact in the situation – that Habiba's husband is playing no part. Habiba's husband is from a neighboring village, where he has another wife and a number of children. He does not spend much time in Changani with Habiba. Habiba, too, is acting quite independently from her husband. Tumbu would normally never do a cure without the husband's permission and presence, but he makes an exception in this case because Habiba is a relative.[3] Habiba's independence from her husband is also apparent in her aim to become a curer in her own right. However, at the moment this independence is matched by a corresponding financial dependence on the members of her own family, especially her brothers. It is in part the degree of Habiba's dependence on her family that is behind the spirit's emphasis on the returns that will accrue to them. It is made clear to all concerned that these returns consist of the advantages in having a curer in the family. Neither Habiba nor her spirit can state this directly yet, but Tumbu strongly reinforces the implications of the spirit's words.

Tumbu even begins to make use of the spirit's curing skills himself, seeking advice about other cases on which he is currently working. This reliance by a curer on the spirit of his patient is unusual and represents an inversion of the normal curer/patient relationship. However, in this case, the patient is the daughter of Tumbu's sister (a category of kin with whom a man can have an open and easy relationship) and the spirit inhabiting her is Tumbu's own major spirit, Mze Jabiry. Furthermore, Tumbu has already had opportunity to observe that Mze Jabiry has chosen to rise in Habiba as a dependable curer, much as it does in himself.[4] In its response to Tumbu's queries, the spirit reinforces Tumbu's own belief in the particular manifestation in Habiba. The spirit also exhibits the consideration with which it holds Tumbu and the intimate relationship it has with him. It enjoins him not to be so modest and ready to accept low fees for his services. This is the kind of personal message that Tumbu could expect from his own spirit.

The skill and maturity of this particular manifestation of the spirit is evident to all. Most spirits do not choose to exhibit themselves as curers in their hosts, and even when they do, they usually wait until the curing ceremonies have been performed. From the point of view that the spirit is none other than Habiba speaking in trance, the rapidity with which Habiba has picked up her new role and the skill with which she plays it are most impressive.

Final settlement of the date, October 18

> Habiba arrived in Lombeni, bringing four meters of white cloth, two pots, a white plate, and a glass bowl, seven kilos of rice, two kilos of sugar, and several bottles of cologne. She claimed to have spent CFA5000 ($25.00). The *patros* rose when the incense was lit and said immediately that it wanted the ceremony held that Monday, in two days' time. It called for Tumbu's sister Marie. While waiting for Marie, the spirit sang a song. It announced that it needed only one small cake. Mohedja scolded the spirit as if it were a child, saying that of course the guests would want cake too and that there would have to be more than one. The spirit then stated that it wanted to hold the ceremony at noontime. Mohedja pointed out that during the daytime no one would show up; people only have time at night. Marie arrived and the spirit asked her to put ointment on Habiba's skin and to do her hair before the ceremony. Finally, the spirit told Tumbu to accept CFA500 as his fee for the ceremony.

Commentary. Now that all the items have been gathered for the ceremony the final date can be set. Normally the date is selected according to the curer's convenience. In this case, the approximate date had already been agreed upon on Habiba's previous visit to Lombeni.

The spirit continues to act childish and difficult about the ceremony. Although it is customary to make several cakes to feed all the guests, and although the festivities are always held at night, the spirit makes contrary demands. Knowing that these ideas will be rejected, it suggests them merely in order to express its willfulness.[5]

Marie is of an appropriate kinship category (MoYrSi) to Habiba to anoint her and dress her hair. The cosmetic, *mwina,* is a fragrant paste applied to women at key moments in the ritual life cycle. It is valued for the smoothness it gives the skin.

The curer who is in charge of a spirit's ceremony receives a cash payment as well as the cloth under which the medicine is inhaled, the two pots used to cook it in, and the bowl and dish. This represents a substantial amount of goods. Whereas Tumbu will receive these even though Habiba is his sister's daughter, a curer who is not a relative might be less willing to coax the spirit into lowering its original demands.

The emergence of coherence

We have observed in this chapter the first stages of rapprochement between the spirit, on the one hand, and the host and her curer and family, on the other. These episodes have the manifest aim of arranging the spirit's curing ceremony and feast, but they are significant in other ways as well. They begin the establishment and acceptance of the host's possession and of the identification of the possessing spirit, and they initiate communication and exchange among the various parties. They also illustrate the first stages in a spirit's socialization, in its career from chaos to clarity. The emergence of coherence is visible on two planes, the physical and the moral.

Physical coherence

A spirit often enters its host roughly, causing the body to tremble or thrash about, producing burping, coughing, whistling noises, sobs, shrieks, or splutters of short nonsense syllables. This kind of behavior during the transition phase does not occur randomly but is culturally constrained in a number of ways.[6] First, particular kinds of spirits appear with their own levels and forms of violence. An individual possessed by more than one kind of spirit will thus exhibit more than one kind of agitated behavior. Second, the violence tends to decrease in intensity with the progress of the cure. It is particularly noticeable during the first stages of cure, when a cure has been long delayed, and at moments of special excitement: during the inhalation of medicine and in the presence of other spirits at a feast. Spirits who have finished their ceremonies, spirits who have been visiting their hosts over a long period of time, and spirits who have been called up for private consultations all tend to enter their respective hosts with far less noise and fuss. Consequently, whether voluntary or involuntary impulses dominate in the control of trance behavior, the behavior has significance for those observing it. The degree and kind of violence exhibited is part of the communicative process. Shrieking is not simply an uncontrolled expression of emotion but an indexical message concerning the species and conditions of the spirit.

This is also true of the changes in behavior visible over the sequence of the curing rituals during the full trance state. The patient may be learning to control herself in the new state or simply following an established cultural model for trance behavior, but the increase in calmness visible in the spirit over time has definite significance to the observers. The broad stages of this development are regular across all patients and are expected and infused with culturally determined meaning. At the very least, it may be said that the symbolic process co-opts the neurological adjustments and uses them to its own ends. However, it is probably more accurate to say that the culture provides a model for behavior, according to which such adjustment is carried out from the first onset of possession.

The first occasions of trance indicate by the exaggerated behavior of the individual that there really is a spirit present and how different the spirit is from the human host. As well as convincing others of the actuality and authenticity of the particular case of possession, the lack of bodily control is an indication of the uncooperativeness of the spirit. The spirit is unstable and inarticulate, often incoherent. It may not even completely rise in the host on the first occasion, so that neither host nor spirit is fully present and confused signals are emitted from each, like a radio tuned between two stations. The spirit here is expressing quite directly its power to abuse the body of the host and its lack of intention to do otherwise. As well as being outside human culture, its incoherence demonstrates that it outside society as well.

Gradually, first the incoherence and then the obstinacy dissolve. The spirit moves from silence, heavy breathing, or dry sobbing to singing, riddles, non sequiturs, impossible demands, and outrageous complaints. Social interaction with the spirit becomes at least conceivable; it is coaxed and remonstrated with until finally – sometimes only after several sessions with the curers – it agrees to set its demands for a first ceremony. Stating its demands is an indication that the spirit accepts the conventions of the exchange process and is committed to it; a common language and a common goal between spirit and humans is established. At the same time, by entering into the negotiations themselves, the humans have acknowledged that they are dealing with a spirit. From this point on, the spirit no longer has to act in a particularly wild or unusual manner to convince them of its nature; but it may still do so from time to time in order to express its impatience or outrage with human inaction regarding the curing process. The degree of violence with which the spirit rises in the host is henceforth an index of its satisfaction with the proceedings.

The original incoherence and unwillingness to communicate culminates finally in the grand symbolic gesture, the announcement of the spirit's name. From this point, the spirit may move to the opposite extreme – to the impartation of esoteric knowledge to the host. However, although the arrivals and departures of the spirit become stabilized and the spirit no longer punishes the host's body with pain or wild movements, the spirit does not relinquish those other features of its behavior that mark it as different from the human host. What is food for the one is forbidden or of no interest to the other. Whatever agreement host and spirit come to, the spirit will not abstain from the pleasures dearest to it. Quite the contrary, the very reason a spirit enters its host in the first place is to find support for its pleasures. Thus, the practice of these customs, which contrast so vividly with those of humans, does not decrease with the progress of the cure, but, if anything, becomes more evident.

Moral coherence

Not only do spirits have different habits of consumption from humans, but they also have a far greater interest in adherence to the rules of expression of relative status and a far weaker interest in Islam and in the maintenance of morality. Spirits are pleasure seeking and operate unabashedly from positions of self-interest. These characteristics too are markers, although less categorical ones, distinguishing between the spirit world and the human one.

However, spirits are not immoral so much as amoral. Their greed and selfishness stem from a weak character rather than a bad one. In matters of responsibility they are like small children. They don't set out deliberately to do wrong; they are merely indifferent to the distinctions between right and wrong. Although at times they can be tempted to bad deeds, often they are coaxed into taking the path of reason and showing consideration for the welfare of others. Sometimes an older spirit who has established strong ties to its host, like Mze Bunu with Mohedja, even enlarges its notion of self-interest to include the host's extended family (*mraba*).

The notion that spirits are powerful yet amoral has a number of interesting implications. If spirits are amoral then blame for their actions in those cases where they have not acted alone must be reserved for the humans who have instigated or employed them. Responsibility is placed squarely on the shoulders of human beings. Furthermore, the new appearance of a spirit among a group of humans establishes a forum where correct moral behavior can be expressed. The carelessness and cruelty, the unformed quality of the spirit's behavior, demand reaction on the part of the humans. The host's family and the curer exhort the spirit to take a righteous course of action and explicitly lay out such a course for it. The spirit is admonished not to act without appropriate concern for the rights and welfare of others. For example, in the interchange between Mohedja and Habiba's spirit when the latter suggested making only a single cake for the feast, Mohedja promptly reminded it that the other spirits would want to eat as well.

The members of the host's family are not only preaching moral behavior but, in their active concern for, and intervention over, their suffering wife or daughter or sister or husband, are engaging in it as well. The spirit's behavior forces the close kin to take a stand, to demonstrate the virtues of solidarity. Together they exert themselves on the patient's behalf. This is not a system where a self-righteous preacher or saint or angel exhorts the mortal sinners to reform from afar; in Mayotte it is the mere mortals who, in the context of practical activity, assume the advocacy of moral behavior. Thus, unlikely as it may seem at first glance, the amorality of the spirits is, by reflexion, a moral force in the community. In this sense possession is a highly significant dimension of social life.

If spirits are powerful and amoral, that is, potentially dangerous, the humans upon whose lives they impinge must develop a strategy for dealing with them so as to ensure their own security. Logically, two courses would seem to be open: to convert the spirit's amorality to morality or to reduce or neutralize their power. Neither of these courses could be successful in an absolute sense; the spirits' power is incontrovertible and their amorality is simply a part of their natures. The strategy adopted by the humans is not to attempt to create an absolute change but to mark off a context in which the individual spirit who has made its presence felt will not exercise its power irresponsibly; that is, they try to reach a balanced alliance with it.[7] Outside these relationships, the spirit can continue to act according to its nature, but within them it is expected to act according to the norms of the alliance. Of course, the spirit may prove to be an untrustworthy partner. No relationship with a spirit is free from tension and ambiguity. However, faced with the arrival of a spirit, humans find no reasonable course open to them other than the pursuit of an alliance.

The proposition behind this picture appears to be that morality is a social construction. Morality does not exist in the abstract, outside particular social relationships, but rather depends upon such relationships to be activated (or is synonymous with them). Because of self-interest, the people with whom one engages in social relationships can never be trusted absolutely, yet, without regular and well-established relationships, they could never be trusted at all. This view of things contrasts sharply with Islam, which asserts the existence of a moral order outside any particular social arrangements and in spite of human self-interest.

In sum, what emerges in the initial series of meetings with a spirit is a physical coherence on the part of the spirit and a moral coherence in the human sphere.

7. Medicine and transformation: the case of Habiba continued

In this chapter we will continue to follow the case of Habiba through the administration of the medicine at her *ishima* ceremony. Following the description and explication of these events, the general role of medicine in effecting a ritual transformation of both host and spirit will be analyzed. Discussion of the amusements at the *ishima* will be taken up in succeeding chapters.

Administration of the medicine at Habiba's *ishima*, October 20, 1975

Habiba arrived in the morning. During the day, she and her female relatives in Lombeni made the cakes and prepared the feast. The table in Mohedja's house was arranged with a dish of sugar, eight raw eggs, and two small bottles of cologne. After dinner Mohedja drew lines in white clay on the inside of the two pots Habiba had brought. Mohedja tore off pieces from a large pile of medicinal leaves and branches Tumbu had collected and stuffed some of every kind into each pot. The radio played pop music as she worked. Habiba and two other clients sat and watched as Tumbu arranged the brazier and lit the incense. People gathered in the courtyard, and Tumbu called to Dady Accua to join the patient in the house.

Habiba sat next to Tumbu on the bed. With throaty growls and gasps her spirit began to rise. The spirit shook hands with all of us, starting with Tumbu and Dady Accua, the two *fundi* (master curers). Someone started drumming in the courtyard. A few girls peered in the doorway.

The spirit chatted with Dady Accua. After awhile, it said it wanted to leave in the meantime. It stretched its limbs and lay down on the mat. In a moment, Habiba sat up, herself again.

A slight pause ensued. Habiba turned off the radio and prepared the cloth she would wear while taking the medicine. Tumbu's small grand-daughter woke and cried from the bed. Very suddenly, old DADY ACCUA gave a shout and stretched her arms wide. A spirit had risen in her. It asked what was going on and shook hands with us. Tumbu explained that we were arranging Habiba's medicine. He went back to fussing over the pots. Mohedja inquired after the spirit's village and children. She asked whether the medicine should be heated up inside the house or in the courtyard. The spirit suggested the courtyard. Rukia and Salima were delegated to help with the application of the medicine. The spirit sang in a low voice, then remarked how hungry it was. Mohedja reminded it of the price of sugar.

Two male drummers, young men from Lombeni Be, arrived and shook the spirit's hand. The spirit told Mohedja to feed them. DADY ACCUA joked with Mohedja and her adult daughter Nuriaty. She led the group in a short song, then screamed once, stretched her arms wide and returned to herself. A moment later, TUMBU started groaning. The spirit was soon well established in him. It did not shake hands, but greeted Dady Accua and then ordered Salima to begin cooking the medicine. The spirit started a song. The women seated around the edges of the room began to clap rhythmically. Bako Ali, who had been fussing over the medicine, now held both pots over the incense and muttered an incantation. TUMBU had a broad grin, an expression he never has when he is himself. Salima took the large pot out to the kitchen fire. TUMBU sat rubbing his hands together, then rose to consult with Mohedja. Habiba went out to change and returned dressed only in a single cloth, wound around her body and tucked in under the shoulders.

The beds were pushed to one side of the room, and the lantern and incense were placed on a mat spread on the floor. Habiba sat to one side of the mat, on a large wooden mortar placed horizontally. Rukia was in one corner with the new plate containing the medicinal twigs and a hardwood block for grating them on. TUMBU and Bako Ali sat on the bed, Mohedja on the floor near them, and Dady Accua on the mat. A few more women crowded into the corners of the room. Others stayed in the courtyard with the drummers. Salima put the large white cloth over Habiba's head, covering her whole body. She carried in the large steaming pot of medicine from the kitchen fire and placed it at Habiba's feet, under the cloth. In this way the spirit inhaled the medicinal vapors. The women clapped and sang, and the drums started up in the courtyard. TUMBU cried out *"Ça y'est!"* the call that a spirit makes when it is very excited. Under the cloth, HABIBA panted, shivered, shook, and uttered little cries. She began to cry. Rukia started grinding the sticks and Salima supervised the inhalation. TUMBU fetched more coals for the brazier and lit more incense at HABIBA's feet. HABIBA breathed very heavily. She sang a song, and all the women joined in the chorus. A large empty kerosene barrel was brought into the courtyard, placed lengthwise, and beaten together with drums. It seemed to make the rhythm even more insistent.

Salima removed the pot. HABIBA stuck her head out of the cloth and began to sing *Galaweny* with great intensity. She sat forward on the mortar, her body draped in the white sheet, one white clothed knee shaking wildly. The spirit looked around the room with sharp birdlike twists of the head. As the drummers paused for a moment, TUMBU called urgently to keep playing. They started up again, always in the same throbbing rhythm.

Salima entered with the smaller of the two pots, which she had been heating up in the meantime. She poured some liquid into the bowl to cool and exited with the big pot to reheat it. (Habiba had to alternately inhale the vapors from the large pot and drink the liquid from the small one seven times each.) HABIBA's knee jerked fast; she appeared full of nervous energy – keen and impatient. HABIBA sang "I am a spirit." BAKO ALI suddenly began shouting as he became possessed. TUMBU rubbed the head of Mwanesha (Chapter 5). HABIBA surveyed the scene from her seat, her body swaying from side to side.

The small child on the bed awakened, cried, and was carried out by TUMBU. HABIBA grinned, drawing back her lips to show her teeth. Rukia took the paste she had ground from the twigs and spread it on HABIBA's face, neck, arms, back, and legs, reaching under the cloth to include the thighs and breasts. HABIBA continued to sing while the paste was applied and reached out to shake hands with the spirit inhabiting Bako Ali. Habiba's spirit looked very self-important, as if it were enjoying all the attention. Rukia went back to her grinding. Salima entered with the large pot, placed it between HABIBA's legs, and draped the cloth to cover both her head and the pot. She then left to reheat the smaller pot.

When the steaming pot was removed and the sheet lifted, Rukia began to rub more paste on HABIBA's body. Suddenly RUKIA started screaming. A split second later, NURIATY and AMINA began to shout as well. All three shrieked and raised their arms. AMINA shook wildly for a moment. NURIATY buried her face first in Dady Accua's lap and then in HABIBA's. The spirits quieted down. NURIATY exited and BAKO ALI soon followed her. RUKIA returned to her grinding, then leaned against the wall, her head in her hands. She cried and put her head on HABIBA's knee, her arms around HABIBA's shoulders. HABIBA continued singing and drank from the bowl. Salima brought in the large steaming pot and rearranged the sheet. NURIATY returned, and RUKIA went back to her grinding.

The next period of inhalation was brief, and each period seemed to get shorter than the one before. Tumbu and Dady Accua started a soft chant together, clapping in time. The drums grew faster and louder. HABIBA looked rapidly from side to side, twisting her body and especially her neck, in time. The steam was reapplied and HABIBA leaned over the pot underneath the cloth. BAKO ALI returned to the room, sat on the bed, and snorted loudly. HABIBA pushed away the pot, stuck her head out, and grinned. BAKO ALI shouted nonsense syllables. HABIBA shook his hand again. HABIBA stretched out her hand and placed it on the head of Mwanesha. RUKIA grinned to herself as she ground the sticks.

HABIBA jerked under the cloth, then stuck her head out, extending her arms over those seated around her. RUKIA gave her more medicine to drink and rubbed more paste on her body. During the fifth inhalation, MOHEDJA began to scream and flail her arms and head. She quieted after a couple of minutes. The other women continued to sing and clap throughout the incident. HABIBA twitched under the cloth. No longer in trance, Tumbu busied himself turning out the puddings from their banana-leaf wrappings onto the winnowing tray.

When the seventh inhalation and drink were over, HABIBA descended from the mortar onto the mat on the floor and reclined against Dady Accua's body, her arms outstretched. In a few moments, Habiba rose slowly, helped by Rukia, and, herself again, went off to wash and dress. DADY ACCUA suddenly became possessed, barking and rising up on her knees and flailing her arms in the air. The spirit stepped outside to exhort the drummers, and then began dancing in the courtyard. Habiba returned, fully dressed, and gave the large white cloth used for the medicine to Tumbu, who put it aside. Tumbu set up the drummers on chairs in the clearing near the house, and the company exited to join the dancing. DADY ACCUA returned to the house and reclined against Habiba, stretching out her arms and singing. The two women exactly reversed positions. As the drums started up again, HABIBA uttered a screech of delight.

Commentary. The first time I observed the application of spirit medicine, it appeared to be a confused event, too many people in too small a room, the smells of incense and sweat and steaming medicine, individuals going in and out of trance, screaming and moving their bodies about in chaotic fashion. However, a closer examination reveals an underlying structure to the affair. Although the room is close and crowded, and although people wander in and out, participation is actually quite controlled. Everyone has some business there, invited because of their connections to Tumbu or their concern for Habiba (Figure 6.1). No one is merely an observer; each person helps in the application of the medicine, if only by singing and clapping. Of those present, some are Tumbu's *mwana fundi*, that is, individuals who are in the process of undergoing spirit cures with Tumbu or are learning to be curers from him. He appoints Salima and Rukia their tasks because he knows he can trust them not to interfere with the medicine. Rukia is the wife of Mohedja's brother and a patient of Tumbu's (and the subject of the second *patros* cure to be described). Salima, Mohedja's classificatory child, is an older woman with an extensive knowledge of spirits. She frequently exerts herself during cures officiated by Tumbu and Mohedja and plans, I suspect, to become an independent practicing curer herself. She is the only person present with a *patros* spirit who does not go into trance during the application of the medicine. Of the others present, Bako Ali learned to be a *patros* curer from Tumbu, and the two men always attend one another's events. Dady Accua shares the same spirit with Tumbu and is likewise always present at his events. She was the curer who officiated when Tumbu held his own ceremonies. Hassan Kombo is an older man, considered slightly simpleminded, who attends

Tumbu's and Mohedja's spirit cures although he does not have a spirit himself. Mwanesha is a classificatory older sibling of Mohedja's, only visiting in Lombeni and undergoing her own cure. The other women present, with the exception of Bako Ali's wife, are all relations of Habiba's. They include women, such as Marie, who do not have spirits of their own and are present only to support their kinswoman. In all, there are some fifteen adults, twelve women and three men (not including me), present in the room during some portion of the activities; four of them do not have spirits of their own.

Coherence is also established by the cycle of treatments. The medicine consists of an assortment of plant species, including both the leaves and stems. Representatives of six particular species are necessary for the *ishima* cure; the same ones plus an additional six are required for the *azulahy be*. The plants are collected by curers, and supposedly it is only the curers who know where they grow and how to recognize them. A curer's spirit will appear in dreams to identify particular species, collecting spots, and appropriate applications. Some of this knowledge is also passed in waking life from curers to their apprentices. In the case recorded above, Tumbu did the collecting and Mohedja then checked to make sure each species was present.

The medicine is administered to the patient in three forms. The leaves are boiled in water in two separate pots. The aromatic vapor from one pot is inhaled and the liquid from the other is drunk in small amounts. The latter liquid is also used to moisten the slab on which the twigs are ground into a paste; this is then applied to the skin. The medicine has to be administered in each of these ways seven times and the methods are rotated, the steam first, followed by the paste and liquid in either order, until seven cycles are over.

Only one fire is lit and the two pots are alternated on it, brought to the boil anew before every application. The vapor is inhaled while the pot is extremely hot. Under the cloth the patient sweats profusely; if she is not in trance already, the hyperventilation helps induce the change of state. I have never observed a patient receiving the steam treatment who did not immediately enter trance. From the local point of view, the spirit is receiving what it wants and there is no longer any reason for it to act difficult and refuse to appear. The steam often excites the spirit to a frenzy under the cloth; the spirit may become so aroused that it sticks its hands into the pot and stuffs some of the scalding mixture into its mouth.

During the periods of inhalation, the spirit is covered by a sheet, but between the bouts of steam it has a better chance to interact with the others in the room. It sits up, makes eye contact, and sings or makes remarks. Whereas the periods of inhalation serve to build up the intensity of the experience in the patient, the periods between inhalations seem to do the same for the other participants. It is during these moments that they too become possessed. The rhythm of the application of the medicine thus appears to influence the intensity of the whole proceedings, although this intensity is also built up by the drumming. Throughout, the interests and energies of everyone within the room appear to be turned collectively upon the patient's spirit. The spirit, in turn, at once both magnetizes the attention of the company and acknowledges their interest. The spirit is caught up in itself but also recognizes those around it, as, for example, when it magnanimously places its hand on the troubled Mwanesha. It appears keen and exhilarated and at the same time cannot turn its head fast enough to take in the evidence of its importance and to express it back to the gathering.

The constraints on the identities and movements of the spirits also provide coherence to the events described. This is most clearly observable in the opening and closing sequences of the narrative. The opening sequence is a kind of overture to the subsequent events. Incense is lit and Habiba goes into trance. The change in identity in "Habiba" is marked by the new arrival shaking hands with the other participants. A short while thereafter the spirit leaves Habiba and she comes back to herself. Then Dady Accua goes into a trance and again the presence of a spirit is acknowledged by the exchange of greeting rituals. The change in identities is made clear when the spirit asks what is going on, an inquiry concerning an activity that just a moment earlier Dady Accua herself was intimately involved in. The others defer to the spirit by asking its advice in procedural matters, and the spirit again expresses its general identity by remarking in a direct manner, which would be quite out of place among humans, how hungry it is. The spirit soon leaves Dady Accua, and immediately after she comes out of trance, Tumbu enters it. Tumbu's spirit greets Dady Accua and then begins to organize the curing session. The trances of each of these three individuals follow each other sequentially, with no overlap. The sequencing is indicated in Figure 7.1.

In each case, the spirit takes care to greet and interact with the other individuals present. To an observer who was not aware of the movements in and out of trance or of the changes in identity that trance signifies, there would appear to be a great deal of redundancy in peoples' actions, particularly a repetition of handshaking and asking after one another's health. Such greeting ritual is a distinctive feature of the interaction between spirits and humans, serving to define and express or keep track of the multiple changes in identity. In this instance it appears to be laying out an inventory of the possible permuta-

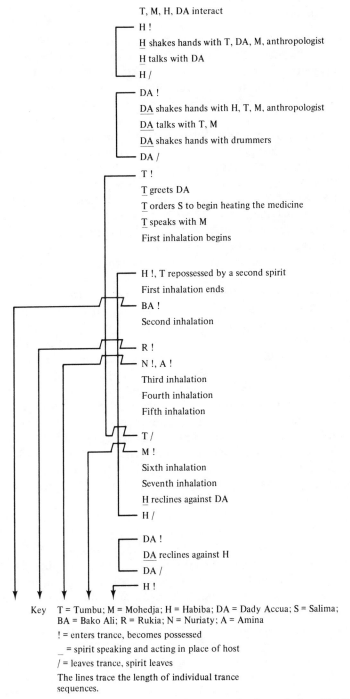

T, M, H, DA interact

H !
H shakes hands with T, DA, M, anthropologist
H talks with DA
H /

DA !
DA shakes hands with H, T, M, anthropologist
DA talks with T, M
DA shakes hands with drummers
DA /

T !
T greets DA
T orders S to begin heating the medicine
T speaks with M
First inhalation begins

H !, T repossessed by a second spirit
First inhalation ends
BA !
Second inhalation

R !
N !, A !
Third inhalation
Fourth inhalation
Fifth inhalation

T /
M !
Sixth inhalation
Seventh inhalation
H reclines against DA
H /

DA !
DA reclines against H
DA /

H !

Key   T = Tumbu; M = Mohedja; H = Habiba; DA = Dady Accua; S = Salima;
BA = Bako Ali; R = Rukia; N = Nuriaty; A = Amina

! = enters trance, becomes possessed

_ = spirit speaking and acting in place of host

/ = leaves trance, spirit leaves

The lines trace the length of individual trance
sequences.

Figure 7.1. Sequence of possessions and communications during Habiba's
cure.

tions in relationships and demonstrating that, in fact, Habiba, Tumbu, and Dady Accua share a single spirit.[1] Nothing of substance is passed verbally between the participants, and, at the surface level, the communication appears to be merely phatic, setting out all the possible channels and demonstrating that they are working and open.

At the close of the performance, two of the participants again run through the permutations. When the spirit is ready to leave Habiba's body, it reclines against Dady Accua. Habiba is no sooner out of trance when Dady Accua falls into it and, in turn, reclines against Habiba. The reciprocity expressed here is perfectly balanced.

What keeps the trance states of these individuals alternating so regularly is the fact that they are each possessed by the same spirit. The maintenance of the integrity of the notion of "person," with the corollary that the spirit cannot be in two places at once, thus provides a major constraint on the action: Individuals with the same spirit must take turns becoming possessed. The spirit first appears in Habiba and subsequently moves from her to Dady Accua and from Dady Accua to Tumbu. There appears to be one exception to this smooth synchronization in the narrative, that is where Tumbu does not leave trance before Habiba reenters it upon the first application of the medicine. I asked Tumbu about this later and he replied that by the time Habiba became repossessed by the spirit that they share, he was already possessed by a different spirit. Tumbu has two *patros* spirits and it was the second one that I then observed. When two spirits of a single individual are of the same species (e.g., both *patros* or both *trumba*) it is not necessary to first withdraw from the trance state and then reenter it when the identity of the possesing spirit changes. The change from one spirit identity to another within the same individual is, therefore, not necessarily marked by elaborate signs. In this case, the switch occurred where I recorded Tumbu calling out *"Ça y'est!"*[2]

The relationship occurring between two or more hosts who share the same spirit (e.g., Tumbu, Dady Accua, and Habiba) is one of "siblingship" in Kelly's sense (1977); that is, the humans are related to one another by the fact that they are all hosts to the same spirit. This is not an identity relationship and there is no fusion or confusion of "self" among them. Such hosts tend to cooperate with one another and frequently they are in curer/patient or master/apprentice (*fundi/mwana fundi*) relationships as well. Thus Tumbu organizes Habiba's cure and, in turn, had his own cure produced by Dady Accua.

If successive possession is a sign that the individuals concerned share the same spirit, simultaneous possession indicates unequivocally that they do not. Simultaneous possession allows for the enactment of another kind of relationship, that between two spirits. Relationships between Habiba's spirit and others are indicated at a number of places in the narrative: Bako Ali's spirit shakes its hand, Nuriaty's spirit buries its head in its lap, Rukia's spirit places its head on its knee. These actions provide messages concerning the relative statuses of the individual spirits. The spirits of Habiba and Bako Ali appear to be indicating that they are peers, while those of Nuriaty and Rukia allow themselves to be comforted by Habiba's spirit, signifying a junior position. Habiba's spirit is an elder and a curer, while those of Nuriaty and Rukia are youths.[3] Sequences of simultaneous possession thus gain coherence from the maintenance of highly conventional role relationships among the spirits. In fact, virtually all of the communication among spirits is concerned with the expression of relative status (i.e., the relative status of the spirits, not of the hosts). Communication of actual substance among spirits is largely restricted to that between the curer's spirit and his patient's spirit.

Medicine and rites of passage

The manifest concern behind the activities we have been examining is with the welfare of the individual who has become possessed. The process is explicitly described as curative, as a transition from illness to relative health by means of active intervention with medicine and other therapeutic techniques on the part of a curer. Whether the patient is actually suffering or not, the spirit has the potential to create havoc in the body it has entered. The treatment thus has the purpose not only of alleviating symptoms that may be present but of ensuring that the spirit does not abuse the host further. It does not provide immunization from future attacks by other spirits, but it does create a situation in which the current spirit will agree to remain or become benign and may possibly even choose to become benevolent. In sum, if the process is expressed in terms of therapy, "therapy" must be understood to indicate not merely an alleviation of symptoms (which, in any case, may frequently be achieved on a short-term basis by simpler procedures) but a change of state.

This "therapeutic" process can usefully be examined as ritual, because it transforms individuals through communicative means. If the aim of the ritual is to move the spirit from amorality to relative morality and the patient from illness to relative health, it is not surprising that the entire process is organized in the form of a rite of passage. But whose rite of passage, whose change of state, is to be celebrated, that of the host or that of the spirit? Why does the spirit receive more attention than the host?

This paradox may be resolved if rites of passage are viewed as changing not isolated individuals but the relations between individuals. The change occurs in the subject's relationships, that is, it affects not only the central individual but also all members of society who must recognize the new identity and interact with the neophyte on its basis. In fact, then, the rite of passage of the spirit cure concerns primarily the change in relationship between host and spirit, the creation of a new identity relationship between them (Goodenough 1965) in which each member has its specific rights and duties vis-à-vis the other. In theory, the patient's relationships to the other members of her society (except the curer) do not undergo change during the ritual. However, as a newcomer to the social field, the spirit must develop relationships not only with the host but also with the curer, with the host's spouse and close kin, and with the other spirits of the same species who rise in the humans of the village. Because it participates in so many new relationships, it is no wonder that the focus of the rite of passage is on the spirit rather than the host.

According to Van Gennep (1960), rites of passage unfold in three phases: separation, margin, and aggregation. Turner (1969, 1967) has emphasized the importance of the second phase, which he calls the liminal period. In the possession ritual, separation from society, or from the patient's old position within it, occurs with either the first onset of trance or the first diagnosis and with the accompanying preliminary medication the patient may receive. Aggregation occurs with the successful completion of the public feasts. In between these moments lies the period in which the patient is neither free of the spirit, nor totally subjugated by it, nor yet in a steady relationship with it. This is a period of transition, during which, by her own actions in seeking a curer, communicating through him with the spirit, amassing the goods needed for the ceremonies, and producing the ceremonies, the patient is actively engaged in changing her condition. She is thus engaged in moving from an identity as an ill and possibly burdensome individual to one whose relationship of reciprocity with a spirit makes her free from the concerns of illness and cure and less dependent on her kinsmen.

During this period, her ambiguous state does not generally interfere with the patient's daily activities; her status as patient/host does not dominate her other statuses – as wife, mother, horticulturalist, and so on. It erupts intermittently, when the spirit rises in her head and replaces her social persona with its own, so that, like all "liminal *personae,*" she is "neither here nor there; . . . betwixt and between the positions assigned and arrayed by law, custom, convention, and ceremonial" (Turner 1969:95); she "passes through a cultural realm

that has few or none of the attributes of the past or coming state"
(Turner 1969:94).

The patient can also be observed in the liminal state at the onset of
each séance, as she crouches, "passive or humble" (Turner 1969:95),
before the smoke of the incense and obeys the curer's demand for the
spirit to rise, and when she sits, practically naked, to receive the first
shock of the medicine, whether of the pungent steam of the *patros* or
the cold deluge of the *trumba*. Until the spirit rises, which it does
almost instantaneously upon receipt of the medicine, the patient waits,
trembling and alone, so that the onlookers are moved to sympathy and
whisper to one another "poor thing!"

We can consider the rite of passage of the spirit in terms of the
model applicable to humans. The spirit first appears in a liminal state,
in a condition of incorporality and incoherence, separated from its own
village and society. But the liminal symbolism is concentrated during
the application of the medicine. When the medicine is over, the spirit
begins the process of aggregation by entertaining and thus fulfilling its
obligations toward its fellow spirits. Its status remains ambiguous,
however, until the formal announcement of the name, at which point it
is incorporated into the body of spirits of that species that is active in
the village and into the extended family grouping of the host.

The period of the application of the medicine appears to be the
primary liminal phase for both host and spirit, a key to their respective
transformations. The significance of this time is evidenced in the strong
emotional reactions of the participants. The saliency of the therapy is
due to the fact that the identities and fortunes of spirit and host are
least clearly separated at this point; their respective paths of transition
appear to intersect or to be superimposed on one another. These moments demonstrate to all concerned how inextricably linked are the
histories of the two main characters. All along, great care has been
taken to establish an understanding of the distinction between spirit
and host and to maintain the notion of a separate spirit society apart
from the human one. Yet now, the two appear to merge, bound by the
process of undergoing the medication.

The ultimate intention of the participants is to cure the host. But at
this stage in the proceedings, the immediate goal is to give medicine
(*audy*) to the *spirit.* That is, the participants, including the spirit, talk
as if the medicine is supplied for the benefit of the spirit itself. The
spirit has been demanding the medicine and becomes cooperative as
soon as it begins to receive it. A closer examination of the medicine
will clarify this ambiguity.

The concept of medicine in general (*audy*) has broad denotations of
efficacy and of prophylaxis as well as of therapy, that is, of the orderly

control over change. Anything from prayer to insect repellent may be labeled "medicine." As such, medicine is found associated with all the rites of passage, and, as in many cultures, its application appears to be a legitimate context for the presentation of a kind of elaborate epistemological inventory (e.g., Turner 1969).

Although many plant species are associated with very specific illnesses or symptoms, the species used in the *patros* cure, particularly a group of the six most important, are administered in the cure of any spirit-related illness. That is, they are applied not only directly to the spirits as in the *patros* ritual but to humans as well, frequently with an intent other than to coax a spirit to rise. Some of the species may be used interchangeably. From the sack of plants collected for Rukia's ceremony, Tumbu distributed smaller amounts to a small boy suffering from diarrhea and to three women suffering from toothache, venereal disease, and severe menstrual cramps. Although all of these cases involved spirits in one manner or another, the purpose of the medicine varied, functioning either to diagnose the presence of the spirit, to weaken the hold of the spirit, or to achieve the cure of the physical ailment once the spirit had already been dealt with. Patients with the same illnesses but without the presence of diagnosed spirits would be given different and more specific medicines. Such medicines might also be used concurrently with some of the more broadly based ones. The method of application of the medicine, which part of the plant is used, and whether it is applied to the skin or added to water and drunk, inhaled, or bathed in also varies with the case. Patients who are suspected of having spirits who wish to rise to their heads will often be asked to follow a week-long regime composed of daily medicated baths, inhalations, drinks, and ointments.

Such medicine is a major weapon of humans in their fight to come to terms with spirits and, as such, may not be appreciated at all by the spirit resident in the human patient. If the spirit is not yet willing to enter into the process of negotiation, it will refuse to submit to the medicine and will fight the curer, sometimes even violently, to avoid doing so. A practiced curer will have a method for forcing a spirit to swallow something against its will.

In most cases, then, the medicine is applied to the host with the intent of weakening the hold of the spirit or of removing the physical ailments associated with its presence. The medicine is applied either directly to the host, so that it will reach the spirit indirectly, or, occasionally, directly to the spirit (who has risen in the host), but against its will. During the *patros* curing ceremony, however, the medicine is given directly to an eager spirit. The spirit is often so appreciative that it rises at the first whiff of medicine and sometimes even stuffs the scalding mass into its mouth with bare hands. At this point, the spirit is stating clearly that the medicine is working to its own benefit. Like the host, the spirit seems to be undergoing a cure. But, the fact that the spirit requires "medicine" does not mean that it is sick; it is said to be hungry. A spirit eats the host's blood or organs, thus making her ill. It will desist in this when satisfied with cologne, pudding, and medicine instead. The medicine is *haniŋ* 'staple' or 'starchy cooked food,' a term whose primary referent for humans is cooked rice. The "medicine" satisfies the spirit's hunger and stops its consumption of the host's blood.

When the plant substances are viewed as food, the rite becomes understandable: The spirit is actively demonstrating consummation of its bargain with the humans by filling itself on plants rather than on the life forces of the patient. But why should the food be referred to as medicine (*audy*)? The spirit itself is not sick, but the reference to medicine draws the comparison between this instance of its use and all others. It serves as a reminder that the ritual of status change the spirit is undergoing is also a ritual of healing for the host, thus drawing attention to the complementary nature of the transitions. It also brings out the contrast between this application of medicine and others. Whereas in most cases medicine is forced upon the symptom-causing agent, here the spirit takes it willingly as a sign of concord. Perhaps most important, the reference to medicine reminds people of the paradox it represents. Plant medicine is the one sure means that humans have at their disposal to control spirits;[4] yet, it is the spirits who own and dispense the medicine and teach humans its use. The medicine thus signifies both the aggressive, destructive side of spirits that must be overcome and the constructive, generous side. It represents both the conflict and the cooperation between spirits and humans and thus condenses the significance of the whole long sequence of events in the illness and curing process.

These points may be clarified considerably by considering the aspect of medicine that is said to have the most impact on the spirits and to be most attractive to them, namely, its pungent herbal odor. Odor has a central place in many other rites as well. Prayers are generally said over a dish of lighted incense, the aromatic smoke bearing the message to God. Spirits are likewise invoked over incense. Powerful, pervasive odors may be channels of communication like incense, dangerous like blood, or merely unpleasant or offensive like distilled ylang-ylang oil or rotten food.

The classification of smells (*haruf*) is paradigmatic rather than tax-

Table 7.1. *Cognitive classification of smells (haruf)*

	Unmarked	Pervasive, enduring, very strong
Fragant	*Maɲitry*	*Mantsiŋ*
Foul	*Maimbu*	*Mantsiŋ*
Fishy	*Malaŋ*	*Mantsiŋ*

onomic. Along one dimension (Table 7.1) are the distinctions between *maɲitry* 'fragrant,' 'perfumed,' 'aromatic,' 'sweet smelling'; *maimbu* 'foul,' 'stinking'; and *malaŋ* 'fishy'. *Malaŋ* refers only to fish and to birds that feed on fish. *Maɲitry* refers in particular to such things as cologne, certain flowers, and lemons, and may include all sweet foods (sugar, honey, syrup, fruit), cooked meat, spices, and fresh coconut oil, and the incense lit to perfume the mosque on Fridays. Fecal matter, corpses, distilled ylang-ylang oil, and a few other plants are *maimbu*. The other dimension has only one marked category, *mantsiŋ*, which refers to an odor that is particularly intense, pervasive, enduring, and difficult to remove. It is the primary term applied to certain odors such as *uban* and *embuku* incense (the former is used both in Islamic ritual and to call up the *patros*, the latter to call *trumba*), blood, and underarm sweat. It also includes: all the smells emanating from things *lu* 'rotting,' whether fruit, meat, body sores, or corpses, thus everything that is also classified as *maimbu;* those smells that would be classified as *maɲitry* were they not so pervasive or enduring, such as "too much" cologne and the dried flowers that women put in their hair;[5] and the smells of such varied substances as kerosene, alcohol, burnt rice, intoxicating palm wine (but not sweet palm wine), and *trandraka* 'tenrec' meat, which are hard to remove.

Mantsiŋ covers both spoiled food, whether by natural process (decay) or cultural (burning), and illicit food (palm liquor, *trandraka* meat). *Mantsiŋ* odors cannot be removed or concealed. They enter the body along with the food as it is eaten and can be smelled thereafter in sweat and urine. *Mantsiŋ* thus carries connotations of strength, endurance, impropriety, biological process, and the inevitable links between things. *Maɲitry*, by contrast, connotes sweetness, pleasure, legitimate satisfactions. It refers to particular times and places and statuses, to things in themselves rather than to the links and processes between them. Despite the fact that they are not "opposites" in the cognitive scheme, *mantsiŋ* and *maɲitry* do present symbolic contrasts (Table 7.2).

The achievement of status and the celebration of social norms are marked by things *maɲitry*, whereas the processes of transition, the

Table 7.2. *Symbolic classification of smells (haruf)*

Maɲitry	Sweetness, pleasure, legitimate indulgence, status, event, convention (culture)
Mantsiŋ	Strength, endurance, illicit indulgence, impropriety, condition, process, inevitability (nature)

liminal periods, are marked by things *mantsiŋ*. Leaving aside food, as it obviously has aspects of importance besides smell, two *maɲitry* substances frequently applied on festive occasions are cologne and *mwina*, an aromatic oily herbal paste. Unlike ordinary cosmetics, *mwina* is only applied on very special occasions. It may be rubbed on a girl's forehead at menarche. A bride is anointed by an older sister and in turn anoints her husband during the week after the consummation of the marriage. No household is without its small bottle of cologne. Cologne is sprinkled on the body and clothing on all major calendrical holidays, including the weekly Friday mosque service. Along with a good meal, a splash of cologne is offered to the Koranic masters who have recited at family rituals, for example at the oration of the *Maulida* during the month of the Prophet's birth. Cologne is also sprinkled on the central participants and well-wishers at the successful completion of weddings and payment of *shuŋgu* obligations to the age group or village. Expressing the achievement of status, cologne celebrates the initiates and sponsors and aims to please, and therefore acquire the goodwill of, the Koranic masters so that their prayers will travel more quickly.[6]

In their immoderate application of cologne, spirits demonstrate their intemperate, sensual natures, their wilfulness and feelings of self-importance in the absence of significant achievement. In contrast to humans, they do not wait for special contexts and deserving occasions but indulge in cologne at any time. The spirits' use of cologne is determined by personal desire, not regulated according to the public system of morality. Their consumption is emphasized by their habit of imbibing as well as applying it externally. The liberal doses leave a heavy scent on the breath – which is *mantsiŋ* rather than *maɲitry* – and serves, along with the inverted use of the cologne in the first place, to emphasize the liminal quality of the spirits.

The steam from the *patros* medicines is also *mantsiŋ*, its pervasiveness contributing to the experience of the ongoing process of transformation and of the liminality of the occasion. The inhalation of the aromatic herbal medicines presents a striking inversion of the heavy *mantsiŋ* odor produced at another important rite of passage. Before

boys are circumcised and before virgin girls consummate their marriages, they must undergo an unpleasant protective ritual that consists
of inhaling the strong and acrid smoke produced by a combination of
burning seaweed, lemon and kapok seeds, black pepper, coconut oil,
and carbon paper inscribed with special notations for the occasion by
an astrologer. The ingredients are burned together in a pot set up over
a fire inside the house. The initiate is forced to remain under a cloth
and inhale the smoke until the substances in the pot are entirely consumed. The process is then repeated with fresh ingredients for a total
of seven times, as in the *patros* ritual. And, as in the case of Rukia's
patros medicine (Chapter 8), the treatment must take place inside the
house, with the door shut and without communication to the outside.
The inhalation of the smoke is a painful and unpleasant experience,
and the initiate may cry or scream and try to escape. Afterward, as he
or she waits for the *wakat*, the auspicious time recognized by the
astrologer for the circumcision or penetration, the initiate is washed
and anointed with *mwina* to offset the smell of the smoke.

The ritual is explained as a prophylactic against *kombelume* 'a kind
of epilepsy.'[7] The smoke removes the *lulu raty* 'bad spirit' (a generalized and vague reference that is not to be confused with the specific
kinds of spirits that rise and speak through humans) that everyone may
be born with and that has the potential for setting off the disease. The
medicine removes this potential, ensuring in particular that a boy will
not be subject to seizure while he is under the circumcisor's knife, nor
a girl during her wedding, nor either of them at any time thereafter in
adult life.

The smoke ritual provides further indication of the association between strong smell and loss of bodily control at significant rites of
passage[8] and stands in metaphoric, inverted relationship to the *patros*
cure. In the former case, in preparation for a weakened condition and
loss of blood, a strong and unpleasant odor is produced in the patient
in order to remove any spirits and to prevent the loss of bodily control.
In the latter case, in the face of a weakened condition, a loss of blood
(eaten by the spirit), and periods marked by the absence of bodily
control, a strong but pleasant odor is produced in order to establish
some control over the spirit's actions.[9]

The *patros* ritual thus makes sense as a rite of passage viewed from
the perspectives of both host and spirit. For the host it is significant as
it contrasts with the "puberty ritual"; for the spirit it is significant as
the two rituals are symmetrical. The spirit, like the child, is undergoing
a ritual of status elevation. The analogy between the rituals suggests
that the medicine is necessary to the spirit initiate in terms of its
prophylactic rather than its healing properties, assuring a successful

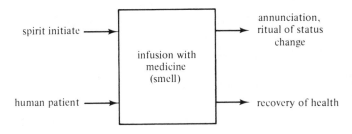

Figure 7.2. Medicine as a logical transformer.

completion of the annunciation and status change. These points may be summarized in the following equations:

Host's view:
permeation with foul smoke : avoidance of ill health and loss of bodily control :: permeation with fragrant steam : recovery of good health and bodily control

Spirit's view:
permeation with foul odor : successful completion of human's circumcision/defloration :: permeation with pleasant odor : successful completion of spirit's annunciation

Combined:
foul smell : pleasant smell :: avoidance of loss : recovery :: circumcision/defloration : annunciation

The apparently contradictory attitudes of the spirit toward plant medicine now make sense. The spirit rejects undergoing medical treatment when the aim is to weaken it and appreciates the treatment when the aim can be interpreted as the successful accomplishment of its own status elevation. It is the fact that in both cases the means are provided by *medicine* that makes this transformation possible. The medicine makes the changes occurring in spirit and host mutually comprehensible, or at least mutually compatible, by orienting them within a single, inclusive symbolic system. Just as it physically permeates both spirit and host, uniting them in a common scent, so the medicine provides a kind of permeation between their respective conceptual worlds. For all their outward differences, humans and spirits share the same scheme for the performance of rites of passage. As incense provides the context for the material transformation between human and spirit, so does medicine provide the conceptual transformer, allowing the participants to move back and forth between understanding the ritual in terms of the changes it produces in the host and understanding it in terms of those it produces in the spirit (Figure 7.2).

8. The hidden name: the case of Rukia

Before completing our analysis of the syntagmatic structure of *patros* activity, it will be useful to examine a second case. Rukia's history complements that of Habiba in a number of interesting respects. First, it concerns the second and larger of the curing ceremonies, the *azulahy be*. Second, it centers on an individual whose problems and social position are quite different from Habiba's and whose relationship with her spirit is of a somewhat different quality. Consequently, the atmosphere of the two cures presents a striking contrast. The speed with which Habiba's rituals were conducted and the lack of emphasis on the imposition by the spirit of pain and suffering on the host mark Habiba's case and her immediate relationship with her spirit as somewhat unusual. In fact, when Habiba actually did fall ill, some months after the performance of the *ishima,* the spirit rose and forthrightly denied all responsibility for the illness and made no claims of any sort on her relatives. Habiba's cure went so smoothly that even her curer had a hard time believing it. Rukia, on the other hand, was very unsure of herself, and her cure was fraught with tension.

Most important, Rukia's history provides us with the material to understand the process of construction of the spirit's personal identity and the significance of the spirit's announcement of its name. In contrast to Habiba's case, where the tacitly acknowledged identity of the spirit added a rich layer of allusion to the action, the identity of Rukia's spirit (as well as that of her sister Kuraishiya) was a matter of suspense until the last minute. We can take advantage of the fact that where the performance of the key actors is problematic, the principles of competence are made more explicit.

The two cures serve to show the range of behavior that possession can encompass in Mayotte. The contrast also suggests that there is no single motivational pattern underlying possession, that its onset has no single psychological cause, and that it serves no specific psychological function (cf. Chapter 4). Possession exists as a symbolic system organized in a fairly rigorous way; nevertheless, the personal messages that are communicated through it vary with the users.

The account is divided into the following sections, interspersed with commentary:

1. Background
2. Certification of the spirit's demands, October 28, 1975
3. Scheduling the ceremony, November 7
4. Administration of the medicine, November 10
5. Performance of the *azulahy be,* November 12, 1975 (excerpts)

The theme to be emphasized throughout the account is the problematic emergence of the identity of Rukia's spirit. However, a full analysis of the process of identity construction will be postponed for the general discussion of the nature of the *azulahy be* in the following chapter.

Background

Rukia was a handsome woman in her mid-forties. Her parents were dead and she had two younger half-siblings. She had been married nearly twenty years to a man who, although kind, was a heavy drinker. Whereas most males drink during their youth, they tend to stop when they reach maturity. However, Rukia's spouse, Sula, had been unable to do so despite numerous attempts to persuade him. Unlike many women, Rukia tolerated her husband's habit, although she was concerned when he drank in public. Sula and Rukia also had trouble disciplining their older children. The two boys were reluctant to assist on the family farm; the daughter brought disgrace by becoming pregnant before marriage and continued to live with the father of her child despite her parents' strong and sustained objections. One of Rukia's younger children appeared to have a debilitating ailment. In sum, Rukia's situation was not a particularly happy one.

Rukia had had a *patros* spirit for some years and had already held the *ishima* ceremony. Sula had promised to produce the *azulahy be* in 1975. I first observed Rukia's spirit at the *patros* ceremonies of other individuals in the village. During the public dancing at one ceremony, Rukia, in a state of possession, began to cry. When a bowl of goat's blood was carried into the arena, she dashed up and fell on her face over the bowl and greedily lapped up the blood. On the occasion of Habiba's ceremony, Rukia's spirit again began to cry and later had an angry conversation with Tumbu, its curer, over the size of the goat Sula was providing for its ceremony. The spirit announced that if Tumbu couldn't talk Sula into providing a larger goat, it might just decide not to go through with the cure at all. The behavior of the spirit indicated its troubled and impatient state, how sorry it felt for itself, and how badly it wished to draw attention to itself.

As her spirit was unhappy and concerned over the fate of its curing ceremony, so was Rukia herself. In a private conversation some days after the successful completion of Habiba's ceremony, Tumbu and Mohedja commented upon Rukia's anxiety and, to my astonishment, attributed it to the fact that she didn't know her spirit's personal name. Although the moment when a spirit reveals its name in public is supposed to be the climax of the whole affair, in fact, patient and curer are both extremely nervous if they don't know the name beforehand. The question in their minds is: What if, when the moment of climax arrives, the spirit isn't able or doesn't want to announce its name? The spirit might rise in Rukia, climb on the chair, and, surrounded by an eager audience, be speechless or say simply, "I am –" and not be able to continue. Or it might give the wrong name and be immediately challenged by someone in in the audience, their own spirit rising in them to prove that the neophyte is lying, as a spirit can't be two places at once. Any one of these events would be very embarrassing to both the patient and the curer. The patient would not get well and would have to go through the expense of producing another ceremony. The curer would have failed at his job and would be disparaged accordingly. I have never observed such a failure myself, but people say they are not infrequent.

There was one clue to the identity of Rukia's spirit. Each *patros* spirit demands a certain color of offerings, either white, red, black, or tricolored. For example, the *patros* spirit Mze Marwan demands black animals. Most spirits ask for "red" (i.e., red or brown) animals. Rukia's spirit had demanded a white goat and chickens. This narrowed the possibilities. Tumbu asked Mohedja to review the spirits that required white. They recalled that Lahadjy, a young male *patros* who visited Mohedja, wanted white, and also the spirit – they didn't recall its name – who visited a woman at the far end of the village. Tumbu asserted that he would call up Rukia's spirit and have a long talk with it to see if he couldn't bring out the name for her. He could not, of course, ask it directly, because, first of all, it was the spirit's prerogative not to reveal its name until all its conditions had been met and, second, if it really didn't know its name, asking it outright would create a deadlock.

The whole business suggests that the public announcement of the name is a validation of the status of the patient (and that of the curer) as well as that of the spirit itself. Successful completion of the naming indicates that the patient's troubles are over, that she has succeeded in mustering the funds and assistance to produce the ceremonies for her spirit, that these ceremonies have proceeded without a hitch (*nefa tsara*), and that, in return, her spirit will now treat her with a certain amount of respect. A Western analyst might say that the patient has been able to impose control over her somewhat chaotic behavior and to stabilize it in a formal identity. She has gained a handle on her behavior by naming it. The affirmation of the name is also an indication, both to the curer and the patient herself, that control has been established and that the spirit is behaving in a coherent fashion by maintaining a discrete, autonomous identity. Ideally, this fact should be tacitly or privately established between the spirit and the curer and the patient before it is announced to the public.

Certification of the spirit's demands, October 28, 1975

> Tumbu, Mohedja, and I went to Rukia's house in the neighboring hamlet of Bevatu in order to call up her spirit. Her husband, Sula, and her younger sister Kuraishiya were present (Figure 8.1). Rukia's spirit arrived slowly after the incense was lit, an increased rate of breathing the only evidence of the transformation. Suddenly the spirit spat[1] and then reached out to shake our hands. Tumbu explained that we had gathered to arrange the impending ceremony. Then Sula held up the incense in front of Tumbu and called upon his spirit to rise as well. When Tumbu's spirit had appeared, Sula addressed it, again stating the purpose of the assembly. He showed what he had already bought for the ceremony: two meters of white cloth that the spirit would wear around its head, two large and two small bottles of eau de cologne, some sugar, and fifteen eggs. He even led in the white goat. Sula said he still had to acquire two pots, a plate and a bowl, the four-meter cloth under which the medicine would be inhaled, and the two large chickens the spirit had asked for. The latter was a particular problem; because of a recent poultry epidemic, there were few to be had, and the *patros* insisted on a white cock. No date was set for the ceremony, and Tumbu's spirit suggested they leave the scheduling up to Tumbu. In none of the discussion did Tumbu appear to throw out to Rukia's *patros* any suggestions concerning its identity. Rukia's spirit, however, was quite clear on demanding that the goat, chickens, and headcloth all be white.

Scheduling the ceremony, November 7

> Juma Hassan, a well-known spirit curer with kin in Lombeni, was in charge of the *patros* cure of Rukia's sister Kuraishiya. He approached Tumbu and suggested holding the spirit feasts of the two sisters jointly. Although suspicious of his motives, Tumbu took the only polite course and accepted the invitation, flattering Juma Hassan by

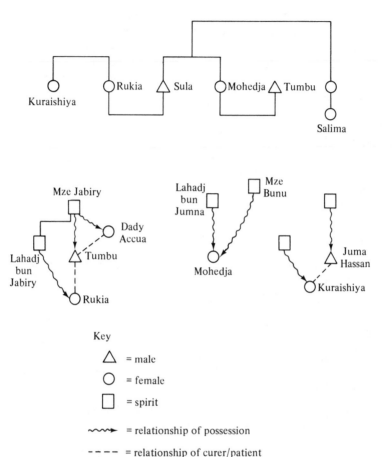

Figure 8.1. Relationships among the individuals mentioned in Rukia's cure.

saying that he, Tumbu, would act as the *mwana fundi,* the 'apprentice' or 'junior curer.' The two men then tried to select an appropriate day for the ceremony, avoiding days that, according to astrological considerations, were considered bad luck. They settled tentatively on the coming Wednesday.

Tumbu and I then went over to Rukia's. Tumbu recounted to Rukia his conversation with Juma Hassan. Sula lit the incense and called both Rukia's and Tumbu's spirits to rise. Tumbu sat waiting for Rukia to go into trance first, but she gave no indication of doing so. There was a long pause. Tumbu lectured Rukia's spirit on not keeping the curer and the people who wanted to help it waiting. Another pause. Tumbu suggested holding the meeting another day. At this, Rukia switched into trance and Tumbu berated the spirit again. Ru-

kia's spirit called for more incense and then waved it in front of
Tumbu, calling upon his spirit to rise and muttering about people
with "quick tempers" (*malaiky meluku*).

When Tumbu was in trance as well, Sula brought out the things he
had bought for the ceremony. Tumbu's spirit was very pleased to
learn that two additional bottles of cologne had been contributed by
Sula's daughter, who was normally at odds with her parents. Mohedja
had entered the room in the meantime, and Tumbu's spirit called
upon her spirit to rise as well, saying, "Let's all work together."
Tumbu's spirit asked if there were any dates they objected to. Sula
pointed out that the village had forbidden spirit events on Thursdays
and Fridays. Mohedja's spirit suggested Wednesday, and they all
agreed to this. Tumbu brought up the idea of sharing the ceremony
with Kuraishiya, and Rukia's spirit again assented. Mohedja's spirit
then remarked that Rukia's medicine should be given on an earlier
day when it would be easier to maintain privacy and restrict participation to the family members. They settled on Monday.

The conversation stretched on. Sula asked the assembled spirits for
medicine for his sick child, and Rukia then left trance and asked the
remaining two spirits for medicine for a second child. Tumbu and
Mohedja were the last to leave trance.

Commentary. The reason that the scheduling of the medicine is of such
concern is that this is a time when it is very easy to practice sorcery
against the patient. All one needs is a single leaf of the medicine and
one can disturb things so that the *patros* will not be able to announce
its name. Tumbu and Mohedja have already been worried about the
possibility of failure, and now, with the participation of Juma Hassan,
they suspect that their fellow curer, out of a sense of competition,
might attempt to cross them. Therefore, they establish the precaution
of holding the medical part of the ritual privately and well in advance
of the feast.

It is interesting to note here both the sense of competition and
suspicion that prevails between Tumbu and Juma and the contrasting
cooperation between Tumbu and Mohedja. Tumbu's spirit calls upon
Mohedja's for reinforcement and Mohedja's spirit responds admirably,
being the one to make all the substantive suggestions and thus conceal-
ing from the company the unease that Tumbu feels about cooperating
with Juma. In this way, Tumbu and Mohedja, and their spirits, operate
in perfect and subtle solidarity.

Two other points of note are the role played by the patient's husband, Sula, and the degree of redundancy in the conversation. Sula
plays a major role in the whole business, acting as responsible agent
for his wife. First he calls upon the spirits and then he demonstrates to
them that he has observed their wishes and produced the requisite
products. The trouble between Rukia's spirit and Sula over the size of

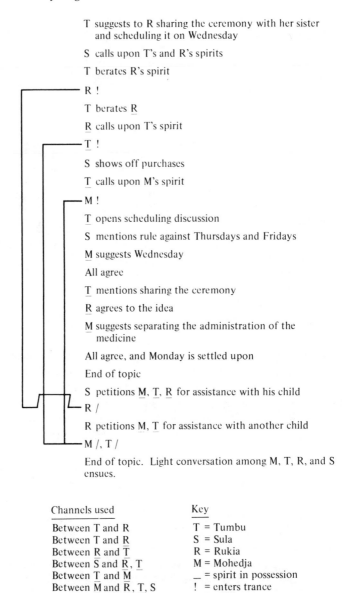

T suggests to R sharing the ceremony with her sister and scheduling it on Wednesday

S calls upon T's and R's spirits

T berates R's spirit

R !

T berates R̲

R̲ calls upon T's spirit

T̲ !

S shows off purchases

T̲ calls upon M's spirit

M !

T̲ opens scheduling discussion

S mentions rule against Thursdays and Fridays

M̲ suggests Wednesday

All agree

T̲ mentions sharing the ceremony

R̲ agrees to the idea

M̲ suggests separating the administration of the medicine

All agree, and Monday is settled upon

End of topic

S petitions M̲, T̲, R̲ for assistance with his child

R /

R petitions M̲, T̲ for assistance with another child

M /, T /

End of topic. Light conversation among M, T, R, and S ensues.

Channels used	Key
Between T and R	T = Tumbu
Between T and R̲	S = Sula
Between R̲ and T̲	R = Rukia
Between S̲ and R̲, T	M = Mohedja
Between T̲ and M̲	_ = spirit in possession
Between M̲ and R̲, T, S	! = enters trance
Between R̲ and T̲, M	/ = leaves trance
Among T, R, M, and S	The lines trace the length of individual trance sequences.

Figure 8.2. Summary of scheduling discussion with Rukia's spirit.

the goat appears to have been resolved, the spirit having been talked into accepting what was available. The spirit remains adamant about the white cock, however, requiring a lengthy search on Sula's part.

The redundancy in the communication is summarized in Figure 8.2. It is produced by the passage of the same key messages between virtually every possible set of identities. Thus Tumbu first tells Rukia about the scheduling decision, and then his spirit consults with Rukia's spirit about it. Tumbu also refuses to enter trance until Rukia's spirit is already present, and this opens yet another channel of communication (i.e., between Tumbu and Rukia's spirit), as well as establishing who is dominant. It is almost as though what is being highlighted is not the substance of the communication (the message) but the act itself. In this regard the exchange is similar to the scenes at the beginning and close of Habiba's medicine inhalation and, indeed, to most contexts in which spirits and humans are both present. The redundancy in the transmission of a particular message may serve to impress the patient; simultaneously, the metamessage that individuals in a relationship must communicate with one another works in the same direction.

Administration of the medicine, November 10

> Various precautions were taken to ensure that the administration of the medicine would be a success. It was held in the afternoon, two days before the public ceremony, in Tumbu and Mohedja's own home, well out of the way of the rival curer. To help administer the medicine, Tumbu called in his loyal *mwana fundi* 'apprentice,' Salima, from her husband's village. Furthermore, it was announced that the medicine would be applied entirely behind closed doors. No one could enter or leave the house during this time, and I was severely warned that if I wanted to observe I wouldn't be able to change my mind part way through. Although Rukia was accompanied to Mohedja's part of the village by her husband, daughters, and sister, only Tumbu, Mohedja, Salima, and I entered the house with her. The door was shut firmly behind us.
>
> Tumbu explained the contrast in procedure to Habiba's case in the following way. Whereas Habiba's spirit was already a mature adult (*ulu be*), Rukia's was not. Tumbu likened the situation to a first marriage, in which bride and groom have to stay in the house for a week-long honeymoon; anyone who wishes to see them during this period must enter the house as well.[2]
>
> Tumbu lit the incense and spoke over it to the absent spirit, saying that he expected it to announce its name. A supply of wood had been brought into the house, and Salima started a fire. As in Habiba's cure, there were two pots, one large and one small, filled with leaves. But the pots were of clay and they were heated inside the house, which rapidly filled with smoke. Salima retained the job she had

fulfilled during Habiba's cure, and Mohedja began to grind the sticks. Tumbu lay back on a mat and fell asleep, exhausted by his busy schedule of curing and agricultural activities. Rukia undressed to a single cloth and sat slightly above the rest of us, on a mortar placed horizontally.

As the water in the large pot began to boil, Salima draped the new white cloth over Rukia's head and pulled the sticks back from the fire. Pronouncing the Islamic formula, "In the name of Allah, the compassionate, the merciful . . .," she set the pot down in front of Rukia, placing the white cloth so that it covered both the pot and Rukia's face. Then she added water to the second, smaller pot and placed it on the fire. Under the cloth, Rukia uttered deep gasps. After each of the seven inhalations she was given some of the liquid to drink and then had the paste rubbed on her body.

The atmosphere was much quieter and more matter-of-fact than during Habiba's session, and I took the opportunity to ask some questions. Mohedja and Salima appeared ready to oblige, and explained to me that *patros* spirits enter people precisely so that they may be fed medicine and other foods. As we talked, Rukia's spirit became very agitated under the cloth, thrashing about and thrusting its hands into the steaming pot. Salima pointed out to me that spirits are not affected by such hot temperatures. Suddenly, from under the cloth, the spirit broke into our conversation, announcing that it wished to eat my liver! For once, I was at a loss for questions. After a momentary pause, Salima and Mohedja advised me not to let it have my liver, but to give it cologne instead. Were the spirit to acquire my liver, I should have no strength left. The spirit would enter my body, and I would have to go through the cure myself (and thus have the spirit enter my head and possess me) in order to regain it.

With the completion of four of the seven rounds of medicine, the women started some low singing, "in order to make the spirit happy." Tumbu awoke and joined in. The spirit asked for more incense. On the seventh round they sang louder, and Tumbu lit even more incense. The spirit cried out "*Ça y'est!*" a couple of times and then proceeded to tell us its name: "Lahadjy bun . . ." The name of the father was muffled but appeared to be Jabiry, Tumbu's own spirit.[3]

Tumbu asked it to repeat, "Lahadjy son of whom?" He began to giggle. Mohedja remarked that this could not be the same Lahadjy who possessed her because it had a different father. Tumbu said that they must be the same. He wavered, confused by the turn of events; the spirit did not produce a name that was known to them. Mohedja said emphatically that her spirit and Rukia's were different, that they only happened to share the same name. Tumbu then agreed, the new Lahadjy must indeed be Mze Jabiry's son.

Rukia's spirit started a song as it waited for the last drink of medicine to cool down. Tumbu and Mohedja both entered trance. At once TUMBU rose from the mat to sit in a chair. Rukia's spirit leaned its head against the knee of its "father" and the father gently rubbed the shoulders of its "son" and uttered syllables in spirit language (*kilulu*). Next Salima inclined her head to TUMBU, as a sign of respect appropriate to her own curer spirit. RUKIA crawled across to lean her head against MOHEDJA. RUKIA groaned and MOHEDJA laughed in reply. Salima bowed to MOHEDJA. The two new arrivals (Tumbu's and Mohedja's spirits) then shook hands with me, and the greetings were completed.

Mohedja's spirit began to take over. It told Rukia's spirit reassuringly that the ritual had ended well and without mishap. MOHEDJA instructed Salima to take some liquid from the pot of medicine and pour a little over each of the four corners of the house door in order to remove the restriction (*maŋaboka fady*) against opening it. Salima did so and then opened the door, admitting the first smoke-free air we had breathed in two hours. A crowd of curious small children peered in from the other side. MOHEDJA ordered Salima to prepare water for Rukia to wash in and sent Rukia's daughter home to fetch clean clothing for her mother . . .

Sula entered, shook hands with all, and was apprised that the name had come up. MOHEDJA turned to RUKIA and asked, "What's your name? I've forgotten." RUKIA replied firmly: "Lahadjy bun Jabiry, Faez" (Faez = the spirit's village). Sula did not quite catch it, and the spirit was forced to repeat itself for a second time. Attention then turned to Sula and Rukia's sick little daughter. As Rukia went to wash, MOHEDJA, assisted by Tumbu, attempted to cure the girl of sorcery. I was admonished not to repeat the name announced by the *patros;* so far it had told only us and not the world at large.

Later in the day, Tumbu, Mohedja, and I discussed the cure. Tumbu admitted that he was astonished by the name the spirit gave. He said that he hadn't heard it too well the first time. Mohedja asked if Mze Jabiry really had a son named Lahadjy. Tumbu answered, a trifle quickly, "Well, you've just seen him."

Commentary. This sequence contains a number of fascinating exchanges. The spirit's challenge to me was presented in mock seriousness. Rukia had always held a somewhat ambivalent attitude toward me; she found me an object of amusement but never appeared very sure whether or not it was safe to express it. Her spirit discovered the perfect moment and was not afraid to make use of it. My questions, with which it had to put up during the ceremony, led to an explanation that spirits enter human bodies in search of food. The spirit then announced that it was going to eat my liver, the tastiest organ and perhaps the seat of the life force. What a perfect illustration of both the point that Salima and Mohedja had just made and of Rukia's feelings toward me! To the women, the comment also had a perfectly ordinary meaning: The spirit expected me to give it something in return for letting me observe the cure. The women suggested the most common gift to spirits, cologne.

Despite its humor and apparent extravagance, the attitude that the spirit took with me was in no way different from that taken with everyone else in its surroundings: childish and extortive. Sula spent great sums of money on the ceremony, Tumbu and Mohedja were devoting their whole afternoon to pleasing the spirit, and there was I, the foreigner, remaining aloof, continuing to ask irrelevant questions and drawing the attention of the company away from the spirit. The challenge the spirit presented me with was essentially the same one it had presented to Sula, Tumbu, and the others: get involved, show concern. The women answered in the sympathetic but businesslike way with which they usually responded to the demands of a spirit: give it something, but don't let it get away with demanding too much.

A second exchange of interest is, of course, the announcement of the spirit's name. It would appear that Rukia was in a state of some confusion, as had been predicted. She desired to identify her spirit both with that of her sister-in-law, Mohedja, and with that of her curer, Tumbu (Figure 8.1). With Mohedja's young spirit Lahadjy she wished a relationship of identity and so chose the same color of offerings (white) and the same personal name. With Tumbu's spirit, she wished a relationship of clientship and attempted to achieve this through the idiom of descent. Unfortunately, however, the combination could not work, because Mohedja's Lahadjy was emphatically not the offspring of her husband's Mze Jabiry. This is why Tumbu was confused and "didn't hear right." Later, in order to make sure they all did have it right, Rukia's spirit was encouraged, without prompting, to repeat its name to Sula.

This incident shows how, in what is ideally a closed universe of spirits, new spirits come into being. In this case the new spirit took on the name and color preference of one previously existing spirit and the kinship affiliations of another. In order to ensure a smooth continuation of the cure, Tumbu and Mohedja made a quick decision to accept and reinforce the new identity. Tumbu's dry final comment to Mohedja managed to sum up the skeptical underpinnings of the whole affair. Where the conclusions of reason contradict the evidence of the senses, doubt may legitimately arise. Acceptance, however, is a public attitude and, as such, a matter of convenience.[4]

Both Habiba's and Rukia's cases serve to show why the emergence of the identity of the spirit in the process of the cure is exciting. In Habiba's cure it is a matter aesthetic satisfaction. The identity is built up surely; the signs are clear to those who know how to read them and everything fits in its place. The final announcement of the name has the satisfaction of a confirmation. The last piece falls into place and confirms our understanding of the whole. Rukia's case highlights the other side of this – the tension of uncertainty, the excitement of surprise.

A third point of interest is what occurs after Tumbu and Mohedja both go into trance. A series of actions then expresses the relative statuses of all of the participants. Rukia's spirit reclines briefly against Tumbu's, expressing in action the status relationship stated earlier in the language of kinship. Rukia's spirit is also in a position of relative inferiority to Mohedja's, because Mohedja is currently possessed not by her young male spirit, Lahadjy, but by the elder, Mze Bunu. Salima, currently unpossessed, in her role as apprentice also acknowledges the superior position of the two curer spirits. Later she carries out the orders of Mohedja's spirit with no hesitation. The two curer spirits shake hands with me, affirming our relationship of friendship and approximately equal status.

Performance of the azulahy be, November 12, 1975 (excerpts)

By late afternoon the food was cooked and prepared for display. After sunset Kuraishiya fed her small children and put them to sleep in the back room. She was then taken to the house of Juma Hassan to receive her medicine.[5] Kuraishiya had already gone through the expense of an *azulahy be,* but her spirit had given a false name.[6] Tonight was thus an extra event, outside the normal ritual sequence. Kuraishiya killed a chicken, and the spirit was expected to announce the correct name.

After dinner, sixteen people congregated in Kuraishiya's front room. Dady Accua passed lighted incense in front of the two sisters and called on their spirits to rise. Mohedja led the women in spirit songs. The women clapped loudly and the two men present hummed along . . .

Tumbu entered, having set up the drummers just outside the door. Rukia's spirit knelt with its head in Tumbu's lap, then placed the incense directly in front of him. The drums started up, loud and steady, and the women began clapping again. Someone called urgently for a song. Tumbu made whistling noises as his spirit rose. RUKIA panted heavily, breathing in jerky movements in time to the music, and sat in the lap of Dady Accua. TUMBU took RUKIA to look over the food on the table. It included four dishes of sugar, six bottles of cologne, two plates of congealed chicken blood, six puddings, and a pile of eggs. Under the table were stashed a big basin of goat blood and pots of rice, chicken, and goat meat. Together they counted the items, as TUMBU explained that everything the spirit had asked for was present . . .

The room was hot and smoky and jammed with people filling the beds and mats and crowding in at the doorway. There appeared to be a common focus of individual energies in the room, as if everyone were, through their singing and clapping, straining mind and body to the task of curing the ill. Juma Hassan and his patient, Kuraishiya, both in trance, were the focus of attention. KURAISHIYA leaned against the curer spirit's knees, crying. The latter, swinging its arms dramatically, addressed the gathering, volubly reciting the details of the past delinquency of Kuraishiya's spirit and assuring it that everything would turn out fine this time. JUMA HASSAN switched back and forth between Malagasy and long stretches of *patros* language. From the spirit's gestures and tone could be gleaned the general import, if not the substance (if indeed there was any), of what was being said.[7]

Kuraishiya's spirit lay back, legs and arms outstretched, now against JUMA HASSAN's legs, now against DADY ACCUA's. It was having a lot of trouble announcing its name. Either it lay with lips firmly shut, or it babbled incoherently. Everyone looked very concerned. JUMA HASSAN urged it on in a loud clear voice. The spirit gave forth a series of "*ça y'est . . . ça y'est . . .*" ending in nothing. Tears rolled down its face. Finally it managed to utter a name. JUMA then led KURAISHIYA to examine her portion of the food . . .

Most of the women went outside. A few spirits, those of Rukia, Kuraishiya, and Habiba in particular, began to dance to the drums. The next few paragraphs represent a composite picture drawn from the observation of several *patros* ceremonies. At the sight of the dancers another woman became possessed and exuberantly threw her arms about her neighbor. In a few minutes there were five possessed women dancing. They moved in short steps or hops, a kind of light bounce, as if they were not touching the ground. Each dancer faced in one direction, moved two or three steps to the right, then, rotating the upper part of the body, went two or three steps to the left, rotated again and returned to the right, so that the eventual path was a series of sharp zigzags. Two drunk youths joined the dancing. They were able to replicate the style of the *patros* spirits so exactly that I considered them to be possessed until apprised of my mistake by a fellow spectator. A few nonpossessed girls also danced but at some distance from the crowd of spectators.

Tumbu paced the edge of the clearing. He carried the incense into the midst of the seated women and passed it in front of their faces, inviting their spirits to rise and join the partying. Occasionally, one of the seated women, stimulated by the incense, the persistent beat of the drums, and the general heady atmosphere, complied. If the entry of the spirit into the host showed signs of violence, Tumbu or Dady Accua tried to calm the individual. Habiba, Dady Accua, and Tumbu alternated possession and passed the blue shawl among themselves, as it belonged to Mze Jabiry, in whomever's body the *patros* might be. Clients could locate the spirit by means of the shawl.

There were some forty to fifty people present in all, but never more than seven or eight on the dance floor at a time. Lit by the full moon, the dancers pursued their pleasures. Although all the dancing was unmistakably *patros* fashion, each dancer added a personal touch as well. HABIBA dashed up to the four drummers and danced facing them, often just a hair's breadth from their bodies. From time to time she backed off, only to come rushing up again. BAKO ALI moved restlessly back and forth across the clearing, covering much more distance than any of the others. His style included very sudden and complete pauses, split-second moments of freezing in time to the beat, giving the impression of a dancer in a fun house or discotheque where the lights keep flashing on and off. MOHEDJA and SALIMA

A group of possessed women dance in front of the drummers toward the end of a nightlong festivity. (Photograph courtesy of Jon H. Breslar.)

danced more sedately, each in her own space. Suddenly, SALIMA jerked her spine, screamed, laughed, raised her arms wide, and then bowed her head and hollered, moving her legs rapidly in place: The older spirit possessing her had just been replaced by a younger one. The most common dance style was the one described earlier, elbows and torso moving hard as the body executed a series of tight turns in a short and entirely self-defined space. Occasionally, however, a spirit seemed to explode out of this tense equilibrium and dashed wildly out of the clearing and off into the village.

Mze Jabiry left Tumbu for Dady Accua, who immediately began to dance holding the blue shawl. A youth, grandson to Dady Accua, called the spirit aside for some personal advice concerning the attacks of sorcery to which he had recently been subject. Other people held similar conversations with Tumbu, each person choosing his own confidant. RUKIA lead fellow spirits by the hand to the buffet table. SALIMA, meanwhile, sprinkled cologne on everyone.

The male curers spent most of their time inside the house, eating, chatting, and dozing. At first cockcrow, Tumbu went outside and roused the lagging women, many of whom were asleep on the mats. As the call to prayer sounded from the mosque, he motioned the drummers and dancers to silence. The participants left trance for the duration, but the scene livened up again the minute the worshippers were observed leaving the mosque. RUKIA started screaming and

"Ça y'est!" A spirit announces its name. (Photograph courtesy of Jon H. Breslar.)

crawling around the arena on hands and knees. A few other spirits began to dance. The circle of spectators widened with the addition of newly awakened villagers. A middle-aged man, momentarily diverted from his expedition to his fields, entered the circle and danced, machete and basket in his hands.

Rukia's spirit was led away in order to prepare for the annunciation. It returned at the head of a small procession, with a piece of white cloth fixed around its head, turban fashion.[8] A chair was placed in the center of the clearing and smeared with medicine. As the drummers paused, the spirit mounted the chair. The audience watched attentively, and some began to cry. RUKIA stood erect, threw open her arms, and cried in a loud voice, *"Ça y'est:* Lahadjy bun Jabiry, Faez!" In a moment it was over. The spirit was helped down from the chair and began to stagger around the clearing as the high screams of a number of other women entering trance were heard.

The drums started up and a number of dancers entered the ring. It was daylight now. The drummers and dancers played up to the crowd. The drummers introduced sudden pauses to throw the dancers off-balance. The audience laughed at the spirits' discomfiture. Some of the dancers drank greedily from a basin of goat's blood. Two danced arm in arm, distributing pieces of pudding to the other spirits. When all the spirits had indulged, Tumbu passed pieces of pudding to the spectators. The entertainment continued until midmorning.

Commentary. This period is intended as a public entertainment (*soma*) hosted by the spirit who has been receiving medicine for all the other *patros* spirits. The role of Rukia's spirit thus changes from patient and recipient to host and donor. It invites the other spirits to dance, eat, drink and be merry; it even leads them individually to the table of offerings.

The spirits amuse themselves, but at the same time, many of them use the opportunity to vent their feelings about the state of their own ceremonies. The curers switch their attention from the spirit receiving the medicine to all the other client spirits who have not yet finished their own treatments. In private consultations with the curers and curer spirits, both spirits and humans air their personal concerns. Many of these discussions will be acted upon at later dates.

With the announcement of the names of their respective spirits, Rukia's and Kuraishiya's cures each end successfully. The significance of the naming, as well as the role of the spirit as feast sponsor, will be analyzed in the next chapter.

9. Of affines and annunciations

This chapter continues the analysis of the ritual sequence, focusing on the period following the application of medicine and, in particular, the announcement of the spirit's name. The argument in Chapter 7 led to the proportion: Inhalation of smoke is to circumcision/defloration as inhalation of steam is to annunciation. From the point of view of the spirit, it is the similarity between the former terms of each pair (i.e., inhalation, permeation with smell, heat, sweating, prophylaxy) rather than the dissimilarity (stinking/fragrant, burning/steaming, repelling/attracting) that is significant. This assumes a similarity between the latter terms of each pair as well, namely that the spirits view annunciation as a significant and necessary rite of status change. This point will first be demonstrated by considering the codes that possession shares with other rites of passage.

Codes of status elevation

The rituals of circumcision and defloration produce changes in initiates so that the latter are incorporated into their respective adult sexual classes. At whatever age circumcision takes place (the age ranges from infancy to early adolescence), the immediate consequence for a boy is that he must henceforward dress modestly. Exhibition of his circumcised penis is said to be equivalent to exposing the penis of his father; it is extremely shameful. Father and son are thus classed together as men. Circumcision is also a prerequisite for sexual activity, which can then begin as soon as the boy is physically ready. The immediate consequence of legitimate defloration (i.e., by her husband, after he has legally contracted the marriage with her parents or sponsors and not before the time set by the astrologer consulted by the parents) is a girl's freedom henceforward to engage in sexual activity.[1] The adult women of the village gather outside the marriage house immediately after the defloration is accomplished to congratulate the couple and to celebrate women's sexuality, performing dances miming the sex act and mocking men. The prohibition on the circumcised boy's behavior and the bride's new freedom each indicate the achievement of new status and involvement in new identity relationships.

In similar fashion, the announcement of its name produces the social recognition of a spirit's identity as spirit, incorporating it into the body of spirits of that species that rise in the village. Just as the social recognition and classification of the human initiates's sexuality has consequences for his relationships with the members of his own sex and those of opposite sex, so the initiation of the spirit has consequences for its relationship with the members of its species and with the human villagers.[2]

The analogy could be drawn further, but upon completion of the medicine, a different metaphor of status change becomes dominant. The spirit is likened not only to a child entering the adult world of sexuality but also to a man engaging in marriage. As with the medicine, the analogy is not commonly made explicit in exegesis (although isolated comparisons are drawn from time to time) but is implicit in the underlying structure. Two comparisons between spirit and groom are particularly striking: fulfillment of obligations toward, and achievement of full status within, a peer group and incorporation into an "affinal" group. The point here is *not* that the spirit "marries" the host but rather that the process of incorporating the spirit into the family group is similar to the incorporation of that other kind of outsider, the husband. Just as the uxorilocal household[3] must take in the husband, so too must it accept a spirit.

The metaphor emerges primarily through the fact that in the production and performance of the feast and entertainments (*soma*), the spirit, like the new husband, is paying its *shuŋgu*. This analogy is quite explicit; spirits worry about paying their *shuŋgu* much as humans do and consider such payment a major aim of their feasts. The *shuŋgu* is a formal obligation of hospitality that each member of a designated group must perform for all the other members of that group. In human society, *shuŋgu* obligations occur within the entire village, within each age/sex group, and, occasionally, within specifically constituted groups of friends. *Shuŋgu* groups are not based on kinship or descent. A member of the group who has partaken of the hospitality of others but has not yet offered his own feels shame; conversely, an individual who has paid his or her *shuŋgu* feels at ease among his peers, knowing that no one has the right to make any more claims. Payment is expected from all members and is rewarded with respect. However, it would be correct to say that proper payment of a *shuŋgu* obligation does not so much raise the status of the performer as it fulfills it.

Among humans, *shuŋgu* exchange is highly formalized. Each *shuŋgu* group has its elected leaders who count and measure the particular payments, keep records of all past payments, and adjudicate internal disputes. Membership in a *shuŋgu* is clear cut, and, for age and friendship groups, it is eventually closed. The particular requirements of each group, set at the outset by the members, are precisely defined. The requirements usually include a certain quantity and perhaps cut of meat, varying from as much as two large cows per couple or individual in a village-wide *shuŋgu* to a thigh of beef and a certain amount of rice or tea and cakes in a small age group of women. Every ingredient used in the cooking is measured precisely, so that each member provides exactly the same number of coconuts and onions and amounts of salt and other specified spices per person. In some cases the accumulation of sufficient food may require planning over a number of years. *Shuŋgu* payments frequently cause anxiety among those individuals who are in the process of paying or who have not yet paid. The members of the *shuŋgu* group have the right to refuse acknowledgment of payment if they consider it to be either insufficient in quantity or deficient in the quality or number of ingredients. Successful payment is a matter of great relief, the occasion for self-satisfaction and the acceptance of the congratulations and esteem of others.

Among spirits, payments are not controlled nor are redressive measures ever taken by the group. Indeed, the *shuŋgu* group is permanently open, its membership changing as new spirits arrive and older hosts die. Regulation of standards is maintained not by the sanctions of the group but by the internalized desire of each spirit to produce a fitting feast, a feast large enough to allow it to consider its obligations to its fellows fulfilled.

Each spirit specifies and demands of the host and her kin that they provide the means for the affair. The spirit's only role in the production is to make its demands known and to ensure that they are met. The spirit takes over as master of its own ceremony only after the medication has been administered and the curer has shown it all the delicacies exhibited on the table at the beginning of the feast. The spirit then invites its fellows to come and help themselves. Among humans, by contrast, an individual is generally responsible for the production of his or her own *shuŋgu* feast. However, there is one major exception to this rule: At a wedding, it is the obligation and privilege of the parents of a virgin bride to provide on behalf of the groom the *shuŋgu* payment that he may owe to the members of his age group. It is this structure of exchange, whereby an individual develops a relationship with one set of people insofar as the latter take over his obligations to another set of people, that is similar in weddings and spirit cures. The total set of exchanges at a wedding is more complex and also more balanced than at a spirit feast,[4] but the underlying structure is identical: The family of the host (bride) produces a feast on behalf of the incoming spirit (groom) in order to settle the latter's scores and to announce his new status vis-à-vis his peer group.

The analogy between spirit and groom is of the form: spirit is to host's sponsors as groom is to bride's sponsors. In other words, the relationship being expressed between the spirit and its host's relations is an affinal one. Like the groom, the spirit obliges its affines to pay the *shuŋgu* and is concerned that they provide enough to properly satisfy its associates; like the groom, the spirit is expected in return to treat the affines and their charge (the host or wife) according to the norms of kinship. It is important to note here that the possible relationship – spirit is to host as groom is to bride – is irrelevant. No mention is made of the spirit actually marrying the host, nor did I ever hear of a spirit indulging in sexual relations with its host.[5] Although most spirits are male and most hosts female, the *shuŋgu*-like exchange holds true even in those cases where the spirit is female or the host male. What is important is the nature of the relationship, not the sex of the partners; what is stressed is not a "conjugal" bond but an "affinal" one. Whereas the ritual might appear on the surface to be most concerned with the relationship between spirit and host, in fact, it is largely concerned with that between the spirit and the host's sponsors.[6]

Weddings and spirit cures also resemble one another in the order and process of events that they entail. The sequence of events at a wedding for a virgin bride is briefly outlined here. Shortly after the legal transaction conducted between the groom or his representative and the bride's father before the representative of the *kadi* (regional Islamic judge) and the witnesses, and at an auspicious moment ascertained by the astrologer, but not made public, the marriage is consummated. The defloration of the bride is immediately celebrated by the women in licentious dancing, and the couple then begin a week-long period during which they must stay inside the new house that the bride's father has built and furnished for his daughter and is now her property. Here, often from the bed itself, they receive visitors. Throughout this period, the new couple, their visitors, and the groom's parents must be well supplied with good food by the bride's family. On the eighth day, the groom is secretly whisked away, hidden in another house, and dressed in finery by his closest friends. Upon his discovery, a flag is raised above the house and everyone gathers to conduct him in triumphant and joyous procession through the village and back to his wife's home. He is flanked by two close male associates and preceded by a long line of male dancers. The women provide an appreciative audience, approaching to fan the groom, light cigarettes for him, and the like. One of them carries on her head the suitcase full of gifts that the groom is bringing to his bride: gold jewelry, clothing, cloth, soap. On the same day, the groom's *shuŋgu* animal is slaughtered, cooked, and consumed by his age group, thus completing the *shuŋgu* payment.

The dancing and festivity is referred to as *soma*, just like the spirit feasts. The procession celebrates the fulfillment of the groom's status as a man capable of meeting his various obligations: to his age group by paying his *shuŋgu*, to the bride and her family by bringing suitable and expensive gifts, and to society in general, and his own family in particular, by marrying a virgin.[7] The change in the social identity of the groom from "bachelor at large" to husband of a specific woman is vividly demonstrated in the passage through the village.

The wedding moves from the private consummation through the honeymoon stay in the new house, where the couple are attended by the bride's family and visited by kin, friends, age-mates, and other well-wishers on both sides, to the triumphant procession and dancing across the village. This transition from domestic to public, from indoors to outdoors, from consummation to celebration, is paralleled in the spirit possession rituals.[8] All the early attempts to negotiate with the spirit take place within the house in the company of the host, the curer, the spirit, and their close associates. This period culminates with application of the medicine, which may admit a somewhat larger group of participants, all of whom must provide active support.

But then, like a groom on the eighth day of his wedding, the spirit is led out to face the admiring crowd. Out of doors anyone is free to observe. As the groom's procession to the bride's house demonstrates the identity of the girl's husband to the entire community and, in turn, expresses the community's acceptance of the match, so does the spirit's public appearance in the body of the host and its annunciation proclaim its identity, its relationship to the host, and the community's (both of spirits and of humans) acceptance of these facts. And, like the groom bearing gifts, the spirit is publicly acknowledging its debt to its "affines," that is, to those who sponsored the ceremony, and its acceptance of responsibility toward the host.[9]

The significance of naming

Spirits jealously guard their identities and will not reveal them without suitable recompence. Two examples illustrate this nicely. Whenever I asked for the name of a spirit who had made its name public before my arrival in the village, the spirit would invariably retort with, "What will you give me if I tell you?" On the other hand, a spirit angry at the deferment of its ritual mischievously tempted the host's kin with an offer of its name then and there. The host's mother refused the offer with alacrity, explaining to me that to accept it would be to remove the humans' bargaining power. Having received the name for nothing, the patient would surely stay sick and might even go mad. This point indicates that it is not the name itself that has value so much as the spirit's right to retain or reveal it where, when, and to whom it sees fit. A public annunciation in the context of the fulfillment of the *shuŋgu* is a source of pride to the spirit. The spirit has the right to wait for this occasion; an earlier revelation of the name deprives it of the opportunity. It is for this reason that people who have guessed the spirit's identity through its behavior keep the knowledge to themselves.

The importance attributed to the annunciation can be clarified by viewing it as a member of the class of utterances that Austin (1962) has labeled performatives (Rappaport 1974). A performative utterance is one that accomplishes something in the uttering. Like the phrase "I apologize," it does not report on an object or state of affairs but creates one. From this perspective, the spirit is not reporting or revealing its name but is, in fact, *investing itself with a name*. Standing on a chair above a crowd of spectators and calling out "*Ça y'est . . .*" is the equivalent of the Queen lowering a sword and saying "I dub thee . . .," a part of the conventional procedure by which the effect is achieved. In other words, although the name or title may have been selected earlier, it does not actually become established until the enactment of the ritual. It is thus not only the spirit's pride that is at stake but the very success of the whole enterprise. Without the proper completion of the ritual, the spirit can have no satisfactory identity at all.

Following Austin, the name uttered can be judged as neither true nor false; the investiture is judged, rather, as more or less "felicitous." That is, there are no false names, merely those that fit more or less well into the system of conventions that governs the identification of spirits. A name that works very badly will be challenged and rejected by the audience; in Austin's terms it is a "misfire." During the course of the ritual activities, great care is taken by all parties to avoid the infelicities of which Austin speaks. The spirit who offers to give its name before an agreement has been reached is threatening a "misinvocation." Tumbu attempted to coach Rukia's spirit before its ceremony in order to avoid the choice of a name in violation of the codes of selection (a "flaw") or the inability of the spirit to utter a name at all (a "hitch"). The spirit of Rukia's sister Kuraishiya had already created a flaw and nearly caused a hitch as well. The care taken not to attribute a name to the spirit before the ceremony and the concern on the part of the spirit over any attempts to encroach upon its rights in this matter illustrate the consideration given to following correct procedure.

But if these concerns show an implicit understanding of the performative nature of the investiture, the explicit remarks of the participants display a different perspective. In this view, the name exists beforehand and the spirit merely reveals it. In other words, there is a mystification of the performativeness. A name that works badly, that clashes with the previous clues that have been given, or that replicates the identity of another spirit already present in a member of the audience will be treated as a lie on the part of the spirit. It is particularly interesting to note, then, that one of the chief attributes of spirits – their reputation for deceit and dissimulation – is actually fed by a logical mistake. The complexity of the system in which they operate is such that errors are inevitable, yet among spirits there can be no "honest mistakes."

The significance of the utterance of the name is not fully revealed by describing it as an act of investiture. Investiture itself is a highly condensed ritual act with many far-reaching implications, several of which are also of a performative nature.[10] A successful investiture establishes the authenticity of the cure and the spirit. It changes the status of both host and spirit, uniting in a single act the reaggregation of all concerned parties. As it has done in its previous appearances, the spirit admits its presence and its responsibility for the host's illness. Now the spirit is no longer simply trying to convince people; by fixing itself with a spirit name it certifies its spirit identity. Having a name, indeed, investing oneself with a name, is intrinsic to being a spirit. The spirit is thus no longer simply claiming to be a spirit but is displaying the fact. Also, that the patient's return to health is effected in this manner is demonstrable proof that the spirit has indeed been the cause of her illness. And, at the same time, the act of annunciation is a commissive (Austin 1962), a promise on the part of the spirit to refrain from harming the patient in the future, a pledge of its good faith, and a seal on the process of exchange through which the spirit has been able to perform its *shuŋgu* obligations. From this point forward the behavior of the spirit and the condition of the host will be judged according to the standards established by the performance of the investiture (although this is not to say that the spirit will necessarily live up to its end of the bargain).[11]

The investiture thus validates the complaints of the patient, the expenditures of the patient and sponsors, and the skill and sincerity of the curer, as well as the status of the spirit among its fellows. It reintegrates the patient among her sponsors, the curer with the patient and sponsors, and all of them with the rest of society. Through their participant observation, through comforting the spirit, humoring it, and refraining from challenging its utterance, the members of the public are accepting the significance of the event.

This analysis appears at odds with the action of Rukia's spirit in uttering its name to the curer and close kin of the host before the public ceremony. Here private acceptance occurs before public. Yet the discrepancy between the official version of the affair, in which the identity of the spirit is first revealed at the public ceremony, and the facts, in which a select group is earlier made privy to the information, is only apparent. The restrictions imposed on the privy group concerning further communication of the identity serve to emphasize the importance of eventually following the full set of conventions. Furthermore, the private announcement creates, as nothing else could, the new basis of the relationship between the spirit and the host and her kin. In revealing its name before the *shuŋgu* payment, the spirit places its confidence in the curer and host's kin and thus demonstrates its acceptance of a relationship of cooperation and solidarity with them. The humans experience the degree of their interdependence with the spirit; they have the power to give the name away, but were they to do so, the health of the patient would be lost. The fiction of common ignorance thus strengthens the feelings of attachment between the spirit and those who secretly share in the knowledge of the name it will invest itself with.

Conclusion

The distinction between those who are secretly in the know and those who must gain their information through public channels, and between the official version and the facts, is comparable to the situation at the consummation of a marriage, where the consequences of a lack of proof of the bride's virginity can be quietly adjusted among the parties concerned and a public front of purity maintained. Although the order of events at the possession curing rituals parallels the outline of major events at weddings, both rituals follow a basic structure found in all major rites of the life cycle in Mayotte. The distinction between domestic and public contexts is always important. Ultimately then, although spirits are strange beings with strange customs, the rituals that incorporate them into society follow the same model as do the human rituals of incorporation. To the degree that they are successful in this regard, the spirit rituals are comprehensible and satisfying to humans. Underneath the twitching and dancing, the vacant stares and odd laughter emanating from otherwise familiar bodies and faces, the gorging on unlikely and unpleasant foods, the ritual follows an orderly, sensible progression.

To argue that possession ritual is orderly is not to say either that this order accounts for every aspect of possession or that the order must be merely a reflection of the social structure. Both these latter assertions would be incorrect. The disorderly aspects of possession will be confronted in subsequent chapters. As regards the second point, there is no indication that the spirit interactions reflect kinship arrangements (or, for that matter, Islamic ritual and procedure). Rather, the social life of spirits is comprehensible from the perspective of human social life and vice versa. This is so for two reasons. First, there are certain general principles, codes, or idioms that appear to underlie both spirit and human life. These include notions of exchange, of egocentricity, and of private versus public domains. Second, although human and spirit domains are kept separate in peoples' minds, they are also applied metaphorically to each other, so that each informs the other.[12] Thus, on the one hand, human–spirit relationships are interpreted in terms of human kinship norms, so that, for example, a spirit is considered to be like an affine and is expected to become cooperative. On the other hand, idioms of human–spirit relations may inform cultural conceptions of kinship. The spirits serve primarily as a model for how not to behave with kin; they also provide a means by which human relations of brute force or of selfishness can be interpreted.

It is important to understand that most of the possible associations are not intrinsic to spirit possession. In the preceding chapters we have considered how possession is constituted as a system of meaning. We have focused on its underlying structure and its relationship to other such meaning systems (or, perhaps more correctly, subsystems) within the culture. Once constituted, possession operates as a kind of cultural resource from which individual interpretations and experiences can be constructed. The choice of interpretation or kind of experience is likely to depend on the social position and personal circumstances of the individual at any given time. The possession complex is broad enough and esoteric enough to allow for numerous personal significations to be constructed from it, above and beyond those that are central to its own construction.

For example, although it is not an integral part of the structure of the ritual, the comparison between spirits and husbands that might be generated as a sort of by-product of the affinal structure could provoke thoughts concerned less with the process of getting married than with the married state itself. Husbands, like spirits, are frequently demanding and untrustworthy and might be considered more trouble than they are worth. Like spirits, they do not always carry out their responsibilities consistently. Spirits often impose certain dietary restrictions on their hosts, as do men on the women who bear their children. Yet the issue is considerably more complex than the mere expression of anger or envy toward husbands. Although women feel that they cannot do without the support of a man, it is not difficult for them to rid themselves of any particular one. However, although hosts may feel they would be much better off without spirits, they cannot rid themselves of particular connections. Thus, whereas possession might be used to formulate an expression of anger at a particular husband, it could also be seen as suggesting how reasonable the institution of marriage is by comparison to that of possession. The curing process might also suggest to participants that just as host and spirit engage in communication and compromise to work out their difficulties, so should wife and husband. Then too, spirits may also express the negative aspects of wives. For example, female spirits are said to be more difficult to handle than male ones, and their demands for new clothing are often considered exorbitant.

In sum, the major point of Part II has been to demonstrate how, despite the fact that humans and spirits are so different, the curing rituals can make sense to both the human and the spirit participants. This is not to suggest that a conceptualization of the spirits is directly or necessarily dependent on notions of human social structure.

Finally, it is no coincidence that the climax of the ritual sequence involves naming. The curing process sees the emergence from the rather vague and abstract category of spirit of first, a representative of a particular spirit species and then, a distinctive, named individual spirit. As such, it can be viewed as a paradigm for creation in general, "the informing of substance and the substantiation of form, a union of form and substance" (Rappaport 1974:43). Communication with the spirit is first established by means of formless substance – incense and other odorous vapors. The spirit too has substance as it attacks the host but lacks form. In the beginning it is inarticulate, not clearly present, not specifically identifiable. Gradually, as the cure progresses, the spirit takes on form, the progression climaxing, as do many creation myths around the world, in "the extraordinary human achievement of *naming*" (Bateson 1972:xxiv).

In an intriguing analysis of *zar* spirit possession in the Republic of the Sudan pursued along these lines, Byrd (n.d.) has suggested that the curing ritual represents an ordering of the chaotic and fearful world of nature ignored by orthodox Islam's one-sided concern with form. However, the ritual in Mayotte seems to be more concerned with social than with natural order.[13] The spirits are not merely classified, they are socialized; they develop particular identity relationships with particular people, and they are taught the norms of social intercourse. Furthermore, spirits are not wild creatures to be domesticated and classified by man; the most significant aspect of the name is perhaps that it is announced by the spirit itself. The naming is thus a commitment on the part of the spirit to cooperation, although carrying with it, as we shall see, all the uncertainty that alliance brings.

The spirit possession cure is concerned with the outward forms of interpersonal behavior, with the social conventions requisite for living in an organized society and relating to other people in orderly, conventional ways. There is nothing more basic to such participation than the establishment of a social identity. Nor is there a more basic form of acceptance of the conventions of identity construction and performance in a given social field than the taking on of a name. The establishment of the name is a ritual act that expresses acceptance of the universe that has created the conventions for naming; it is the acceptance of social responsibility. Rappaport has argued that it is ritual itself that creates these conventions and that, therefore, ritual "contains within itself not simply a symbolic representation of social contract, but a consummation of social contract" (1974:38). Whether or not this is true at the general level for all ritual, the spirit cure is a highly concrete and explicit example of such consummation.

The curing ritual thus demonstrates what appears to be a basic proposition of Mayotte culture. This was poignantly expressed by a madwoman who wandered the countryside in rags and repeated with approval by those who heard her: *maŋka uluŋu uluŋu, uluŋu* 'what makes a person a person is [other] people.' That is, we are created and humanized through our relationships with other human beings; our essence is social.

Part III

The paradigmatic dimension

But we should remember that this precarious balance between seriousness and pretence is an unmistakable and integral part of culture as such, and that the play-factor lies at the heart of all ritual and religion.

Johan Huizinga, *Homo Ludens: A Study of the Play Element in Culture*

10. The *trumba* spirits

In Part II we demonstrated the intelligibility of spirit rituals and concluded that the cures aim, and partially succeed, in bringing the spirits into society. Yet this is not the whole picture. Spirits do not thereby turn into humans; they continue to visit their hosts and to invade new generations of hosts. We must not present an oversocialized picture of the spirits. Having considered the relationships that develop between spirits and humans, we now turn to the relationships of the spirits to one another, both the formal orders that distinguish the various species internally and externally and the dynamic of the amusements with which the spirits celebrate the initiation of their fellows. Part III aims to identify the symbolic inversions that organize spirit behavior. The two dimensions of activity, syntagmatic and paradigmatic, are then brought into convergence in order to discover the central import of possession as a whole.

In order to elucidate the paradigmatic dimension of possession we turn to the *trumba* spirits, because the corpus of roles among this species is elaborated to a greater degree then among the *patros*. The *trumba* come from Madagascar, where they are common today in the northwest and where the practices associated with them are broadly similar to those found in Mayotte.[1] Although certain beliefs and rituals concerning the *trumba* or similar spirits may go back to a period before the Sakalava incursions into the northwest in the seventeenth century (Ottino 1965), today the general belief in this part of Madagascar is that the *trumba* are deceased Sakalava sovereigns. In fact, the *trumba* were institutionalized in the Sakalava politico-religious system and served as the official voices of the deceased rulers. Associated with the *mahabu* 'the royal funerary villages,' the *trumba* were used to legitimize decisions of the living rulers and to mediate conflicts, particularly over succession.[2]

The *trumba* that appear in Mayotte can be divided into those that represent deceased Sakalava sovereigns and their associates and those that represent other Malagasy ethnic groups. The different classes are unified by their common origin in Madagascar and by their appearance at one another's feasts. The former are by far the most common and will be discussed here. The latter are described in the Appendix.

The historical basis of the *trumba* in Mayotte

In 1831, Andriantsuly, the Sakalava king of Boina on the northwest coast of Madagascar, together with his loyal retainers, fled from the invading Merina to Mayotte.[3] Andriantsuly died in Mayotte in 1847 and was buried on the promontory beyond Mamutzu, known today as Mahabu. His *trumba* spirit, called 'Ndramaɲavakarivu, is said to be the leader or king (*ampanzaka*) of all the *trumba* spirits; the older spirits represent his ancestors. Andriantsuly's descendants returned to Madagascar and, despite their continued activity there, are not part of Mayotte consciousness. Elements of traditional Sakalava political structure and genealogy dating back to the seventeenth century are kept alive within the *trumba* ritual (Lambek 1978:285–8) but have no significance outside it; the *trumba* today present a world of spirits, not of kings.

At one time Mahabu was the center of a ritual cult associated with the *trumba* and spread throughout Mayotte, at least among the villages of Malagasy speakers. The tomb of Andriantsuly is still recognized as *tany masiɲ* a 'sacred spot' from which prayers are particularly likely to be fulfilled. In the past, people would promise to leave gifts if their wishes were granted, and the cattle acquired in this way, as well as through annual contributions (*tetibatu*) were used to honor the deceased king. Today more people frequent the tombs of Islamic learned men, which are also said to be *masiɲ* 'sacred,' 'efficacious.' A single elderly guardian cares for the tomb at Mahabu and contributions are still collected, via the local hosts of 'Ndramaɲavakarivu, from the hosts of all the senior *trumba*. Some *trumba* curing ceremonies, known as *rombu,* are still held there, but most *rombu* now take place in the host's or the curer's own village. The *rombu* have decreased in scale and draw more limited segments of the island's population than in the past. Likewise, the political functions of the *trumba* in leadership and social control have declined in importance.

Contrasts with the *patros*

Although the nature of the *trumba* is rooted in Sakalava history, the *trumba* operate today in the context of a wider system of spirit species,

Table 10.1. *Contrast in dietary habits between adult and child trumba and patros*

	Trumba	Patros
Adults	Eat poorly	Eat well
	Restrict category of edible foods	Enlarge category of edible foods
Children	Eat well	Eat poorly
	Prepare edible foods	Prepare inedible foods

which may be analyzed synchronically. As argued earlier (Chapter 3), the various classes of spirits are distinguished from one another and from living humans on the basis of a series of concrete representations. Here we will briefly consider the oppositions maintained between the *trumba* and the *patros*.

The *trumba* are deceased humans, not a separate species. Hence, unlike the *patros*, they do not consume substances defined by humans as nonfood. They contrast with both the *patros* and the current inhabitants of Mayotte by consuming that which is defined locally as forbidden or foreign. The *trumba* indulge in packaged cigarettes and bottled beverages: wine and spirits, forbidden by Islam, and sweet soft drinks. They also drink a honey brew, which is especially prepared at a *trumba* ceremony, and cologne. Most *trumba* disdain local palm wine, chewing tobacco, and snuff.

The adult *trumba* eat no solid food, yet, like the *patros*, they make use of food to indicate their presence. Whereas the *patros* extend the diet, the *trumba* narrow the diets of their hosts by establishing restrictions that must be followed even when the host is out of trance. These restrictions refer most commonly to chicken and eggs[4] but may include such substances as chili peppers, shellfish, and leftovers that children have eaten from. Unlike the indiscriminate eating habits of the *patros*, those of the *trumba* are based on a principle of exclusivity. Chicken products are "dirty" because chickens eat everything and everywhere; leftovers are "dirty" when children have stuck their hands in and mixed up the relish and base in unappetizing fashion.

This contrast in dietary habits between the *trumba* and the *patros* is heightened when the child spirits of the two species are considered (Table 10.1). The child *trumba*, unlike the adults, talk of nothing but eating and consume large quantities of rice and chicken, which they frequently prepare themselves. The child *patros*, on the other hand, are said to spend their time making mud pies.[5]

The *trumba* set up a series of other restrictions on their hosts as well. A host may be forbidden to work in the fields on a certain day of the week or to pay condolence visits at funerals and eat the food offered at such occasions. These restrictions are a matter of the individual manifestations of the *trumba* spirits. Sometimes they will be so severe that the host will petition the spirit to decrease them, which it will generally do. The more senior the *trumba* spirit, the more restrictions it sets on the hosts. The restrictions appear to indicate the client status of the host toward the spirit.[6]

Trumba spirits contrast with *patros* in a number of other ways as well. Their home is in Madagascar rather than Mayotte, and they live on land, not under the water. The *trumba* are called up by a different form of incense from that of the *patros,* and their music is characterized by clapping, guitar, accordion, and rattles rather than drums. Whereas *patros* normally inhale and drink their medicine steaming hot, *trumba* medicine, made from a virtually identical set of plant species, is poured over the body and drunk cold.[7]

The Sakalava *trumba*

Informants classify the Sakalava *trumba* into three types: the *trumba maventy* 'elder' *trumba; the chaŋgizy* 'youths,' and the *trumba madiniky* 'child' *trumba.* The sex of a particular spirit[8] is partially dependent on its age category. All *chaŋgizy* are male, all child spirits female; the senior spirits can be either sex but are predominantly male. The age and sex categories also signify differences in authority. The elder *trumba* explicitly represent deceased sovereigns and nobles; the youths, somewhat less clearly, represent commoners; and the child spirits tacitly signify slaves. From this perspective, it is a whole cross section of Sakalava society and not merely the family structure at its apex that is maintained in the *trumba.* However, the symbolization of class becomes increasingly ambiguous and is less readily expressed in native exegesis as the social position represented becomes less desirable. The child spirits tend to deny that they are slaves, preferring to consider themselves the infant children of the senior spirits.

The representation of authority by elders, energy by youth, and servitude by childhood may have developed originally as an idiom to conceal or rationalize previously existing class relations.[9] However, it is also a faithful representation of current Mayotte kinship norms and views about the life cycle. In Lombeni, authority is based on relative age and generation; deference is made to the energy and enthusiasm of youth; and respect, obedience, and service are expected from children.

A more detailed description of each of these categories of *trumba* spirits will clarify the picture.

Trumba elders

These *trumba*, who, for the most part, represent historical individuals (Lambek 1978), are said to be very old and are sometimes referred to as *dadilahy* 'grandfathers.' Unlike humans, *trumba* neither die nor become senile but retain their wits forever. The youngest of the senior *trumba*, because he represents the most recent Sakalava monarch in Mayotte's memory, is the leader of the spirits. Although it is well known that the actual monarch died some generations ago, the *trumba* leader is considered to be at a stage of life equivalent to that of the mature village leaders in their forties and fifties. The older *trumba* maintain their ritual precedence, however, and, unlike extremely old humans, do not withdraw from society. The system thus maintains a distinction between "hierarchy" and "power" (Dumont 1970).

The senior *trumba* indicate their rank as well as their age in their bearing and costume. They hold either an iron war spear or a special wooden *trumba* wand (*aŋgira, kakazu ny trumba*), decorated with bands of silver, in one hand. These are considered the personal possessions of the spirits. The wand or spear is not part of the inheritance that a host passes on to her children. Rather, when the same *trumba* rises in someone else, it can send for its possession from the deceased host's heirs, who must give it up.[10]

The costume of the male *trumba* elder is completed by a *lamba* 'shawl,' which is made of four meters of cloth of a red hue, signifying royalty, and draped around the upper part of the body. The female *trumba* elder demands a whole new outfit of clothing, including plastic sandals, at a cost, in 1976, equivalent to some $27.00. Although the clothes may be in current style, the spirit will under no circumstances allow the human host to wear the clothes herself (i.e., when not in trance). Women with several *trumba* may have stashed away on a back shelf an extensive, and expensive, wardrobe that they cannot touch. Even more characteristic of the female *trumba* is the fact that they require a cloth placed over the head and face. The cloth is held away from the mouth with one hand in order to permit talking and drinking.

Senior *trumba* demonstrate their powers by taxing their hosts more than do the junior ones. The host will be sicker during the first stages of the association and will have more restrictions (*fady*) to keep after the ceremonies are over. Should the host break any of these restrictions she is liable to become ill again and will have to mollify the *trumba* in some way. However, although the senior *trumba* can be troublesome to their hosts, they generally maintain a decorous demeanor in public. The senior *trumba* are treated with deference and are often asked to dispense advice or criticism and protective medicine.

The male *trumba* tend to have deep voices, forthright stares, and erect posture, whereas the female ones sigh, utter very high-pitched cries, and whisper or have trouble speaking.[11] The female *trumba* are considered fussy, causing a lot of *zistoires* (Fr. *des histoires*). They often enter a host concurrently with a male *trumba* but then rise in the host less frequently than the male and stay for shorter periods of time. On the other hand, one elderly lady of my acquaintance was possessed by a senior female *trumba* who was active as a curer.

Trumba youths

The *trumba* youths (*chaŋgizy*) are believed to be the equivalent of human males aged between about fifteen and thirty. The word itself means literally "not good children." They make up the most numerous and lively segment of the *trumba* population apparent at a *rombu*. Although the individual spirits vary in degrees of indulgence and energy, all of them drink heavily, dance wildly, and are generally on their feet throughout the night of a *rombu*. These are the spirits who drink the European wine and hard liquor and smoke the French cigarettes that must be supplied. They disdain cologne as *manintsy* 'cold' (i.e., 'weak'). By contrast, the *trumba* elders drink cologne, only occasionally taking a secret nip of the harder stuff.

The young spirits tie their cloths across their chests like bandoliers and often wear straw hats. Sometimes they erupt in wild body movements, calming down again to a steadier, but still frenetic, pace. Their habits and movements seem to indicate unharnessed energy. The *chaŋgizy* may represent the Malagasy pirates who raided Mayotte in the last century, and the idea of power is also exemplified by the association made between *trumba* youths and Western foreigners (*vazaha*). Alone among the categories of spirits, they frequently take the form of Europeans in dreams. They enjoy Western wine, liquor, tobacco, and bottled soft drinks, disdaining the local equivalents. And, "like the *vazaha*," they indulge beyond their capacities, until they are drunk.

Youth, virility, piracy, the West, indulgence, incredible energy – all these references form a coherent symbolic whole. The underlying theme is power, but it is power of a particular sort, uncontrolled by, and largely unconcerned with, society. In this respect, the youthful *trumba* present a striking contrast to their elders, who are symbols and representatives of a historically legitimate authority.[12]

Child trumba

Child *trumba* are all female; they are the equivalent of humans between the ages of about three and eight, but, in fact, they act much more childishly and irresponsibly than girls of that age are permitted to behave. The little *trumba* skip, giggle, and utter shrieks of mischievous delight (*Shiguly!*). They speak with heavy childish lisps and observe none of the proprieties of adult speech.[13] Like the other kinds of *trumba,* they are extremely self-indulgent, but they express this somewhat differently. They are the only spirits to refuse alcohol; instead, they are always concerned with food. They consume great quantities of rice and meat and other foods preferred by humans, eating with so much haste and greed that inevitably they manage to soil their garments. Sometimes they even place the food inside the folds of their clothing intentionally, announcing that "it tastes better this way." In sum, they do all the things for which mothers are always scolding their children. The antics of these *trumba,* risen in the bodies of dignified matrons, many of whom have small daughters of their own, are uproariously funny.

The little *trumba* are also extremely hard workers. They dust the feet and perform services on behalf of the senior *trumba* and, alone among the spirits, they do their own cooking. They may also rise in their hosts during the agricultural season and work with extreme diligence in the household fields, demanding in return a portion of the harvest. Sometimes they husk rice for the *trumba* master curer in the village, the woman who hosts 'Ndramaṇavakarivu.

Child *trumba* are among the most fascinating of all the spirits, presenting at one and the same time both a submission toward authority and a complete disregard for it. They will be described in further detail in Chapter 12, where I will argue that they form an interpretation of possession internal to the system itself.

The Sakalava *trumba* as a structure

The various Sakalava *trumba* share what may be considered a common "culture," that is, a symbolic system, traditions, and norms of mutual interaction. For example, they all respond to the same kind of incense and to the same medicines and music. Most important, when two or more *trumba* are present together they interact in regular, patterned ways that display their relative statuses. A younger *trumba* will always show deference toward an older one, and an older *trumba* will always demand precedence and signs of respect. The following account is particularly interesting because it shows that matters of relative status are an issue even when only one spirit is present at a time:

> Mohedja was host to a number of Sakalava *trumba* representing each of the classes, but, of course, only one of them rose in her at a time. During a period when I was conducting some business with her child spirit it was sometimes necessary for me to request its presence. This was accomplished by entering the house in the evening after dinner, lighting the incense in front of Mohedja, and requesting the presence of the spirit by name. Within a few moments, Mohedja would go into trance. However, on most occasions not her child spirit but the male elder would put in an appearance, with much straining and coughing as was its habit, which, as I knew, was of some discomfort to Mohedja. After a few minutes of inconsequential conversation, the older spirit would leave, to be replaced, after a pause, by the child spirit. The child spirit entered, complaining volubly how the "grandfather" spirit had held it back, that the older *trumba* were attempting to stop it from coming because it hadn't asked their permission, that it had to give way before the elders, and the like.

The representation of status differences is an integral part of spirit identity and behavior. It is always apparent and frequently made the object of elaborate play. In other words, the spirits form a "structure" as Dumont has defined it, in which the parts do not exist as independent entities in themselves but are defined entirely according to their relationships to the other parts. In Dumont's words:

We shall speak of structure . . . when the interdependence of the elements of a system is so great that they disappear without residue if an inventory is made of the relations between them: a system of relations, in short, not a system of elements [Dumont 1970:40].

It should be clear that the interpretation of spirits cannot be based on viewing them as isolated and independent symbols whose meanings can be read off. Rather, it is the relationships among the parts and the nature of the system as a whole that must be understood.

11. The world of possession

Although the curing ritual aims to socialize the spirit, it is precisely during the accompanying amusements that the spirits act out their spiritness to the utmost. Building from the description and analysis of such behavior, this chapter sets forth the central paradox of possession and attempts to grasp the nature of possession as a whole.

The *rombu* at Melekavo

Trumba spirits cause more pain to their hosts, are harder to propitiate, and are a great deal more expensive than *patros* spirits. Nevertheless, the order of events in a *trumba* cure is broadly similar to the sequence discussed for the *patros*. The *trumba* ordinarily require a series of three ceremonies. The first of these, the *fanuiŋ*, consists of the administration of medicine to the spirit. The *rombu be* 'great' or 'large' *rombu* is the occasion for the revelation of the spirit's identity. Finally, the *valu hataka* (lit., 'appeal for pardon' or 'arbitration'), similar to the *rombu be* but smaller in scale, is the context in which the restrictions that the host must henceforward follow in order to maintain the spirit's goodwill and patronage are established. Like that of the *patros*, the *trumba* ritual can be interpreted as a rite of passage that produces and documents the establishment of a contract between host and spirit. However, rather than elaborate the ritual details,[1] let us examine the revelry that takes place at a *rombu*.

The *rombu* to be described was held for a youthful *chaŋgizy* spirit. It took place in Melekavo, a village of Comoran speakers. Three of my friends from Lombeni were present: Mohedja, Salima, and Vola. Each of them was host to *trumba* spirits, and both Mohedja and Salima were somewhat experienced at performing the appropriate curing rituals.

> The public aspect of the *rombu* started around 9:45 P.M., after the patient had been doused, *trumba* fashion, in buckets of cold, medicated water. The space under the awning, lit by a pressure lamp,

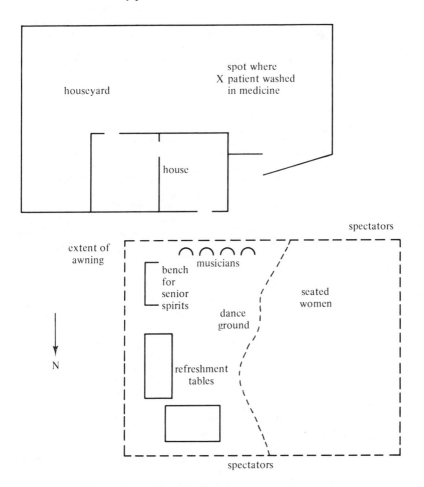

Figure 11.1. Ground plan of a *trumba* ceremony.

contained a noisy crowd of some fifty people, sitting on the mats or
standing around the periphery (Figure 11.1). On the table were eight
soft-drink bottles filled with mead, two cans each of beer, Sprite, and
Coke, a few packs of cigarettes, a dish of local chewing tobacco, one
bottle each of Réunion rum and cheap red wine, several bottles of
cologne, and dishes of incense, white clay, and liquid herbal medicine.

The four musicians took chairs on the south side and began to play
accordion and rattles. The curer danced a couple of steps in front of
the musicians, and the seated women began to sing and clap. The
patient was led in and put into trance. The *chaŋgizy* spirit announced
its name as Bota . . .

Soon a woman (*A*) sitting next to Bota began to enter trance, squealing and throwing her arms about. Bota helped to calm the new arrival, and the woman on *A*'s other side untied her hair. *A* continued to shriek for a few moments and then sat arm in arm with Bota, nodding in time to the music. The curer sat on the bench chatting with the patient's husband, who jokingly mimed a seizure. The curer passed a white handkerchief to Bota, and the spirit placed it on its head. The handkerchief was passed back and forth during the night to indicate which of many possible hosts was possessed by Bota at any given moment . . .

The bottles on the table remained unopened, although the drummers, some of the younger male spectators standing on the fringes, and a single spirit had started drinking the local palm wine supplied discreetly by the patient's husband. One of the younger men called out a flirtatious greeting to a spirit who fixed him with a hard stare in return. This male spirit suddenly gave way in the body of the (female) host to a young female. The new arrival squirmed, wiggled her hips, blew kisses in the air, and danced in an exaggeratedly sexy fashion in front of the man who had called out. The crowd roared with laughter at the antics of the spirit.

The curer opened a pack of cigarettes and offered them to the spirits. The men dancing on the fringes begged the spirits for cigarettes. The spirits made a big show of lighting up, wielding their cigarettes with overly precise and perhaps inexperienced gestures. Sometimes they passed them on to the men. One spirit teased a young man. Keeping in eye contact with him, the spirit went through all the motions of selecting, lighting, and offering the cigarette, only to draw back its hand just as he reached for it! The child spirit performed the same comedy with cooked rice contained messily in the folds of its garments. Moving among the onlookers, the child spirit invited them to share, quickly withdrawing again on the rare occasions when somebody actually reached out in acceptance. Then the spirit would stuff the handful of rice into its mouth and cross its eyes in evident satisfaction.

Between 11:00 P.M. and midnight, the number of spirits present at any given moment rose to between ten and fifteen. One of the inebriated unpossessed males was drawn gradually into the group of dancing spirits. He paired off with a spirit, the two first simply making eye contact and then dancing opposite one another and timing their periods of loud stomping to coincide. The mischievous child spirit approached and deliberately danced in and out between them. The couple began holding hands but danced so violently that the older spirit fell down; sprawled on the ground, it continued to shake its limbs in time to the music.

The curer approached Salima, who was sitting among the other nonpossessed women on the mats, and made a concerted attempt to put her into trance. She placed the incense in front of Salima and led the surrounding women in singing and clapping. After some ten minutes, Salima's senior spirit rose and was assisted to the bench. There it sat, heaving slightly, for most of the rest of the night. Vola uttered a series of high-pitched trills and the women around her began clapping hard. She leaned forward and back, twisting her head around.

Arriving with virtually no turmoil, her child spirit grinned, extended its arms, and began a graceful dance. Then it went over to Salima's spirit and began to wipe the latter's feet with Vola's own headcloth. The seated women continued to clap loudly around Mohedja, who soon started to smile and shake her head. Her spirit, evidently a senior female, laughed and spoke in high, hoarse tones. VOLA approached and wiped its face, and the curer helped MOHEDJA over to a seat on the bench next to SALIMA. One of Mohedja's clients[2] knelt with her head in the lap of Mohedja's spirit, and the latter, swaying gently and laughing, stroked her head. The woman then rejoined the other spectators on the mats, and VOLA placed her headcloth over MOHEDJA's shoulders and chest. Mohedja's spirit, now a senior male, sat wrapped in its shawl, its head making small rotations and nodding, and said a couple of words to another client who had been trying to catch the spirit's eye. MOHEDJA called for some cologne to drink, and when this was supplied, shared it with SALIMA.

In the meantime, the other spirits were not so quiet. One spirit poured a whole bottle of mead down the throat of another. The patient's husband brought a bottle of palm wine to a dancing *trumba,* who proceeded to drink half with wildly exaggerated gestures and then hand-fed the rest to the members of the band. Another senior female *trumba* was led up in mincing steps from the back of the group of seated women and leaned back on the bench, sighing and trilling. Then, in a sudden frenzy, it jumped up and, ripping the cloth from its head and tying it around its waist, began a fast dance. A *changizy* spirit had just replaced the female elder in the body of the host . . .

The number of dancers remained unstable, now shrinking to a minimum of three, now suddenly rising to a maximum of about a dozen. One spirit danced with a bottle balanced on its head. The curer, briefly possessed by a *changizy,* danced so wildly that the spirit had to be restrained from striking the other dancers. Another spirit put its arms around VOLA to dance. Mohedja's spirit called to VOLA, and the latter approached the bench, knelt in front of the senior spirit, opened the bottle of proffered mead and began to drink. Then VOLA rose again and began to dance with the bottle . . .

The rum was opened at 1:00 A.M. and finished by 2:00. One of the *trumba* carried the bottle around, pouring shots for most of the spirits, the members of the band, and the favored males among the few who still remained. The liquor was gulped neat. MOHEDJA sent VOLA to fetch me from my post of observation and offered me a drink as well. The dancing and singing continued, and the spirits moved back and forth to the drinks table. At one point, Mohedja's spirit stood to lead a song. But I was not the only one to feel fatigued. By 2:00 A.M. the area was cleared of all male spectators except those few actively carousing with the spirits. Most of the women and children who remained had gone to sleep on the mats. Vola left trance and sat down on the mats. Salima, Mohedja, and even the curer, one by one disappeared into the patient's house for an hour's nap. The patient herself actually spent most of the night out of trance and in the house tending her baby.

A certain "hard core" of *chaŋgizy* spirits remained on the dance floor, becoming steadily more drunk as the night progressed. Somewhat before dawn they were rejoined by the others. A bottle of white wine and some more beer, cola, and cigarettes were brought from the house to supply the insatiable spirits. Both the patient and Mohedja became repossessed by their respective spirits. The former danced awhile and then came, as many of the other junior spirits had previously done, to put its head on the latter's knee. The senior spirit took the opportunity to sternly admonish the junior to refrain from causing its host any further illness; it had received what it had asked for (i.e., the *rombu*) and should now leave the patient alone. Mohedja's spirit then called to the curer to repeat the message to the patient's spirit. The curer added an appropriate remark and the patient's spirit nodded humbly.[3]

Discussion: hierarchy and inversion

From the detail of individual behavior, a general picture of the entertainments can be drawn and an attempt can be made to discover the underlying structure. The behavior is exciting or amusing for the spectators. The class identity places severe constraints on the spirit's behavior; it becomes sharply defined by the manner in which the spirit enters the host and is calmed down and, in the equilibrium stage, by means of the dress, comportment, and manners of the spirits and by their displacement over space. The *chaŋgizy* move to the dance floor and begin their vigorous amusements there. The senior spirits, both male and female, pass the time sitting on the bench provided for them, watching the dancers and the individuals going through the transition phase. On occasion, an elder *trumba* rises to perform a song or stately dance. The few child *trumba* move in and out among all parties. It should be emphasized, however, that part of the complexity of the affair is created by the fact that a given individual can move in and out of a state of possession and can be possessed by different sorts of spirits in turn, these transitions often taking place very rapidly. Furthermore, as was described in some detail for the *patros,* a given spirit can move back and forth among a number of hosts. There is thus a great deal going on at once, often by means of subtle, not explicitly articulated, cues, which are thus difficult for the neophyte observer or participant to catch.

In order to characterize the period of the spirit entertainments, we may turn to Turner's distinction between rites of status elevation and rites of status reversal (1969:166–88). The former, involving the temporary humbling of the novice who will ultimately leave the ritual with a higher status than that which she entered it, is characterized by "the liminality of the strong (and getting stronger)" (Turner 1969:68) and by a model of relationship among the participants of "communitas." Communitas involves the replacement of ordinary social identities and status relationships with an undifferentiated social homogeneity and equality (Turner 1969:96). By contrast, rites of status reversal are characterized by the "liminality . . . of the permanently weak," involving "a symbolic or make-believe elevation of the ritual subjects to positions of eminent authority . . . The liminality . . . of the weak represents a fantasy of structural superiority" (Turner 1969:168). Later in the same work, Turner suggests that a group of people structurally inferior vis-à-vis the wider society may create a "pseudo-hierarchy" among themselves, one that remains more expressive than instrumental (Turner 1969:190–4). This notion is actually a departure from the idea of a simple reversal, because the participants may take on not merely the roles at the top of the structure but create a whole structure, containing higher as well as lower positions.

We have already seen how the curing sequence may be considered a rite of status elevation both from the point of view of the spirit, who is thereby introduced to society, and from the point of view of the patient, who moves from an original state of illness and an ambiguous relationship to a state of health and a clear-cut, if still slightly precarious, relationship with a spirit familiar. However, if the large public ceremonies are examined in synchronic perspective and the behavior of the majority of the participants is considered apart from the intentions of the central characters, it becomes apparent that the ceremonies also resemble Turner's second class. Most of the participants, both spirit and human, are attracted to an event of status reversal, of entertainment and license. In short, the *rombu* (or the *azulahy*) contains a distinction similar to that of Turner's ideal types but combines their performance on a single, larger occasion and is thus more complex than either. It is this combination and opposition of themes that makes the ceremonies so fascinating.

The key aspects of the status reversal and the "pseudo-hierarchy" may be elaborated. The hierarchical aspect of the relationships among the *trumba* is continually and consistently brought to the foreground in their activity. Interaction between members of different *trumba* classes is more frequent and more formal than between members of the same class. The *chaŋgizy* and child spirits show respect to the senior *trumba*. A junior spirit kneels in front of a senior *trumba* and places its head in the latter's lap. A child spirit may also wipe the brow or dust the feet of a senior. The senior spirit, concerned with maintaining face, expects to receive these signs of respect and, in turn, acknowledges them graciously. The distinctions in rank are primarily expressive in nature, but they have instrumental significance as well. Senior *trumba* dispense blessings, advice, and reprimands, whereas the junior *trumba* (and humans) must pay attention. During the *rombu* sketched above, I observed a senior spirit separate and scold two quarreling *chaŋgizy*, admonish the patient's *chaŋgizy* to stop making her ill, and warn a child spirit of the dangers of behaving flirtatiously in the presence of men. In each case, except perhaps the last, the younger spirit took on a humble and attentive attitude and appeared to act upon the elder's advice.

That this hierarchy is integral to spirit behavior is undeniable. Yet there are also indications that, as Turner suggests, the hierarchy is simulated, mock, unreal. Whatever its basis in historical fact, the political aspect of the scheme today has no significance outside the limited contexts of possession. Furthermore, there is beneath the hierarchy a sense of something shared by all the participants. This is noticeable in the voluntary way in which the gestures of respect are performed, in the concern shown by all for those having trouble reaching the equilibrium state, in the comfort the spirits provide one another, and in the degree of physical contact. The hierarchy is also subverted by the fact that a given host can consecutively represent all the positions in it (cf. Chapter 4).

The notion that the hierarchy is a simulation indicates that it is no mere reflection or reversal of ordinary society but a symbolic construction upon it; it must have significance of its own. What is presented appears to be more the *idea* of hierarchy than a concrete hierarchical system. Furthermore, the idea is countered (or bolstered) by the simultaneous suggestion that the relationship of those of upper status to those of lower status is, or ought to be, one not of exploitation but of nurturance, governed by considerations of relative dependency and responsibility. In other words, the exaggerated self-interest and concern for prestige exhibited by the spirits individually and between the members of a single spirit class is balanced by the selfless nature of the interaction between members of different classes. The message appears to be that, given the naturally selfish nature of individuals, it is vertical authority ties, ideally of parent-child nurturance but more commonly of patron-clientship, rather than horizontal ones, that hold people together. It is not clear whether this is a critique or a support of existing social relations; its strength may lie in that it can be interpreted either way.

So far we have restricted the discussion to the behavior of those participants in the festivities who are in active states of possession. These are virtually all women, and it may be that as a group spirits represent a reversal of the status of women in ordinary life. In order to examine this question we have to understand the nature of the relationships between the spirits and the nonpossessed participants and spectators, particularly the male ones.

It should be obvious that most of those present at a spirit feast who are not themselves in trance at any given moment cannot simply be dismissed from consideration as an "audience," with the implications of passivity that the term implies. In particular, those men who engage in direct communication with the spirits become an integral part of the affair. Men are attracted to the *rombu* by the chance to enjoy free liquor, live music, and dancing in the company of women.[4] Many young men are heavy drinkers of palm wine, yet because drinking is frowned upon, ordinarily they have the opportunity to drink only in the company of other male drinkers. The *rombu* provides a rare occasion for drinking in mixed company.

The most common *trumba* spirits to appear, the *chaŋgizy,* are male, and male spirit elders are also more common than female ones. In taking on these roles, the female hosts do undergo a role reversal of sorts. The *chaŋgizy,* like young human males, can carouse publicly and engage in extroverted and boastful behavior. The *trumba* elders, like male human elders, can display their authority publicly. In fact, the spirit elders, being nobles of inherited position and widespread reputation, are entitled to even more respect, and, in theory, wield even more authority than their human counterparts, who are merely informal and local leaders. In practice, they rarely encounter one another, because senior human males tend to avoid the spirits on public occasions.[5]

During the *rombu,* the greatest part of the interaction between spirits and men thus occurs between the carousing youths of both species. This relationship between the spirits and the intoxicated male participants is more interesting than might first appear. It is not simply a transformation of the ordinary relationship prevailing between women and men, but a transformation of the relationship between spirit and host. Just as the spirits are parasites on their hosts, so are these men parasites on the spirits. But the relationship is inverted. Whereas spirits are powerful parasites, able to set their own conditions on the hosts, the men are weak. They try to attract the attention of the spirits and wheedle gifts of alcohol and tobacco. The spirits, in turn, engage in the interchange with relish, making the men perform for the gifts. Furthermore, just as women in trance imitate patterns of male behavior, so too do men, intoxicated, then imitate the behavior of the spirits.

In sum, the mediation of opposition between the sexes is not achieved simply by role reversal, although such reversal takes place. Rather, each sex takes a step toward an intermediary liminal state where the women transform themselves and the men then imitate that transformation. Although each sex appears to enter the liminal state by different means and for different reasons, once there the two are somehow united. As one young male informant explained it to me, women who are in a state of trance (*menziky*) start drinking and become inebriated (*mamu*), and men who are very drunk (*mamu*) are high, raging (*menziky*) as well. The two then enjoy playing together. Although one is human and one spirit, they have reached the same "wavelength" (my metaphor).

It is important to note that the common wavelength selected belongs primarily to the domain of spirits rather than of humans. Here again there is an inversion. Just as elsewhere spirits are encouraged to interact with humans in terms of human social rules and values, so here do the human males interact with spirits in terms of spirit values. The inversion apparent in the *trumba* amusements contrasts not only with everyday life but also with the aim of the curing process viewed as a whole. As well as mediating between the sexes, it provides a balance to the perhaps unrealistic goals of the cure; if spirits must learn to behave like humans, there are times, too, when spirits predominate and humans will act like spirits. In this way, neither side, spirit or human, finally wins out; rather, a dynamic tension is maintained.

Conclusion: the dialectics of possession

One theme that emerges from the description of the *rombu* is the special place of the well-established senior *trumba*. Few in number, seated on their chairs next to the refreshment table and dance floor, they provide a kind of axis around which the youthful spirits and human clients revolve. More powerful, seemingly more rational and reasonable, less openly selfish and self-centered than the younger *trumba,* they provide a control on the activities of the junior spirits and mediate between individual spirits and concerned humans. But the senior spirit is a spirit nonetheless, and if its power provides it with increased legitimacy, it also lends it increased dangerousness and unpredictability. All the attributes of spiritness are drawn together and magnified in the senior *trumba;* the resultant contradictions demonstrate in condensed and powerful fashion the central paradox or problematic of the whole affair.

The paradox becomes most evident at the sequence of events that, some time after dawn, draws the *rombu* to a close. Once this final ritual sequence has been conducted, most spirits disappear to their spirit homes, and most human hosts stumble off to breakfast or bed.

With the advent of dawn at the Melekavo *rombu*, a few women brought their children or grandchildren to receive a taste of the spirit medicine. Each child was offered a drink from the plate of liquid containing crushed leaves and a silver bracelet, and then Mohedja's senior spirit rubbed a little in the child's hair. Various of the youthful *trumba* had received the identical treatment at the hands of Mohedja's spirit during the night. The treatment was clearly considered preventive in nature, sought and accepted in confidence from a potent source.

At about eight in the morning, small children, mothers with babies, the patient herself (no longer in trance), her children and husband, and many of their younger relatives were seated on the mats underneath the awning, facing toward Mecca. A dish of liquid medicine was brought forward and each senior *trumba*, in order of precedence by age, dipped the long and narrow leaves of the *hasiŋ* plant into the medicine and, mumbling an incantation, flicked droplets over the seated company. This is considered a potent blessing and, indeed, is referred to as a *dzoru*, a term that otherwise refers to the recitation of Koranic prayers. The form of the ritual parallels that of the Islamic *shidjabu*, which is practiced frequently in both public and domestic contexts. In the *shidjabu*, the Koranic masters toss grains of rice and blow over the assembled company as they recite verses of blessing and protection. For a *shidjabu* to be effective, the masters must be paid a token sum, and at the *rombu*, too, the *trumba* receive small amounts of money. In this case, Mohedja, as the most senior of the *trumba* present, received CFA250 ($1.25), and those that followed her, CFA25 each.

However, despite the Koranic association and the eagerness with which mothers push their children forward to receive medicine, a certain ambiguity envelops the whole affair. The performers, after all, are not pious or learned men, respected by the community, but spirits. And although the performance of the *shidjabu* is a male prerogative, the spirits appear in the bodies of women. As the spirits deliver their potent medicine, the band continues to play and the youthful spirits continue to carouse a few feet away. The spirits themselves squabble over precedence. Mohedja, ostensibly possessed by the most senior *trumba*, accepted the invitation to go first. She was followed by the curer, two other possessed women, and then Salima. When Salima's turn came, her spirit loudly uttered a series of syllables in *trumba* language (of the sort *da-da-da-di-da*) and thrust its spear several times into the roof mats for emphasis before accepting the dish of medicine and the *hasiŋ* leaves. The *trumba* was asserting its importance and expressing anger that its right of precedence had been usurped. The problem was that Salima's *trumba* was actually senior to Mohedja's, but because it had not celebrated its own *rombu*, its identity was not yet open knowledge. When the curer asked Mohedja's spirit to go first she was unaware of the identity of Salima's spirit. Mohedja's spirit, knowing full well its relative status, did not choose to protest the injury to its comrade. Such openly undignified and ungracious behavior as exhibited by both the spirits would have been unthinkable during a Koranic recitation.

Because I could never hear what the spirits were whispering as they sprinkled their medicine, I asked Mohedja's spirit afterward whether it had uttered a blessing of health or good fortune. To my amazement, the spirit responded with a chuckle that I could hardly expect the *trumba* to wish that people remain healthy and untroubled by spirits; after all, people are the means by which *trumba* acquire sustenance and entertainments!

On this extraordinary remark, contrasting as it does with the eagerness and confidence of the human crowd and the elaborate formality of the affair, seems to hang the whole crux of the matter. I suspect that the spirit was pulling my leg. Certainly, no one would place themselves in the hands of the spirits if they did not trust them. Yet the fact that the remark was possible is significant in itself.

The opposition that is set up here is dialectical, turning back upon itself. First, the licentious revelry forms, as we have seen, an odd contrast to the aims of the cure taken as a whole. Then, the apparently generous and responsible action of the blessing ritual contrasts with the night's selfish hedonism. The blessing is perhaps an indication of the office of *trumba* in the old Sakalava religion[6] that has been largely replaced by Islam. Through their past association with the monarchy, in fact, as the source of the legitimate authority of that monarchy, the senior *trumba* continue to evince a power and a sense of social responsibility that is greater than that attributed to their junior colleagues. However, this impression is immediately challenged by the remarks of the *trumba* themselves. *Trumba* have the power and the means to do good but are lacking the will. The ritual is held, but the performers are insincere. Performance brings one message and one set of results, the whispered asides of the spirits another message – and possibly another set of results. Like a pair of mirrors, the oppositions reflect each other to infinity.

What is established, then, is not morality, and what is represented is not simply amorality. Rather, the possession drama is a kind of reflection upon morality and social responsibility. From the point of view of those who gather to receive the "blessing," the *trumba* are satisfied with the feasting with which they have been indulged and are temporarily willing to show their goodwill. From this perspective, the socialization and education of the spirits is a realistic goal; the establishment of ties of reciprocity and contract can have positive results; power can be channeled productively, and social relationships based on human models can provide the means of access to it. The spirits, on the other hand, maintain the notion of the self-serving or irresponsible class or individual, ultimately motivated by selfish ends. In previous chapters we analyzed the process by which the former attitude is acted upon and made self-evident. But concurrent with it runs the second perspective. The axioms of the spirit complex reduce to neither the one nor the other. The richness of possession is derived precisely from the paradox that it faces courageously and does not pretend can be resolved: the individual versus society; the ideal functions of the powerful versus their actual imperfections; public acceptance versus private dissent. Imperfection is inevitable, a part of spirit (read "human") nature, but so are the attempted means of social redress. Neither is reducible and neither triumphs. The result, an uneasy tension – the actual state of human affairs – is represented brilliantly in the dialectic of human ritual and spirit behavior.

12. The spirits as children

The safest and most satisfying way to summarize the spirits is to present the society's own interpretation of them. I argue that such interpretation can be found in the activities and characteristics of the child spirits. That is, the child spirits are not simply another spirit form but a means by which the people concerned with possession interpret it to themselves. In presenting a class of child spirits what is being said is that spirits are children. Like children, spirits are irrepressible and irresponsible, full of untamed energies and unachieved drives. The child spirits are tricksters; of all kinds of spirits their duplicity is most explicit – and yet, at the same time, its consequences are least severe. In fact, the consequences are so harmless as to be merely comic. Far from being treated with fear and respect, the child spirits are objects of affection and intimacy. The child spirits make it clear that spirits are the children within each of us.

Although communication between adults spirits and humans is generally of a serious nature, it can also be interpreted playfully. The incongruity between the face and body of a familiar person and the voice, manner, and identity of a spirit lends itself very well to humorous interpretation. The humor is not necessarily restricted to the eye of the beholder but can be developed by the spirits themselves. Humor is a quite conscious, if tacit, aspect of spirit behavior.

However, even though it is intrinsic to the possession form, humor is regularly only made explicit by the child spirits. For example, immediately following its problematic act of benediction described in the last chapter, Mohedja's senior male *trumba* was replaced by her playful child spirit. The spirit settled down to breakfast but ate very slowly, interspersing large mouthfuls of food with chatter about how it wished to go outside and dance but was afraid of the men present, uttering breathlessly explicit remarks about just which parts of their anatomies it feared. One of the chief characteristics of child spirits is that no matter how much they eat, they leave their hosts feeling extremely hungry. Vola and I were both quite anxious to set off for Lombeni, but we couldn't convince the child spirit to leave Mohedja so that the latter might sit down to her own breakfast and fortify herself for the road. We coaxed and threatened as the spirit chattered gaily on. Finally we rose and pretended to set off on our own. At this, the spirit rather abruptly left its host, Mohedja attacked what from one point of view might be considered her second breakfast, and we soon set off.

The playful, greedy, sexually precocious little spirit sheds a new light on the activities of the ancient and dignified Sakalava monarch from whom it took over. In order to elucidate this aspect of possession, let us consider the occasions at which the child spirits are the center of attention. The example is drawn from my own dealings with such a spirit.

Treating the spirits

Monday, April 12

> I had mentioned a few times that I wanted to offer Zayata's little *trumba*, named Tamtamu 'Yellow' or 'Turmeric,' a meal. Her elder male *trumba* appeared spontaneously to talk to her husband, Vita, as is its wont, and asked if I had really meant my proposal. Vita, in turn, reported to me that if I was serious I should call up the little *trumba* to make arrangements. Tonight after dinner the door was shut and the incense lit. Zayata sat with a half smile, somtimes still, sometimes stretching, until she entered trance.
>
> Tamtamu spoke with a pronounced lisp, especially after I remarked on it. We agreed that I would feed it a meal of chicken and rice. Tamtamu also likes sweet things such as candy, fruit drinks, and cola, but not cologne or liquor, which, it asserted, kill the appetite. The spirit claimed to be about the age of Zayata's three-year-old daughter and stated that it wouldn't ever grow up . . . Tamtamu promised to rise on Friday, when I would have collected the raw materials for the meal. It remarked that it was planning to trap a human to eat with it, so that it could than go to the guest's mother to beg for more food. The reason would not be hunger but simply the desire to make mischief. Claiming to be very hungry, Tamtamu asked if I didn't have anything to feed it immediately. In parting, it told me to call it whenever I wanted to talk.

Wednesday, April 14

> Zayata said that the little *trumba* had given her a message in her sleep for me. But she wouldn't pass it on; if the *trumba* really wanted me to know, it could come and tell me itself. Late that evening, the spirit rose, chatted with Vita, and then came calling at my door. After a moment's disconcertion, I recognized my visitor by the characteristic

lisp. Tamtamu said it wanted to call a friend, namely, Vola's child spirit, for Friday as well. It wondered whether the food would be sufficient, and we agreed on two chickens rather than one. Tamtamu remarked that Vita and Zayata had plenty of chickens to give.

Tamtamu explained that the little *trumba* are very afraid of men, except those they consider their "brothers" (*anadahy*). Tamtamu referred to me, Zayata's sons, and her husband, Vita, all as "brothers"; it considers every male with whom it has made friends in this light. Tamtamu went on to say that it was afraid to come up to my house in the daytime because I often had male visitors. In fact, when it walked past the village meeting place that evening, there were a lot of men present and some called out greetings to Zayata. Tamtamu didn't answer for fear they'd tell by the voice who it was. Tamtamu emphasized to me that the spirits are very small and young and can't fight back. The spirit was hesitant to depart, peeking out of my door and retreating within again. Finally I suggested that it leave Zayata's body from my place and let her walk back home herself. The spirit did so, and Zayata appeared to be rather startled to find herself in my room when she came to.

Friday, April 16

This morning, although Vita wanted to be off in the fields, he stayed at home long enough to get things started. He caught two chickens and set out the three bottles of soft drinks and the loaf of bread I had bought. Bread is a rare treat in the village and one of which Vita is especially fond, yet he refused to touch the loaf when I suggested we leave only half for the *trumba*. He ordered four kilos of rice to be brought from the granary, then lit the incense and called on Tamtamu to come. Zayata wandered in, sat on the bed, and went into trance. Vita greeted Tamtamu, showed the spirit the food, and asked if there was anything else it needed. The spirit replied shyly, onions and spice. Vita immediately pulled out his own money and sent one of his daughters to the store. Vita then left for the day.

Tamtamu announced it was going to visit Vola and asked me not to accompany it. Some time later I noticed the two spirits at the house of Mohedja. There was a lot of laughter as they tried to convince her to go into trance. Mohedja protested that she had too much work to do. Vola's child spirit, Kalu, entered Mohedja's house, lit a piece of incense, and hauled her in. Mohedja laughed and tried to say sternly that they should leave her alone; what were they doing coming to play in a period when there was so much work to be done? They retorted that she should keep quiet and let her spirit rise. But the spirit gave no signs of appearing, and so they left Mohedja behind; the spirit didn't really want to visit or it would have come on its own.

The two spirits returned to Zayata's houseyard to set about cooking. First Tamtamu showed off the table of food to Kalu and the two of them shared a soft drink and the bread. For a long while they cooked peacefully. Zayata's daughter loaned them a big rice pot, salt, and so on. I bought a tin of tomato paste they requested. The two chickens were prepared separately. The larger one, cooked in oil, spices, and tomato paste, was reserved for the spirits; the other, cooked in a water base with fresh tomatoes, was distributed among the children of the compound and portions were set aside for Vita and for Vola's husband. The spirits invited me to eat with them around the table. Zayata's adult neice turned down a portion of food, giggling. A *zuky* 'older sibling' of Zayata's arrived, asked for a portion, and stayed to chat for awhile. She was a *rahavavy* 'friend' of the spirit, because she had given Tamtamu chickens in the past. Anyone who has done so it entitled to receive a small serving whenever the spirits cook again.

The husband of Zayata's niece was also entitled to a serving. Much to Tamtamu's apparent annoyance, Zayata's older sibling and her niece's husband shared their portions with their respective spouses; knowing the trouble it would lead to, the spouses had turned down the food when the spirits had offered it directly, and so, Tamtamu claimed, they should not have any at all. But the spirits did feed Zayata's aged mother without making any claims on her, and thus, in fact, everyone in the compound ended up with something to eat.

It is also customary for the little *trumba* to send food to their *fundi* 'teacher' or 'master.' The *fundi* is an older woman in the village who is the major curer for matters relating to the *trumba* and who is the host to the *trumba* chief. Because the *fundi* doesn't eat chicken (it is forbidden her by her *trumba*), the little *trumba* normally send only rice. This time they forgot to send anything. When the *fundi* learned of their presence, she came to the compound. Hearing her approach, the little *trumba* remembered their omission and began giggling with embarrassment and fright. Kalu ran into the next room to hide, but Tamtamu bravely greeted the *fundi* and heard her announce that she was hungry. Tamtamu said they would go and husk rice for her. After the *fundi* left, Tamtamu stated that it was too full to go pound rice, and the two spirits sat for a long while giggling and debating aimlessly about what to do. Finally Tamtamu remembered an extra plate of cooked rice they had earlier set aside and sent that over to the *fundi's* house.

The spirits spent most of the afternoon eating. They consumed a great deal, but they rationed the meat so that they always had some available with which to entice others to join them. They acted extremely childishly while they ate. Tamtamu dumped rice in its lap and ate from there, saying it tasted better that way. The spirit remarked how the owner of the clothes (i.e., Zayata) would be angry when she saw their condition. The two spirits sang, often with their mouths full, and they rose between bites to do a little dance. They giggled and whispered and spilled food. Whenever anyone entered the houseyard they tried to tempt them to join in. This led to a great deal of loud joking and laughter on everyone's part. The son of Vita's sister loudly told the spirits that there were no creatures worse than they. He chuckled, the spirits giggled, and the teasing went on. The spirits were sad to be unable to catch anyone. If someone had so much as tasted the food, they would have followed him or her home and demanded a chicken and some rice in return. At one point an older man entered the house and agreed to eat with the spirits. But instead, he reached out to fondle them. After a few minutes of shrieking and horseplay, he left.

The younger children stared at the proceedings. When Tamtamu talked to the children, it generally took on Zayata's stern tones and did not protest when the little ones addressed it as "mother." Kalu joked a little with Vola's ten-year-old son, saying it wanted him to give it one of the chickens he was raising. The boy appeared uncertain and Kalu pestered for a moment or two. But when the spirit realized the boy was upset, it quickly became soothing and said never mind, that it could see he was right. All of the children received enough to eat.

In the late afternoon, the two *trumba* visited Vita's mother and were fed again by Vola's husband at his home. When they walked across the village, the spirits tried very hard to pass as Zayata and Vola. The villagers appeared to treat the spirits with affection as well as amusement and told me I had performed a good service in feeding them. The two spirits themselves thanked me before separating.

Later in the evening Tamtamu was still present. A young man came to visit at Zayata's, bearing the spirit a gift of two eggs. The two chatted and joked together. Tamtamu tried to bait the youth, saying it knew he had gone searching the night before for tenrec (the hunting and eating of which are highly disreputable occupations, but ones that many young men engage in). After the disconcerted young man had left, Tamtamu, too, parted company with us. The first things Zayata said on coming out of trance was how hungry she was, and she immediately served herself some food, though less than might have been expected from the way she talked. She appeared not at all disoriented or tired, and we had a lengthy discussion of other matters.

Later I discovered from the young man that it was the *trumba* who had asked for the eggs and that they were actually a gift for me. The youth told me that he really believes the little *trumba* go about at night and see things. Tamtamu presented his tenrec hunting experience quite accurately. He admitted he was now frightened to go hunting alone, though not to sit and joke while the *trumba* possessed Zayata. The *trumba* were out at night looking for food, and although he didn't know what they ate out there, it was not tenrec.

A humorous interpretation of possession

This sequence has a number of interesting aspects. Among other things, it recounts the initial development of my relationship with the child *trumba* Tamtamu. I began with the offer of a meal, and Tamtamu reciprocated with eggs and frequent subsequent visits. A few weeks later the spirit asked me for a gift of clothing. The account also provides glimpses of the much deeper relationship that Tamtamu has with Zayata's husband, Vita. Their relationship appears to be characterized by an open and informal reciprocity. Tamtamu and Vita talk to each other frequently, although they say they had more regular contact in the years immediately after Tamtamu first entered Zayata. Tamtamu's visits increased in frequency again with my own expression of interest but were generally conducted, or at least initiated, in the presence of Vita.

Although the development of relationships between spirits and the close associates of their hosts is general to possession (Chapter 5), several features are particular to the child spirits. The child spirits describe a model of exchange that excludes marriage. Men are either enemies (potential sexual aggressors and victims of trickery) or "brothers." Siblingship ties are created by means of direct gift exchange, which need not involve the host. Child spirits only enter women who have been possessed previously by older spirits,[1] and they refrain from harming their hosts once they have risen for the first time (although they do make their hosts ill before their presence has been diagnosed). Unlike other spirits, the child spirits present their names immediately, requiring neither medicines nor elaborate feasts.[2] The chief manner in which they prove detrimental to their hosts is in causing them embarrassment by their behavior in public. At the *rombu* of the older *trumba,* the little ones distinguish themselves by doing "stupid" things like carrying chunks of freshly slaughtered meat in their clothing and covering themselves with blood.

The energies of the child spirits are not directed against their hosts but outward. Their major preoccupation concerns food. In contrast to the older *trumba,* who indicate their presence by severely restricting the diets of their hosts, notably by denying them chicken, the child spirits love nothing better than to gorge themselves on hearty meals of chicken. It is also the case that the little *trumba* tend to rely on charm and guile rather than violence and extortion to achieve their ends. They coax people for the means to prepare their meals, tempt others to share their food, and then demand recompense. With those who provide food freely, they establish close bonds of friendship, calling their benefactors by the terms for siblings of equivalent status[3] and providing gifts and labor in return. Thus Zayata's child spirit formerly appeared every year at the beginning of the new horticultural season and put in such long hours clearing the fields that Vita felt sorry for it and also had to beg it to leave so that Zayata could nourish herself. In return for its labor, Vita offered the spirit rice from the harvest whenever it wished to visit during the year. One year the spirit insisted on his setting aside a bushel (*vurohu*) of the rice harvest for its exclusive use, but Vita felt the household could not afford it, and so the spirit stopped working for them. Such horticultural service on the part of the child *trumba* also provides another interesting contrast with the senior *trumba*, who frequently restrict production by demanding that their hosts stay home and do no field labor on certain days of the week.

Whereas the child spirits assist their friends, to those who accept their invitation to eat without first having provided raw food, they are merciless. They will follow such people to their homes, crying and whining and demanding to be repaid. No one who was not already a friend would ever knowingly eat food offered by a child spirit. The spirits attempt to meet this dilemma and trap their victims by disguising their voices and pretending to be the hosts whose bodies they occupy. Such attempts at trickery contain an intriguing inner tension, because a spirit must first establish its presence by distinguishing itself from the host before it can begin to imitate her. Because imitation of the host must remain secondary to distinction from the host, the spirit's attempts at disguise are not generally very successful. Sly strategies of deceit are inevitably transformed into rich comedy.

Wherever they appear, the child *trumba* are figures of fun. In the child spirits the latent humor of possession is fully and explicitly realized. At the *rombu* the little *trumba* perform the role of clowns (Chapter 11). They move freely among the other participants and comment on the action. Their powers of recontextualization, of shifting boundaries, are similar to those of the comic figures in Shakespearian drama. The child spirits also rise in the context of regular domestic life. And although they come infrequently, they like to make a full day of their visits. Despite their shyness with male strangers, the child spirits are highly gregarious and establish friendships with large numbers of people. From the safety of their hosts' houseyards, they laugh and joke and chatter with one another, with the families of their hosts, and with all passers-by.

The situation is an inherently comic one. Mothers, normally the models of propriety, hospitality, and selflessness, become suddenly the very opposite, indulging in all the bad habits from which they habitually try to wean their children. Domestic relations and roles are abruptly skewed: sons, husbands, and in-laws alike become siblings, mothers become children. The joke grows richest when the spirits attempt to set their tricks. Little girls in the bodies of familiar adult women try to imitate those women; spirits press the most generous offers of hospitality, all the while never quite managing to conceal their underlying selfish intentions. The potential victims respond in kind. Instead of graciously accepting, they tease or taunt in turn, sometimes pretending to fall for the trap until, at the last moment, they make their escapes.[4] The whole business suggests that hospitality, a dominant idiom of proper social intercourse, is, in reality, pursued with selfish ends. Just as the older spirits parody the *shuŋgu* and the values of public life, so too do the child spirits treat the norms of household hospitality. The paradox is that success and social respectability at both the public and the domestic levels are achieved at the expense of violating the very social norms from which they are supposed to be constructed.

At the same time it is apparent that the relationships of the child spirits to their hosts and to their hosts' communities are quite different from those of the older spirits. The behavior of the child spirits is at once more transparent and of less consequence. Adult spirits aim to fulfill their status obligations to other spirits but do so at the expense of human health. In the process, they develop ties with humans as well. The burdens of the child spirits are lighter and their immediate aim is to achieve, not prestige among their peers, but friendship with humans. As children or slaves (Chapter 10) of the older *trumba,* the younger ones labor for them, wash their feet, and cook their food at feasts. But they seem equally willing to work for humans, clearing fields and husking rice. True, the child spirits are demanding and unpredictable, deplete their hosts' stores, and dirty their clothing. But if they are frequently unreasonable, they have the excuse of their age; they are too young to know any better. The child *trumba* are naughty rather than evil, amusing rather than fearful – although their pranks and powers serve to remind of greater transgressions and larger dangers. In short, they are like the older spirits, with the sting removed.

Clifford Geertz, in his masterful essay on the Balinese cockfight (1972), says that "societies, like lives, contain their own interpretations." These interpretations, or aesthetic forms, he argues, do not merely express subjective experience or sensibility, they create and organize it. It is in this light that we have been viewing spirit possession, but here we go further. Interpretations, too, contain their own interpretations; the child spirits may be seen as an interpretation of the larger institution of possession. This view is plausible for several reasons. Child spirits are secondary because they only enter hosts who have previously received older spirits. Their qualities are transformations of the model that underlies the older spirits. If all spirits are characterized by their amorality and irresponsibility, by being not fully socialized, what better way to state it than to compare them with those creatures who are necessarily not fully socialized, that is, with young children.[5]

Most significant, the visits of the child spirits are always received with humor. In a sense, all the spirits, old as well as young, are humorous, but it is only the child spirits who make people fully aware of this. All possession deals in paradox. Although structured in a hierarchy, the spirits point most clearly to the discrepancy between hierarchy and sentiment, between power and responsibility, between the mystifications of social structure and the actual relations between people. But if possession is a joke about all this, it is the sort of joke in which people catch their breath but do not dare or wish to laugh. Through the child spirits, this laughter is released. Here the weakest spirits are made to stand for the most powerful, the less harmful for the more harmful, the spirits on the lowest rung of the hierarchy for the hierarchy itself. In this way, the danger and the pain inherent in the awareness of the discrepancies that the spirits present us with is defused, and the spirits can be recognized for what they are: transformations of ourselves.

Humor is, by definition, interpretive. Whatever approach we take to humor, whether we see it as the spontaneous in human life reduced to the mechanical (Bergson 1913) or as "an opposition of suitableness and unsuitableness, or of relation and the want of relation, united, or supposed to be united, in the same assemblage" (James Beattie 1776, quoted in Milner 1972), the potential for humor can only exist in the contrast to an ordinary or accepted state of affairs. The realization of the potential occurs when we allow ourselves to accept the contrast or paradox, when we "get" the joke, when we experience the "joke form" in the social structure (Douglas 1968) – and express our evaluation in laughter. In the case of possession, however, the ultimate joke form is the entire social structure; spirits are about the experience of social life.

Conclusion

Trance behavior in Mayotte rests on a coherent, articulate, and highly sensitive cultural system, which we call spirit possession.

Spirit species and classes are organized according to a "science of the concrete." A contrast is maintained between spiritkind and humankind; in addition, possessing spirits are systematically distinguished as separate persons from their human hosts.

Possession operates as a system of communication, which must be viewed as an integral, although semiautonomous, part of the social structure. Messages are exchanged between spirits and humans and between humans and humans via spirits.

The system of communication transmits certain typical or standardized texts, which are interpreted according to the conventions that mark possession as a particular genre within Mayotte culture. Simultaneously, it is the performance of these texts that constitutes or reproduces the system of communication.

The ostensive context of the texts is illness and cure. Illness is a reference of possession, not a constituent element or link in a causal chain. Whether or not a host is first ill and then cured, possession is spoken of in this idiom. Possession may provide a means through which therapy is effected in particular cases, but such therapeutic efficacy is neither necessary nor sufficient to explain possession.

The syntagmatic dimension, or plot, of possession texts concerns the emergence and stabilization of the identity of the spirit inhabiting a specific host. The persona of the spirit is created through the elaboration of social (exchange) relationships with significant others and is established in a ritual of public validation. The ritual sequence operates to make possession natural, intelligible, and meaningful to both the host and the members of society at large.

The career of the individual spirit runs from muteness to candidness, confusion to clarity, formlessness to form, nature to culture, psyche to society. However, along the paradigmatic dimension of the texts, these oppositions remain unresolved. That is, chaos and order, senselessness

181

and sense, malevolence and beneficence, are not only brought into play sequentially but also exist simultaneously throughout; a fully socialized spirit would be a contradiction in terms. The discrepancy between what is syntagmatically and paradigmatically achieved provides the texts with an inner dynamic, a force that continually challenges the performers and observers.

Therefore, we cannot mechanically ascribe a particular meaning or set of meanings to possession. Meaning must be drawn by each individual confronted with the experience or knowledge of possession and will change over time. Possession relates to social experience at a highly general level. It is not a code whose meanings can be read off once we discover the key, but a context or ground from which meaning can be generated. The meaning is open, "in suspense" (Ricoeur 1971:544).

Following Ricoeur (1971: 557), "the depth-semantics of the text is not what the author intended to say, buṫ what the text is about, i.e., the non-ostensive reference of the text. And the non-ostensive reference of the text is the kind of world opened up by the depth-semantics of the text." The world that possession opens up is a troubling one, a world of contradiction, in which psyche and society are seldom in accord.

But this is not, of course, the total universe open to the people of Mayotte. Other texts, notably those of Islam, provide other perspectives, and we must consider how these perspectives coexist. It may be that the view of the world offered by possession is too realistic (cf. Murphy 1971) to exist comfortably in a society that does not also have the support of as staunchly moral a system, as meticulous a model of and for the pursuit of social life, as Islam. Possession and Islam operate in Mayotte in a kind of dialectic, each providing the context against which the other can be considered. Although neither is of immediately obvious importance to the other, each provides the other with a foil and with an ultimate reference point.[1]

We can argue, then, that possession is not a reflection of certain aspects of society. Possession considers the experience of social life as a whole. And because it views the human condition dialectically, it cannot be a simple reflection at all. Possession interprets the experience of social life, and, in turn, shapes, indeed becomes, a major part of that experience. The general conditions of life are made apparent through the particular events that strike individuals; the careers of individuals are a product of the general conditions. Possession and kinship mutually inform each other. For example, kinship presents possession with the analogy between spirit and affine and with the notion of spirit as sibling. Possession describes both the pull between individualism and collective ties and the formation of strategic alliances characteristic of a society based on nuclear family household units in villages that maintain a corporate ideology in the face of internal stratification and differentiation. At the same time, possession informs social structure, providing both a model of amoral individualism and a context in which such individualism has to be put aside for social ends. Possession invests social life with moral debate and activity.

Finally, the reader is entitled to ask what relevance this work has for the study of trance is general. The major conclusion is that trance must be approached in terms of its cultural particularity. The codes and constraints underlying trance behavior and according to which it is interpreted, the forms of articulation between trance and other social, cultural, and psychobiological subsystems are not the same from one society to the next. General properties of trance behavior lie at a more abstract level than has been commonly assumed, a level that can only be grasped through the detailed account of a specific case, such as the one that has been presented here.

Having started this work with a consideration of the biases against trance, we may also briefly examine its creative potential. Given cultural form, altered states of consciousness provide a medium for the transmission of messages that are not apparent in the ordinary everyday world of "unaltered" consciousness. They help to establish the meaning and meaningfulness of culture by providing controlled experience of what it is not. They provide empirical evidence for the fact that culture is primarily a matter of convention. This understanding can be applied either to subvert or to support the culture at hand. At the same time, the immediacy of the particular possession case, viewed in the emotional idiom of illness and cure, hides the conventionality of the trance structure itself and protects it from challenge. Possession thus maintains the power to impose order, even while engaged in an active contemplation of disorder. Perhaps the dramatic element and the suspense that some observers have noted in traditional trance performances is a function of the playing out of this tension between acceptance and rejection of the conventional order. Whatever the outcome, which need not, of course, be determinate, and which will usually support the side of convention to the degree that convention controls access to trance and the behavior within it, it is always the case that the ordinary world is illuminated by its contrast with the extraordinary. To borrow a phrase from Lévi-Strauss and one from Becker (personal communication), respectively, trance structures are "good to think" and "good to think in the context of."

These points can, of course, be made with regard to the liminal periods of ritual in general (cf. Turner 1969). It might be useful to compare the liminality produced by spirit possession with that found in other kinds of ritual, particularly those that rely on different means of manipulating the neurological and psychological processes. In this sense, the construction of the liminal state in Mayotte lies between that of societies relying primarily on chemical substances (e.g., Harner 1973) and that of societies depending on the active human creation of a radically new material and social environment, for example, through the use of masks, seclusion, and the reversal of established role relationships in initiation rituals (e.g., Turner 1967). A key difference between these means of producing altered states of consciousness concerns the matter of how much control the conventional order is able to maintain over the outcome.[2]

Trance, masking, and drugs all contrast with certain means of altering consciousness with which we are more familiar, for example, reading, writing, and watching television.[3] The former emphasize the change of state, the radical contrast with the ordinary world. The subjective experience of this contrast and of the movement back and forth between two different worlds is highly significant. In reading and writing, on the other hand, the focus is less on the subjective experience of the change of state (exceptions might include the writing of certain kinds of poetry, the reading of "escape" fiction, and the recitation of sacred liturgy) than on the information transmitted. As the act of reading does not usually strike the reader as a special experience, so it does not directly challenge the conventional order. The potential for challenge comes from the fact that the reader has so much leisure to reflect upon what he is learning and also from the fact that writing generally conforms to ordinary discursive logic. The facts and theories presented in written form may challenge specific conventions, but they are not likely (with the exception of certain trends in modern literature) to challenge convention itself. Control over the flow of information, of backtracking or repeating a stimulating message is not possible to anywhere near the same degree in chemically induced states. Trance, as it occurs in Mayotte, lies between these extremes and thereby gains in flexibility. The flow of information between those in trance and those out of it can be largely controlled by the participants and is presented, for the most part, according to the conventions of everyday discursive logic. As in regular speech, there is the possibility for repetition, reflection, remaneuvering.

Possession and masking[4] present an interesting structural contrast. In the former, spirits appear, in theory, in the bodies and shapes of men. In the latter, men hide, in fact, in the bodies and shapes of spirits. However, whereas the actor/role or guest/host relationship is denied or concealed in many masking cultures, it is emphasized in possession. What is emergent in Mayotte is the integral identity of the spirit, distinct from the host it inhabits. The contrast between the alien spirit and the familiar body of the host provides a paradox or tension that is a central and striking aspect of possession. Tension of quite a different sort must be generated between the informal speculation and conventional ignorance on the part of the spectators associated with masking.[5] The social organization of belief is quite different in the two cases. In the former, the authenticity of individual manifestations of spirits can be tested and challenged by the public. In the latter, authenticity may go unchallenged and rests upon a division in the society between those with access to privileged information and those without, a distinction that frequently runs along age or gender lines.

Appendix: Additional classes of possession spirits in Mayotte

Mugala and rewa

Two kinds of spirits that come out of the same cultural matrix as the *patros* are the *mugala* and the *rewa*. Like the *patros*, these spirits require an *azulahy* 'drumming ceremony.' However, each kind has its own particular dancing style. The drums for the *rewa* are said to be beaten with two sticks, whereas those of the *patros* and *mugala* are beaten with the hand (except for the oil drum, which is turned on its side and beaten with a pair of sticks).

Whereas the *patros* are said to be indigenous to Mayotte, the *rewa* are believed to speak the language of 'Ngudja (Zanzibar). The *rewa* were formerly common in Lombeni but have not appeared in some time. The only two individuals known to me who were possessed by *rewa* are both over sixty. It is supposed that the reason the *rewa* no longer appear is that all their curers have died out and no one knows how to handle them any more. The *rewa* ate their own special form of cake or pudding, sugar, sweet bananas, and other things, but no blood. They particularly liked to listen to the radio (to hear Zanzibari spoken?). The most unique feature of the *rewa* was that after their ceremonies were finished, the spirits (with the exception of those who inhabited the curers) left the bodies of their hosts permanently. A small-scale, toy-sized model of a canoe would be constructed. At dawn, after the dancing was over, everyone trooped down to the beach, where the canoe, filled with bits of all kinds of food the spirit liked to eat, was put out to sea, sending the *rewa* home. An informant remarked that the *rewa* was a relatively good kind of spirit to have, because after its ceremony it went home and bothered you no more.

The *mugala* are said to be native to the neighboring island of 'Ndzwany (Anjouan). They are very common today in certain Shimaore villages of Mayotte. *Mugala* ceremonies are similar to those described for *patros* (Jon H. Breslar, personal communication), and the two kinds of spirits sometimes rise at one another's ceremonies. The *mugala* typically consume salt, flowers, and milk, and chew betel. The salt forms a binary opposition with the *patros*, who exclude it from all cooked food.

Kakanoru

Rather than just entering humans, *kakanoru* sometimes appear to them in their own shape as well. The *kakanoru* are considered indigenous to Mayotte and are supposed to be numerous.[1] Their appearance is anomalous. They are creatures of the forest, shaped like humans yet small, whose entire bodies are covered with long hair. Their left arms are short but very strong, whereas their

186

right arms are much longer and weak. Living out in the country and strongly disliking the light, the *kakanoru* are rarely seen. However, one woman recalled having seen one once when she was a child and living in a small, isolated inland village:

> At noontime, when the sun was shining strongly (and therefore no one was about), Zayata and a friend decided to go fetch water. The stream was very far from the village. As they neared the stream, they noticed a little person standing under a banana plant, stuffing baby lemurs into a bag. He was very short, like a child, yet had adult features. He had long hair, covering even his legs, and one long arm and one short. Zayata wanted to call out *mro!* (the warning call given when approaching a bathing place), but her friend suggested keeping silent. They watched for a long time, not knowing whether the figure was human. Finally, Zayata called out. Startled, the figure turned around, saw them, and then vanished into the forest. When the girls returned to the village and recounted their story, the adults told them they had seen a *kakanoru*. They were admonished not to go to the stream at noontime; the spirit probably frequented it then because it thought it would be undisturbed. Nevertheless, on another day Zayata suggested to her friend that they return to see the *kakanoru*. They went, but saw nothing. Zayata chuckles that children don't have the sense to be scared; today, she would be far too afraid to even think of revisiting such a spirit.

Although Rusillon (1912) reported that the *kakanoru* were the most feared of all the *trumba* in northwest Madagascar, in Mayotte they are neither classified as *trumba* nor more feared than other kinds of spirits. In fact, there are stories concerning *kakanoru* who befriend humans. The members of a Malagasy-speaking family, renowned throughout the island for their skill at setting broken bones, are said to be aided in their profession by a *kakanoru* friend. A *kakanoru* may also sometimes warn a friend when representatives of the central administration are coming in search of him or perhaps give a friend a gift of riches or the means to achieve them – a medicine (*audy*), which will make the shopkeepers forget he hasn't paid for his purchases. The following brief story is typical:

> A man in a certain Malagasy-speaking village had a *kakanoru* as a friend. One night when he was asleep in his house, he and his wife in one room and his mother in the other, he was awakened by a noise. It was the *kakanoru*, dragging in a large chest, filled with money perhaps or clothes or . . . ? But his mother lit the lamp in order to see what the commotion was about and the *kakanoru* fled from the light, taking the chest with him.

Although *kakanoru* often simply want to make friends with people and visit them at night, occasionally they choose to enter someone. In this case the pattern is similar to the *trumba* and *patros*. The ceremony is an *azulahy* (drumming) as opposed to a *rombu* (clapping, guitar), is held on a dark night or inside a darkened house, and ends at cockcrow. The spirits consume milk and sweet bananas and sometimes sugar and sweet coconut. A special kind of incense (*maneviky*, a grass that is occasionally also used to thatch roofs) is lit, and the medicine, like that of the *patros,* is inhaled. A *kakanoru* may also rise when *patros* incense is lit. *Patros* and *kakanoru* spirits sometimes rise at one another's feasts. The two kinds of spirits have been known to fight on such occasions, particularly if precautions have not been taken to prepare food pleasing to both. On the other hand, individual *patros* and *kakanoru* may be friends.

The *kakanoru* contrast with the *patros* in that, whereas the latter are associated with the sea and coasts, the *kakanoru* are associated with fresh, running water and with the interior of the island, the forests and mountains. Yet both are considered indigenous to Mayotte. The contrasts with the *trumba* are more numerous. Whereas *trumba* require bright, moonlit nights for their ceremonies, the *kakanoru* abhor the light. The *kakanoru/trumba* contrast also follows a nature/culture opposition. For example, whereas *trumba* subsist on liquor, a culturally processed and foreign food, the *kakanoru* rely on natural, untreated foods – milk and sweet bananas. Thus, to the extent that they are involved in possession activities at all, the *kakanoru* appear to be an example of an original Malagasy form of spirit that developed, by inversion to the *trumba,* into a form akin to the Mahorais *patros.*

Mwana 'Isa

No one in Lombeni is possessed by a *mwana 'Isa,* but they are said to be common in *aranta* 'by the shore,' the area of large villages in the northeastern part of the island, frequented by the French and other foreigners, that form the commercial and administrative hub of Mayotte. Like the *kakanoru,* the *mwana 'Isa* are said to live in the forest or bush and to be shaped like people, but very small: The adults are the size of human toddlers. Like the *kakanoru,* they dislike light and hold their ceremonies in darkened houses and then only until cockcrow. My informants in Lombeni disagree about whether or not *mwana 'Isa* and *kakanoru* are identical. Citing the above similarities, Mohedja claims that they are merely Shimaore and Malagasy words for the same phenomenon. Zayata, however, has observed the following contrasts. She claims that *mwana 'Isa* require a guitar and rattle (i.e., a *rombu*) rather than drums like the *kakanoru,* that they use *trumba* rather than *kakanoru* incense, and that they eat honey and possibly other foods but never sweet bananas. Furthermore, she points out, whereas *mwana 'Isa* are strict in their avoidance of light, *kakanoru* often do participate in lit *patros* events and do not always run from the light as they claim to.

I would explain the apparent contradiction in the two points of view by interpreting both the *mwana 'Isa* and the *kakanoru* possession ritual as emergent and unstabilized. The *mwana 'Isa* is apparently fairly recent to Mayotte. The term itself is Comoran for 'child Jesus' and, although 'Isa is of course present in the Islamic canon as well, it is suggestive that the *mwana 'Isa* spirits are found primarily in those parts of Mayotte that have had most contact with the foreign, Christian community. Of course, I am not saying that the *mwana 'Isa* represent Christ but simply that the figure has become raw material for incorporation into the local structures. The *mwana 'Isa* may be in part a symbol of commonality between the islanders and the French, but the name is also appropriate for beings who are "the size of toddlers" and undoubtedly for a number of other reasons as well. At the same time, although the Comoran name is in use, the ritual features appear to imitate the *trumba:* music, incense, and honey. Like the *kakanoru,* the attempt seems to be to define the *mwana* '*Isa* in terms of the structure of the preexisting spirit classes.

Other kinds of *trumba*

The Sakalava *trumba,* whether they are interpreted as representing age groups, generations, or social classes, form a social whole. Outside of this "society" at least two other kinds of *trumba* are recognized in Mayotte. Neither is currently active in Lombeni, one having gone out of fashion and the other being a recent arrival on the island.

Antaŋala

Antaŋala trumba, whose name means 'people of the forest' or 'wilderness' (i.e., beyond the village), appear to represent the Antandroy, an ethnic group of pastoralists of southwest Madagascar, said to live deep in the wilderness (*aŋala be*) raising cattle. The Antandroy are known because about a generation ago some males came to work on the plantations on Mayotte and had children. At their *rombu,* the *antaŋala* wear loincloths (*sadika*), a form of dress not otherwise found in Mayotte. Their condition for announcing their names is that they stand in a canoe filled with honey that is placed somewhere high off the ground. Although this behavior might delight a structuralist, it is recognized as an extraordinary condition in Mayotte, where it is impossible to amass so much honey. The spirits are willing to stop harming the hosts without fulfillment of the conditions, but what is interesting is that they will not compromise on the conditions for annunciation. It is the hosts who are said to lose out, because they will never know their spirits' names. Thus, the ritual of investiture is preserved intact.

The *antaŋala* are said to appear rarely today (perhaps because they cannot achieve their desires on Mayotte), and I have never seen one.

Be tsiku

I first observed the *be tsiku* (lit., 'big wind') at the *rombu* in Melekavo (Chapter 11), where my Lombeni friends were as impressed by their novelty as I. They are said to be a recent arrival on the island. One informant associates them with the *mgodru,* a secular dance rhythm, performed by humans of both sexes and played on either drums or accordion, that reached its height of popularity some eight or ten years ago and that is similar, but not quite identical, to the dance of the *be tsiku.* No one could tell me whence in Madagascar the *be tsiku* come; their original ethnic reference is, therefore, in some doubt. The entry of the *be tsiku* into the body of its host causes more agitation than does that of any other kind of spirit. The host exhibits severe spasms and foaming at the mouth that my fellow observers liken to (but do not equate with) an epileptic attack. The host lies flat on her back on the floor and calms only after the entire body has been covered in a white sheet and the face anointed with white clay. The spirit then sits up and begins to act in a more coherent, if still quite lively, fashion, similar to the *chaŋgizy,* the youthful Sakalava *trumba.* The host's headcloth is twisted up, passed under the chin and tied at the crown of the head so that the spirit looks to me like one of those old pictures of someone suffering from toothache.

My Lombeni friends feel that although all spirits are unpleasant, the *be tsiku*, to judge by the commotion they create in the bodies of their hosts, may be the worst. What is particularly fascinating about them is that they demonstrate so clearly how even the aspects of possession that would appear to be the most physical or "natural" – the wild and apparently uncontrolled reactions of the body during the moments of transition between a normal state of consciousness and full trance – are actually as constrained by cultural rules as all the rest. Each kind of spirit has a particular somatic reaction associated with its entry, which every individual possessed by this kind of spirit will show (tempered, perhaps, by personal idiosyncracies). In the case of the *be tsiku*, the reaction is an imitation of an epileptic seizure, but when the same hosts are possessed by any other kind of spirit they show the less severe symptoms associated with it.

Notes

Introduction

1   In actual fact the picture is somewhat more complex than this. The memory of class differences prevalent in the nineteenth century still plays a role in certain domains, and new class distinctions are currently emerging. The discussion also ignores the numerically (if not socially) insignificant population of Europeans, East Indians, Creoles, and modernizing Malagasy citizens.

2   The identities of the villages, as of all individuals mentioned throughout the text, have been altered in order to make an effort toward guarding the anonymity of those who so generously provided me with personal or private information. Lombeni Be and Lombeni Kely 'Greater' and 'Lesser' Lombeni have populations of approximately 600 and 300 individuals, respectively. The villages are relatively isolated from the strip of settlements known collectively as Aranta 'By the Shore,' which forms the commercial, administrative, and communications hub of Mayotte and the focus of Western influence today. In 1975–6 the two villages were not served by roads. Like the rest of the island (with the exception of the French Foreign Legion outpost on Dzaoudzi), they were also without electricity; water came in the one case from wells and in the other from a line of bamboo pipes that fed from a spring above the village into a cement basin.

3   I was able to check some of my conclusions during a six-week return visit in the summer of 1980.

4   This is not to exclude the fact that in numerous instances altered states of consciousness are the manifestations of pathology.

5   An alternate view would suggest that "insanity" is our cultural model for interpreting trance.

6   The answer to this question lies far beyond the scope of the present work and the competence of the author. The roots of the Western attitude go back at least to the witch-hunts of the sixteenth century and perhaps even to the original formalization of Catholic doctrine and the institutionalization of the church in opposition both to Hellenism and European "folk" culture. Trance is, of course, common today among certain Protestant sects.

7   In truth, virtually every activity in every society can be described by the intersection of each of these aspects. Sometimes one of them may appear emphasized: for example, "intentionality" in the marketplace, "coher-

ence" in the Catholic Church, "reference" in traditional literary criticism or in Ndembu rites of affliction (Turner 1967), and perhaps everywhere where exegesis becomes professionalized. But the ways in which activity is classified and particular aspects or dimensions of classification are stressed have barely begun to be studied. Arguments about the definitions of religion, ritual, art, and the like tend to be isolated from one another and from particular cultural contexts rather than developed systematically.

8 The question also arises whether to consider spirit possession part of "religion." The answer to this must vary with one's definition of religion. To the people of Mayotte who, without a firm grasp of much of the content of their holy books, entertain a scripturalist definition of religion, the phenomena of possession definitely fall without. In fact, spirits themselves may be Muslims or may follow religious traditions of their own. Practitioners tend not to view their activities as competing with their religious beliefs and observances. I follow the local people in this regard and consider possession apart from religion, especially as possession entertains no view of either the sacred or the numinous.

However, if one prefers a broader definition of religion similar to that of Geertz (1966b), or even a narrower one like that of Spiro (1966), the reader is invited to consider the matter presented as falling into it. What *is* of general significance, and here I do part company with the explicit conceptions of the local believers, whether they actually participate in possession activities or not, is that the spirits and spirit phenomena are symbolic constructions.

9 The identification of "work" and "ritual" is, of course, found in numerous other cultures as well. Rappaport (1974) cites Firth and Ortiz on Tikopia and Tewa, respectively, in this regard and also points out that the word *liturgy* derives from the Greek for "public work."

10 Within the *asa* as a whole, the portion of feasting and entertainment is referred to as *soma*.

1. An overview of Mayotte society

1 The present account draws heavily on, and may be supplemented by, the more detailed analyses of Breslar and Martin. Other relevant work includes Ottino and Vérin. Finally, it should be cautioned that the information presented is valid only until 1976, which constitutes the ethnographic present. Since then, the new French administration has introduced many changes.

2 By 1980 affiliates were purchasing house plots within the village, thereby transforming themselves into *tompin*.

3 The younger male *shikao* are dropping this *shuŋgu*.

4 The ratio of marriages to divorces occurring in Lombeni during the year of study was 8:7. I use the word *divorce* here to mean separation with the possibility of initiating marriage with a new partner.

5 Some readers may find the discussion in this chapter far too succinct and even superficial, especially in light of the position to be taken later that possession informs social life and, indeed, is an integral part of it. However, I argue that possession speaks to highly *general* features of human social experience. Hence, although we would certainly understand possession better if we knew more about social structure, our lack of knowledge

does not hamper or invalidate the analysis to be presented. The material on economic and social organization has been kept brief intentionally in order to avoid throwing a work on spirit possession off-balance. More details and supporting argument can be found in Lambek (1978:464–514) and will be presented in future publications, which will then be supported by the previous work on trance. This is merely the reverse of the traditional anthropological practice of producing one's first book on social organization and moving on to "secondary" domains thereafter.

2. Who the spirits are not

1   God is neither male nor female, and because Malagasy has no pronominal gender system, perception is not biased by grammar.

2   This is not to say that some individuals did not provide me with truncated taxonomies. The Islamic astrologer (*mwalim dunia*), for example, distinguished between land and sea spirits, an opposition that is important in other areas of the Swahili coast (Caplan 1975, Gray 1969) but has little relevance here. The lack of a clear or formal ordering for the spirit world in Islamic Africa has been noted by a number of other students of the subject, for example, by Crapanzano (1973) for Morocco and Gray (1969) for the Swahili coast. Gray cites the *Encyclopaedia of Islam* to the effect that the Koran itself is not clear on the matter. In Mayotte spirits typically are not even described in Islamic terms as created from fire and so on. Perhaps an approach through the analysis and comparison of speech events would prove helpful in other areas of the Islamic world. Part of the problem is no doubt due to the multilinguality of the field. Arabic, Swahili, and Malagasy all have terms for extracultural beings and these terms do not have precise equivalents in the other languages. I presume, therefore, that the terms tend to coexist rather than to cancel one another out. Patterns of use may then also be affected by more general rules of code switching.

3   It is perhaps unfortunate that *extracultural* or some similar term has not more generally replaced *supernatural* in the literature on religion (cf. Köngäs Maranda 1967).

4   Traditional Malagasy beliefs and rituals concerning death are quite contrary to Islamic ones. A major ritual of the Plateau societies, the *famadihana* (Bloch 1971), involves the very handling of the corpse that disgusts the Mayotte sensibility. See also Huntington and Metcalf who write that "the most striking aspect of Malagasy funerals is the bawdy and drunken revelry enjoined upon the guests" (1979:98). The Bara funerals they describe share a similar mood with *trumba* ceremonies in Mayotte. For further discussion of the *trumba* spirits, see Chapters 10 and 11.

5   The partial exception in Lombeni is an elderly woman who claims descent from the Sakalava royal family. Also, there is an interesting parallel to the *trumba* in the custom of long-deceased notables of Mayotte rising in human hosts, particularly Shimaore speakers.

6   In fact, possession activities have been banned in the village that contains the most frequented saint's tomb of the island. However, people expect the proscription to end with the disappearance of the generation of the saint's children.

3. The nature of spirits

1   The spirit classes in Mayotte are not organized so as to present a coherent picture of the range of known ethnic types, as they are, for example, in Nubia (Boddy n.d.).

2   This process has been demonstrated for Mayotte (Lambek 1978). Although the *trumba/patros* dichotomy may be a matter of contrasting traditions stemming from Malagasy and Swahili culture, respectively, the Malagasy spirits may have developed originally from an African model, and today in Mayotte the two traditions appear to be merging again. The culture history of Madagascar and the Comoros is quite complex and the subject of some debate. For the Africanist perspective see Kent 1970; for a more comprehensive Indian Oceanist point of view see Ottino 1974.

3   Of course, not all instances of possession found in this large region necessarily follow the same model. Another pattern, where the medium holds public shamanistic or priestly office, has been defined by Lewis (1971) and is found throughout Africa, e.g., in Eastern Africa among the Nuba (Nadel 1946), the Tonga (Colson 1969), and the Korekore (Garbett 1969). A model similar to that of Mayotte, where possession is a private matter, requiring propitiation through gifts, is apparent, e.g., in the Sudanese *zar* (Barclay 1964; Boddy n.d.; Byrd n.d.), the Somali *saar* (Lewis 1971), among the Tonga and the Korekore (Colson 1969, Garbett 1969), and, closer to the Comoros, among the Segeju (Gray 1969), the Swahili of Mafia Island (Caplan 1975), and various groups in Madagascar (e.g., Althabe 1969, Ottino 1965, Rusillon 1912). The *zar* is also common in Egypt and Ethiopia and has been recorded in nineteenth-century Mecca (Snouck-Hurgronje 1931) and among the African diaspora of Bandar Abbas, Iran (Modarressi 1968). Occasionally, specific details can be traced across wide distances. Thus, an alternate term for *zar* in the Sudan, *ar-rih al-ahmar* 'the Red Spirit' (Trimingham 1949), becomes the individual *patros* spirit Mze Rihu LiAhamar, brother of Mze Nuru LiAhamar. Likewise, *Subiani*, a kind of *Sheitani ya pwani* that brings miscarriages to women on the East African coast (Koritschoner 1936), becomes the individual *patros* Subiany in Mayotte. For an explanation of this, see note 5.

Koritschoner gives a fascinating long list of kinds of spirits that well illustrate Lévi-Strauss's notion of *bricolage*. For example, the *Sherifu* spirit imitates spoken Arabic, the *Masai* spirit imitates the Masai, the *Simba* 'lion' bites and scratches, and the *Ngombe* 'cow' crawls on all fours and eats grass and leaves. The treatments for possession, involving drumming, dancing, and medicines that include steam baths and cold lotions and the drinking of goat blood on the day the spirit receives its gifts, are similar to the Mayotte *patros*. A major difference, however, occurs in the order of events. The Swahili curer sings songs appropriate to each kind of spirit in succession. Whenever a woman hears the song of her particular kind of possessing spirit, she will enter trance and dance the appropriate dance. After a time, the curer will start up the next kind of song and the performers will change over. One interesting aspect is that the spirit begins by answering questions by means of pantomime and signals, similar to the initial refusal or inability to communicate found in Mayotte.

4   Seven public *patros* ceremonies took place during the thirteen months of my residence in Lombeni. For a comparison of the number of individuals

possessed by *patros* and *trumba* spirits, see Table 4.1; contrasts between *trumba* and *patros* spirits are considered in Chapter 10, and features of other kinds of spirits are summarized in the Appendix.

5 *Patros* names only appear in very particular contexts and information about them is limited. I do have one genealogy three generations in length and also several pairs of siblings who appear in humans. These show that related spirits appear to share identical home villages. The names are originally derived from an Arabic book, the *Mutwar il Ayyam*, which lists the original twelve spirits present at the beginning of the world and their numerous descendants. The specialists able to read the book do not generally participate in possession activity and the information is not passed on directly. It should also be noted that the Arabic locations of the spirit towns have been transposed onto Mayotte geography.

6 A few adult and child females also appear. The majority of spirits of all classes are male. Gender is not a means by which the various spirit classes contrast with one another. However, the *trumba*, which are Malagasy and non-Islamic, do include women among their powerful elders. The emphasis on male *patros* is also found in the use of the patronymic form *bun*. *Bun* is not used when naming human beings. The given name of a human is followed directly by the given name of his or her father without any connective, e.g., Hassan Ali and Mariam Ali for the son and daughter, respectively, of Ali. Teknonyms, e.g., *Baba ny* Mariam, *Nindry ny* Hassan 'Father of Mariam' and 'Mother of Hassan,' respectively, are the polite forms of address in use among kin and acquaintances. I have never heard spirits referred to, or addressed, by a teknonym. Some of the older *patros* are referred to by only a single name prefaced by the title *Mze*, e.g., Mze Nuru, Mze Jabiry. The same title of respect is used to refer to Frenchmen, replacing the harder to pronounce *Monsieur*, viz., Mze Dupond, Mze Dupont.

7 This speech is little used, aside from a few words, little known among the *patros*, and not, I suspect, very well developed. There are a few simple phrase replacements and the rest are largely nonsense syllables. Some meaning can be gleaned in context by intonations and emphasis.

8 For a more complete analysis of cologne, and the significance of smells in general, see Chapter 7.

9 *Patros* also disdain the second-rate staples that frequently take the place of rice in ordinary domestic meals: manioc, green bananas, and fish.

10 This is the reason Tumbu's spirit asked me to report back to Mohedja the next morning rather than to Tumbu: Tumbu himself had not been a witness to our conversation. Similarly, Tumbu made no reference to the previous night's activities because he had not been present and, therefore, had no basis on which to talk about it.

11 However, a certain amount of seepage between individual hosts and spirits is conceded. The host who has a particularly greedy spirit may herself be accused of greed, and the spirit of the man who maintains a strong identity of orthodox piety may refrain from some of the wilder spirit activities.

12 The medical system will be discussed in greater detail in subsequent publications.

13 For example, by Marwick 1965. This brings out the general point that explanations of "sorcery" have to distinguish its place in the conceptual system from its place in the system of social action.

14   Possession by a *trumba* spirit is not a qualification for becoming a sorcery extractor. *Trumba* hosts may, however, become medical specialists in their own right. One treatment they concern themselves with assists mothers who have lost several children in succession through miscarriage or infant mortality (*mitrambuŋu*).

15   Generally, in the case of curers, host and spirit share information so thoroughly that the host is perfectly capable of performing the cure herself without going into trance. Sometimes, however, the patient is not satisfied unless he deals directly with the spirit, and at other times a curer may go into trance in order to make a stronger impression.

16   Generally speaking, men are considered to have strong dispositions and women weak ones. This is why most extractors are male.

17   The system of social obligations known as *shuŋgu* is discussed in Chapter 9.

4. The incidence of trance

1   The Mayotte case thus runs counter to the interpretation of much African trance material as a means of granting social acceptance to deviant individuals through integration into a meaningful and socially acceptable role.

2   This deserves to be explored in greater detail. It may be that the demonstration of greed is "legitimate" because it fits into the symbolic pattern of the entire ritual, whereas nakedness does not. It would seem that nakedness is too central a symbolic issue in Mayotte to be played with. Modesty is governed by a system of complex rules concerned with kinship relations and is important even after death (Lambek and Breslar n.d.). The body is considered an integral aspect of the person, such that a violation of the former is a violation of the latter.

3   First the attempt is made to talk the evil spirit into leaving. Evil spirits respond antagonistically to prayer and Muslim amulets. If neither talk nor spirit medicine nor patience solves the problem, exorcism may be attempted. This is a form of shock treatment, involving the forced inhalation of putrid fumes. Exorcism is a last resort, because it is recognized as likely to leave the patient irreparably damaged. During one case when the use of exorcism was being debated, Tumbu likened the situation to a stuck drawer. There are two ways to extract a drawer: gentle maneuvers, which take a long time but leave the frame unscathed, and yanking with full force, which is quick and effective but leaves lasting scars on the wood.

The diagnosis of madness is the recognition that nothing further can be done for the patient; it is applied when exorcism has failed or has had only limited success. Mad individuals who are not regularly violent are left to live their own lives. The most severe cases wander the countryside and are supported by sporadic individual charity. They are the victims of severe forms of sorcery or mystical retaliation, and those who have brought about their condition will be duly punished in the afterworld.

4   Each of these characteristics, except possibly the last, is, of course, extremely reminiscent of Western psychoanalytic therapy. Haley, for one, argues that one of the major factors influencing a psychoanalysis is the patient's realization of change in himself in order to escape from the ordeal of further therapy (Haley 1963:83–4).

5   By 1980, this man had also held his *azulahy* ceremony. Also by 1980, another male spirit curer had emerged in Lombeni.

6   Although Lewis would certainly include Mayotte in his class of societies in which possession is peripheral, it is really the basis of such a notion that is at issue here. Possession in Mayotte is functionally peripheral to Islam (fewer active participants, less apparent overall effect on society, viewed as less important and less valued by the members of the culture themselves, etc.). Possession also appears on the surface to be amoral. However, as I argue in later chapters, possession deals with symbols and issues that are central to the culture. The devaluation of possession may be due in part to the fact that its main adherents are women.

7   The ability to enter trance may itself run counter to male personality (as it is culturally established), with its relatively inflexible ego boundaries (cf. Chodorow 1974 and n. 14).

8   *Viavy tsisy iman. Iman* in Muslim theology means 'faith.' However, in the context cited here, in Malagasy rather than Arabic, it appears to be used in the sense of 'compassion' or 'mercy' and 'morality' or 'righteousness.'

9   The politicization of Islamic observance may be a relatively recent phenomenon in the village, and in the past a larger percentage of men may have engaged in possession activity. The men who do participate in possession today tend to be those who seek alternative avenues to positions of authority as curers.

10   The various deprivation hypotheses may work better in societies in which the overall status of women is lower or polygyny and barrenness are more of a burden to women than in Mayotte, e.g., among the Somali (Lewis 1971). Among the Ga of southern Ghana, where the status of women is relatively high but maternity is a prerequisite for wielding authority, mediumship is particularly common among barren women (Kilson 1972). In Mayotte women also enjoy a relatively high degree of autonomy and play a major role in political life. Co-wives refuse to reside in the same village as one another, and a woman whose husband remarries may threaten divorce and actually carry it out. Barren women quite readily acquire children through fosterage. Although not subject to scorn, they may feel unfulfilled and will worry about support in their old age.

   The incidence of possession also does not correlate in any clear-cut fashion with either relative security of membership in the social group or marital stability. However, such conditions are hard to judge, as they are relatively subjective and also shift over time. In general, relative wealth and marital stability provide a woman with the means to pursue a cure and indulge in possession activity once it has been diagnosed. Because my sample was restricted to the village level, I cannot report on frequency among other social classes.

11   The large number of unpossessed daughters of possessed mothers does not counter the argument at all. It is precisely from this category that we can expect new cases of possession in the future.

12   Because my data on age at first possession are scanty and imprecise, I have not included the matter in the discussion. I would expect, however, that women tend on the average to become first possessed between the second or third and tenth year of marriage, i.e., in their late teens or early twenties, whereas men on average become possessed during their thirties.

13   Haley (1963) argues that entrance into trance may be a response to paradox. It is interesting to note that the converse may also be true. That is, *exit* from trance may also be induced by paradox. An example of such an occurrence is presented by Rusillon (1912:90–1). A colonial missionary who was interested in Sakalava religious behavior, Rusillon describes how he entered a house where a *trumba* ceremony was in progress. Everyone sat on the floor, and the single chair was occupied by an individual possessed by a Sakalava king. Rusillon demanded the chair for himself, and the spirit, faced with an attitude that completely contradicted his royal identity, responded by abruptly leaving the body of his host. The lowly villager who remained readily gave precedence to the white missionary.

14   This approximates the pattern of male versus female socialization discussed by Chodorow (1974). My argument could be supported by reference to her sophisticated discussion of the relative flexibility of female ego boundaries. As she points out, strength of ego boundary need have little to do with overall strength (or health) of the ego. This supports my observations that possession does not correlate with psychopathology of any kind.

15   Women who are accustomed to trance will generally treat their children gently (cf. Chapter 12); novice trancers may ignore them. I have never observed any intentional aggression, verbal or otherwise, perpetrated by the spirits toward children. My point concerns coping with ambiguity, not abuse.

16   Possession may be classified locally as an affliction in part for the reason suggested by Lewis (1971:89), that this protects it from attack from (or allows it to coexist with) the dominant morality system, with which, if it was defined in explicitly religious or otherwise positive terms, it would be in open competition.

5. Possession as a system of communication

1   The importance of the communicative function is also demonstrated by the amount of time given over in any conversation to phatic messages, i.e., to messages that indicate merely that the channel is open and working. Examples of sequences of discourse with major phatic components can be found in Chapters 7 and 8 and are diagrammed in Figures 7.1 and 8.2. Figure 8.2 presents an example of redundancy in which the same message is repeated between a large number of sets of humans and spirits.

2   I am indebted to Ray Kelly (personal communication) for the initial clarification of this point and that of the last paragraph. He is, of course, not responsible for the form they have taken here.

3   Other therapeutic aspects of possession, such as catharsis, could also be discussed, but this would take us away from our focus on communication. In any case, the psychotherapeutic functions of non-Western curing rituals are already the subject of an extensive literature. The interested reader might begin with the collection of essays edited by Kiev (1964). On psychotherapeutic aspects of possession specifically (but differing somewhat from Mayotte), see, e.g., Obeyesekere 1970, Kennedy 1967, and Messing 1958.

      By 1980, Mwanesha had also been possessed by a *trumba* spirit. Her physical ills were over, but she and her spirits were still bothered by Dauda's drinking habits.

4   For further examples of spirit-spouse conflicts, see Lambek 1980 and 1978.

Part II: The syntagmatic dimension

1   For example, if the central problematic of the possession cure is how to deal with beings that are culturally different from yourself and more powerful, one possible message that could be grasped from the performance would be that social interaction is possible without cultural assimilation. This idea, if accepted, might have strong implications for the relationship between the islanders and the intrusive French. Although this formulation is couched in the jargon of Western social science, the point is that in Mayotte the notion is rendered through the actions and interactions of spirits and human beings. My slogan presupposes a whole domain of discourse without which it cannot have any meaning. It is precisely the Mayotte domain of discourse we are after here, rather than any particular messages or meanings that might be generated from it.

2   Culler (1975:131–60) presents an extensive discussion of this process. At the same time, the conventional expectations are maintained and sometimes even transformed through the observation and acceptance of particular cases of possession.

3   This perspective reinforces the point made in Chapter 2 that interaction with spirits is considered to occur not at a mystical level but at a social one.

6. Negotiation and emergence

1   Capitalized names indicate individuals in a state of trance. They are used periodically to remind the reader who is being referred to and at moments of transition between spirits and humans.

2   In Bateson's terms (1958), the humans do not permit a process of "schismogenesis" to develop here. Instead of reacting to the spirit's unsociability by drawing apart themselves, the humans draw closer. They respond to the spirit's aggression neither with aggression of their own ("symmetrical schismogenesis") nor with submission ("complementary schismogenesis").

3   It is not the wife who needs her husband's permission but the curer who wishes to avoid conflict with the husband.

4   Tumbu would have put his questions to Mze Jabiry in any case but would normally have waited until nightfall, lighting incense and asking his questions over it, then leaving the incense by his bedside and going to sleep, to await Mze Jabiry's response in his dreams.

5   All major spirit ceremonies involving dancing and drinking are held at night (although some may continue the next day). The reason given is always that of convenience. The other major forms of entertainment, Sufic chants and dancing and wrestling, are also performed at night. However, kinship rituals, such as weddings and circumcisions, are largely celebrated during the day.

6   Certain individuals tend always to exhibit more physical disruption than others, suggesting that factors of individual psychology, physiology, or neurology are also important. For more discussion on individual variability see Chapter 4.

7   Alliances are pursued with spirits by individuals or small family groupings rather than by larger or more inclusive social units. This pattern is consistent with the conduct of social relations in Mayotte in general. Mayotte is characterized by nuclear family households, cognatic kinship, and egocentric networks.

7. Medicine and transformation

1   Nevertheless, care is taken at this point not to refer to the identity of Habiba's spirit explicitly.

2   This French expression is normally used by *patros* spirits at the climax of their ceremonies, as an indication that they are about to announce their name. Tumbu translates it for me as *zahu navy* (lit., 'I have arrived'). As in the original French, it implies that the moment of climax, the moment that everyone has been waiting for, is at hand. It draws all attention to the speaker.
     It should also be pointed out that Tumbu's two *patros* spirits are unrelated to one another. One is an elder, and one a youth.

3   Nuriaty's spirit places its head directly in the lap of Habiba's spirit, whereas Rukia's spirit only goes so far as the knee. The difference may be attributed to the fact that Rukia's spirit is much farther along in the process of its own cure than is Nuriaty's. Another factor may be that, whereas Nuriaty and Habiba are of the same generation and approximately the same age, Rukia is much older and of their parents' generation.

4   Koranic medicine, by contrast, often has the opposite effect on spirits, making them violent and uncontrollable. Curer spirits, especially, will throw off Koranic amulets.

5   Flowers are selected for their fragrance, not for their color or form. The interest in scent and in cologne has little to do, it should be noted, with the fact that the recent popular cash crop grown and distilled in the village is ylang-ylang oil (from flowers), used as a stabilizer by the French perfume industry. Most of the villagers are ignorant of its eventual use and, in any case, find the heavy, sickly sweet odor most unpleasant. The oil is occasionally used as medicine, applied externally for certain kinds of swellings.

6   The word for cologne is *marash*. Trimingham translates the Swahili word *marashi* as meaning "rosewater and scent in general" (1964:96 n. 2). Knappert, in his discussion of Swahili Islamic poetry, finds that the smell of perfume is an "expression for [*sic*] scholarship and piety" (1971:36).

7   Despite their metaphoric association, the distinction between epilepsy and spirit possession is very clear to people. There are several terms and variants of the former. *Fanafana*, epilepticlike fits in small children that include dizziness or fainting, shaking, and rolling up of the eyes, is said to be fairly common and curable. Cure is effected by means of plant medicine squeezed from a dark cloth into the *nostrils* of the child. *Kifafa* is a disease occurring infrequently among adults, characterized by intermittent periods of loss of control, jerking, eyes rolling up, foaming at the mouth, and falling on the floor unconscious. Together with insanity and elephantiasis, *kifafa* is one of the few diseases that the local curers believe to be incurable. Epileptics are discreet and retreat into their houses when they feel an attack coming on; as a result, most people have never seen a

seizure and may not even know who suffers from the disease. *Kombelume* is used only to refer to the disease that is warded off in adults by means of the smoke treatment. As far as I know, real symptoms in a patient are never labeled *kombelume* in Malagasy.

8 Yet another example of the association of smell with liminality occurs immediately after childbirth, when the mother is said to "stink of bad blood." Aromatic substances are applied in order to ward off any spirits attracted by the smell. The consideration of smell as the main efficacious aspect of the spirit medicines also helps to explain the bewildering variety and variability in the possible means of application – drinking, inhaling, anointing, aspersing, etc. All serve to fix the patient with the odor of the plants.

9 Yet a third permutation is possible. In exorcism, a strong, foul-smelling smoke is used to drive the spirit out of the afflicted host. The symptoms again involve loss of bodily and mental control. Exorcism is considered extreme treatment, a last resort, because it can leave the patient mentally unbalanced.

8. The hidden name

1 Spitting is ordinary behavior, because saliva is considered "dirty" and therefore not to be swallowed. Spitting may serve to punctuate a conversation; here it marks the end of the period of instability and the readiness of the spirit to begin communicating.

2 However, wedding visitors are free to come and go. The wedding metaphor will be traced out in some detail in the next chapter. What is referred to here is the liminal and somewhat vulnerable position of Rukia.

3 On the structure of *patros* names, see Chapter 3 under "*Patros.*"

4 I do *not* wish to suggest that Tumbu and Mohedja are guilty of ill faith, but simply that they recognize the possibility of doubt while believing that it is usually better to take a confirmatory and supportive stand on issues in public. I believe this "management of belief" is an important characteristic of Mayotte social life. The problems it poses are of universal significance; Rappaport (1974:33–5) makes a distinction between "acceptance" (a public act or stance) and "belief" (a private state).

5 Because Rukia had already received her medicine, this evening she merely had to wash in medicated water.

6 When Kuraishiya first became ill she was treated by Juma Hassan and her spirit asked him to organize the *azulahy*. On the day scheduled for the ceremony Juma's mother died and he said they should postpone things until the end of the mourning period. However Kuraishiya's mother insisted that the ceremony be held immediately and called in another curer. Because the spirit did not have the curer it wanted it refused to announce its true name.

7 A few key words definitely have direct Malagasy equivalents. It is fairly common knowledge that *patros* greetings begin with "*Yesh habar!*" the response being "*Kely mwa habar.*" My main informants claimed that they could understand the language while in trance but that their spirits did not themselves actually speak it. It is possible that the "rival" curer, Juma Hassan, could have given me language lessons, but I did not consider it politic to ask him.

8   Jon Breslar (personal communication) reports that during the *mugala* ceremony in Shimaore-speaking villages, a similar white turban is placed around the head of the curer. This is supposed to help the spirit announce the correct name. However, to ensure that the assistance of the curer is not too direct, he or she is required to stand at some distance away.

9. Of affines and annunciations

1   A girl's sexual activity ideally remains within marriage, but indulgence in other sexual exploits have now become the girl's own business. Modesty, however, has been enjoined on her since infancy.

2   A successful defloration or circumcision also has implications for the relationship between the initiate and his immediate family and sponsors. The parents have rights over their children's initiations, the privilege of scheduling and producing them. By waiting until the parents are ready to sponsor the transformation, the child is showing them respect and earning their pleasure. At the same time, the child is grateful to the parents for sponsorship, and the parents earn public recognition for fulfilling their obligations. The successful circumcision or first wedding thus maintains reciprocity and and solidarity between initiate and sponsor. In spirit possession, although it is the initiate (the spirit) who creates the obligation on the part of the sponsors and not the sponsors who claim privileges vis-à-vis the initiate, the same kind of bond is confirmed. It should also be noted that these metaphoric associations do not indicate convergence between possession and Islam. This is so both because the similarities have to do with structure not content and because the customs surrounding circumcision and defloration are not entirely Islamic to begin with.

3   Uxorilocal residence is not prescribed but it is the statistical norm, because women own the houses and most are reluctant to move. Uxorilocality is always part of the wedding ceremony.

4   The in-laws do not actually pay for the *shuŋgu*. According to the agreement reached at the betrothal, the groom will earlier have given his prospective father-in-law the means to produce the feast, either money, or a cow, or both. But it is up to the bride's father to administer these resources and to see that the *shuŋgu* requirements are fulfilled from them. Because the early calculations are not exact and because unforeseen circumstances, such as an increase in the number of guests, may greatly increase the expense, the bride's father may have to add something from his own pocket. On the other hand, he may gain something. The freeness of the exchange and the trust it involves is the source of the bond between father-in-law and son-in-law but may also be the source of ill-feeling, as each side believes it has been taken advantage of by the other. The fact that the relationship is maintained despite such feeling or despite losses is an indication to the participants that it is manifestly one of kinship.

The fact that the spirit's *shuŋgu* is achieved by extortion does not really make it different in kind, but only in degree. Furthermore, that the spirit moves from more to less excessive demands in the negotiating process makes the host's sponsors somewhat beholden to it. The same idea occurs in the settlement of intravillage disputes, where fines and reparations are originally set much higher than intended in order to re-create a relationship between the two quarreling parties by forcing the guilty party to bargain and to appreciate concessions made by the other side.

5   Jon Breslar (personal communication) heard one such story. Such relations are commonly expressed in other parts of the world where some form of spirit possession is recognized, e.g., Burma (Spiro 1967).

6   Some of the implications of this point for the position of the spirit in the family once the cure is over are described in Chapter 5.

7   As it acclaims the feats of the individual, so the procession appears to celebrate the largesse of the male sex in general and the complementarity of the sexes united in marriage. In this way it contrasts with the women's dance, which opens the week of celebration.

8   The distinction between the domestic and public spheres, the concern to incorporate and regulate the position of the individual in both spheres and to balance their conflicting claims are major aspects of all the life-crisis rites in Mayotte. They find their expression and resolution in a spatial idiom based on the binary opposition indoors/outdoors (*antraŋu/antany;* lit., 'inside the house'/'on the ground'). For preliminary discussion of this issue see Lambek 1978:260–6 and Lambek and Breslar n.d.

9   The distinction between domestic and public affiliation that is followed in the order of events is also maintained in the identity that the spirit finally reveals. For example, "Darwesh bun Zakariya, Polé" includes the spirit's personal name and village, signifying the domestic and public poles, respectively. The inclusion of the father's name does not, in Mayotte, signify membership in a lineage. Rather, it serves to contrast this Darwesh from all other spirits of the same name, to locate him firmly at the center of his own network of kin.

10   It may be that just as we recognize the polyvalence of ritual symbols (Turner 1967), so we should speak of ritual "multi-performatives."

11   This point, as indeed the entire argument here, is simply the application to a particular case of the analysis that Rappaport (1974) has made for ritual in general. See especially pp. 14–15 and 39–40.

12   Ray Kelly first suggested this line of argument to me. For a more elaborate explication and application see Kelly 1976.

13   In fact, this is what most recent theory would lead us to believe. For example, Rappaport argues that "it is conventional, not natural, form that is problematic" (Rappaport 1974:44). He goes on to say: "In the primordial union of form and substance expressed in myth and of which ritual may be a representation, the natural order is apparently formed by, and thus absorbed into, a conventional order. But the point of the exercise is not so much, I think, to make nature conventional as the reverse. By accounting for the palpable world of trees and beasts and places the conventional is transformed into the apparently natural and, in becoming natural, to partake of the regularity, necessity, and solidity of natural objects and processes that apparently present themselves directly to the senses. To conventionalize the natural is at the same time to naturalize the conventional" (1974:45).

10. The *trumba* spirits

1   See Baré 1977, 1973a, 1973b; Dandouau 1970; Althabe 1969; Ottino 1965; Aujas 1912; Rusillon 1912.

2   Baré (1977, 1973a, 1973b) has produced the definitive work on the northern Sakalava politico-religious system.

3   Vérin (1972) provides useful historical background to the region and to the conflict that sent Andriantsuly abroad.

4   Some *trumba* spirits do not even allow their hosts to keep chickens in the house without the host becoming ill. Mohedja said she refused to believe that her spirits could prevent her from raising chickens. She kept a laying hen and was subsequently ill for three months. Furthermore, none of the eggs were any good. After the hen died, Mohedja had to be washed in *trumba* medicine before she became well again.

5   I have never seen a child *patros,* and they appear to be few in number in Lombeni. They are said to appear during the festivities of adult *patros,* cuddling simple dolls made of coconut husks. *Patros* children do eat popcorn at these festivities. *Trumba* children are described later in this chapter and in Chapter 12.

    It should also be pointed out that Mohedja could eat chicken without harmful effects only while she was possessed by either her child *trumba* or her *patros.* Her adult *trumba* forbade and punished her for doing so when she was not in trance.

6   The signification of clientage by means of dietary restrictions is also found in other social relationships in Mayotte, e.g., between patients and curers. However, it should be remembered that where the spirit makes the demands, it is actually none other than the patient herself in trance. The power relationship is thus of a rather peculiar sort.

7   The hot/cold distinction is an indication of ethnic or family difference. A large proportion of people of Malagasy descent inherit and pass on a condition known as *ranginalu,* which entails an acute sensitivity toward hot substances (e.g., hot water and air, spicy foods, stinging medicines), and a consequent reliance on cold ones. Most *trumba,* like most Malagasy, follow the *ranginalu* pattern in their medicines. However, in both cases there are just enough exceptions to prove the rule.

8   Note that this is the sex of the spirit, not the host. In fact, hosts of all child spirits and most youth and adult spirits are female.

9   This analysis is supported by Baré's etymology for *andevo* 'slave,' formed from *zanaka* 'child' and *doany* 'village where the living sovereign resides' (1973a:167). It should also be noted that the people on Mayotte were not made slaves to the Sakalava directly. However, slavery was present on Mayotte and it is possible that immigrants to the island included former Sakalava slaves. In addition, prior to the mid-nineteenth century, Mayotte was subjected to Malagasy slave raiders.

10   However, it is likely that the new host will be one of the deceased's relatives.

11   The crying and the veils correspond to the behavior of the *trumba* in the Ambanja and Nosy-Be area of Madagascar who represent Tsiomeko, queen of the Sakalava in that region from 1836 until her death around 1849. The veil accords with the story that the young queen herself hid a disfigured face under a veil, and the signs of weakness and timidity represent, according to Baré, the character and situation of a woman who inherited a very troubled kingdom at the age of eight and thereafter spent her brief life under the control of her ministers (Baré 1973a:61–5). The few female *trumba* I have observed in Mayotte do not go by either Tsio-

meko's living or posthumous names, nor do they show the particular nastiness that Baré attributes to the *trumba* who represent her.

12   It is also interesting to note how Western power has been absorbed into the *trumba* system.

13   For this reason, the child spirits make good, if rather unorthodox and possibly unethical, sources of information.

11. The world of possession

1   For further description of *trumba* ritual see Lambek 1978.

2   Mohedja's senior male *trumba* was patron to the family of a recently deceased woman of Melekavo in whom it had also appeared as a curer. Through her spirit, Mohedja initiated an alliance with this family; some time after her own *rombu* for this spirit, Mohedja married off her daughter to a descendant of the deceased woman.

3   This interchange shows how the hierarchy existing among the spirits may be used to control illness. The authority of the senior *trumba* reinforces the suggestibility already produced in the patient by her trance state in order to produce the desired results.

4   There is also the small chance of a sexual liason, but this would occur with the woman herself, rather than her spirit. The man could petition or bribe the spirit to intercede with the host on his behalf.

5   Such interaction as occurs between senior *trumba* and elder human males is usually of a personal and private nature and is generally characterized by an approximation of equality between the parties.

6   A number of the elements in *trumba* rituals have concrete parallels with royal ritual in Madagascar. Thus, the use of a silver coin in the cure compares with the presentation of an uncut silver coin to a superior in Madagascar. Likewise, the *hasiŋ* plant, with which the *trumba* elders sprinkle medicine on the congregation at the close of a *rombu*, derives its name from *hasina* 'virtue,' 'power,' 'grace,' 'sanctity' (Abinal et Malzac 1955). On *hasina*, see also Bloch's intriguing analysis (1977). In Mayotte, *hasiŋ* is also used, in a ritual virtually identical to that performed at the end of the *rombu*, to heal a breach among consanguineal kin (*razaŋa*), particularly for a senior relative to withdraw anger aimed at a junior relative (e.g., parent–child).

12. The spirits as children

1   Child spirits are relatively few in number and are found, in my experience, only in women of middle age. In Lombeni, out of a total of some fifty-six women with spirits, the number with child *trumba* is probably fewer than ten. On the day of her meal, Tamtamu attempted to call up every other available child spirit in Lombeni Kely.

2   Tamtamu later did make Zayata uncomfortable in order to force me to keep my promise to buy the spirit some clothes. I was thus placed in an analogous position to the spouse and relatives who must pay for a host's spirit cure.

3   Child spirits reduce the human kinship system to four categories, based on dimensions of gender and reciprocity. The speaker is female:

	Male (cross sex)	Female (same sex)
Positive reciprocity ("siblings")	*anadahy*	*rahavavy*
Negative reciprocity (non-kin)	(unmarked)	(unmarked)

Human sibling terms in Mayotte are relatively complex. Actual siblings usually refer to and address each other by *zuky/zandry* 'older/younger sibling' (sex unmarked). A male may alternatively refer to his sister as *anabavy*, and a female to her brother as *anadahy*, marking the distinction in sex. Each of these four terms is appropriate for cousins as well, i.e., for all consanguineal relatives of the same generation. The terms *rahavavy* and *rahalahy* are the counterparts to *anabavy/anadahy*, used respectively between women and between men and marking the similarity in sex. Whereas in Madagascar these terms are found referring to actual siblings, their use in Mayotte is restricted to "friends" and to the spouses of siblings. Thus, a man addresses and refers to the husband of his wife's sister as his *rahalahy* and a woman to the wife of her husband's brother as *rahavavy*. *Rahavavy* is also the polite term between co-wives. *Rahavavy/rahalahy* can thus be understood to mean "siblings" in a general sense, where birth order is irrelevant.

4   I suspect that the most intense joking occurs between the spirits and those individuals with whom their hosts already have joking relationships, that is, with brothers' children, husband's sisters' children, mother's brothers, father's sisters, grandparents and grandchildren.

5   Teaching children not to be selfish with food is a major theme in early socialization. The comparison between children and spirits can work in the other direction as well. A badly behaved child may be told that he is acting *kara lulu* 'like a spirit.'

Conclusion

1   It is clearer that Islam forms an ultimate reference point for possession than the reverse. But, in some ways, the practice of Islam in Mayotte is viewed as an uphill fight against the forces of entropy and egoism.

2   No rigid typology is meant here, and the methods do, of course, overlap in particular societies. For example, although the people of Mayotte do not make use of drugs to induce trance, entranced individuals frequently do consume large quantities of alcohol.

3   If the expression is taken literally, reading and writing may certainly be considered altered states of consciousness. Sartre (1948) has called them states of "nonreflective consciousness." Other examples of altered states common in daily life include praying, singing, and listening to music. The problem with the whole discussion of "altered" consciousness is that the contributors seldom define the "unaltered" state.

4   I am thinking of masking as it occurs in numerous Central and West African societies. In some societies the maskers may go into trance as well. Vern Carroll has pointed out to me that carnival may include forms intermediate between masking and trance possession.

5   For a brilliant evocation of this tension, see Chinua Achebe's novel, *Things Fall Apart*.

Appendix

1   Yet they are also found in northwest Madagascar (Baré 1973a:21, 178; Rusillon 1912:141). Rusillon calls them *kalanoru*. Conrad Kottak has pointed out to me the Betsileo *oronala* (lit., 'people of the forest'), which is cognate with Malay, and more recently English, orangutan. On the other hand, an informant in Mayotte suggests the presumably secondary etymology *kaka ny horuŋ* 'nasal spirit.' The *kakanoru* in Mayotte do speak through the nose.

Bibliography

Abinal et Malzac, S.J. 1955. *Dictionnaire Malgache-Français*. Paris: Editions Maritimes et Coloniales.

Achebe, Chinua. 1959. *Things Fall Apart*. Greenwich, Conn.: Fawcett.

Althabe, Gérard. 1969. *Oppression et libération dans l'imaginaire*. Paris: Maspero.

Aujas, L. 1912. "Notes historiques et ethnographiques sur les Comores." Bulletin de l'académie Malgache IX.

Austin, J.L. 1962. *How to Do Things with Words*. Cambridge, Mass.: Harvard University Press.

Balandier, Georges. 1966. *Ambiguous Africa*. London: Chatto & Windus.

Barclay, Harold B. 1964. *Buurri al Lamaab*. Ithaca: Cornell University Press.

Baré, J.F. 1973a. *Conflits et résolution des conflits dans les monarchies Sakalava du Nord actuelles*. Publication Provisoire, Musée de l'Université de Madagascar.

1973b. "Successions politiques et légitimité: l'exemple Sakalava du Nord (1700–1800)." *Asie du Sud-Est et Monde Insulindien* (ASEMI) 4, No. 4: 91–114.

1974. "La Terminologie de parenté Sakalava du Nord (Madagascar)." *L'Homme* 14:5–41.

1977. *Pouvoir des vivants langage des morts: idéo-logiques Sakalave*. Paris: Maspero.

Barthes, Roland. 1966. *Critique et vérité*. Paris: Seuil.

Bateson, Gregory. 1958. *Naven*. Stanford, Calif.: Stanford University Press.

1972. *Steps to an Ecology of Mind*. San Francisco: Chandler.

Beattie, John, and Middleton, John, eds. 1969. *Spirit Mediumship and Society in Africa*. London: Routledge & Kegan Paul.

Becker, Alton L. 1979. "Text-Building, Epistemology, and Aesthetics in Javanese Shadow Theatre." In *The Imagination of Reality: Essays in Southeast Asian Symbolic Systems*. Alton L. Becker and Aram A. Yengoyan, eds. Norwood, N.J.: Ablex.

Benedict, Burton. 1967. "The Equality of the Sexes in the Seychelles." In *Social Organization*. Maurice Freedman, ed. London: Frank Cass.

Bergson, Henri. 1913. *Laughter: An Essay on the Meaning of the Comic*. Trans. Cloudesley Brereton and Fred Rothwell. New York: Macmillan.

Bloch, Maurice. 1971. *Placing the Dead: Tombs, Ancestral Villages and Kinship Organization in Madagascar*. New York: Seminar.

1977. "The Disconnection between Power and Rank as a Process: An Outline of the Development of Kingdoms in Central Madagascar." *European Journal of Sociology* 18, No. 1:107–48.

Boddy, Janice. n.d. "Spirit Possession and the Anthropological Experience." Paper presented to the University of Toronto Working Seminar in Social-Cultural Anthropology, April 20, 1979.

Bourguignon, Erika, ed. 1973. *Religion, Altered States of Consciousness, and Social Change.* Columbus: Ohio State University Press.

1976. *Possession.* San Francisco: Chandler & Sharp.

Breslar, Jon H. n.d. *L'Habitat Mahorais: une perspective ethnologique.* Paris: Editions A.G.G.

Byrd, Emily. n.d. "The Zar Ritual in a Suburb of Khartoum: A Study in Complementary Ritual Domains." Ann Arbor: Department of Anthropology, University of Michigan.

Caplan, Ann Patricia. 1975. *Choice and Constraint in a Swahili Community.* London: Oxford University Press.

Chodorow, Nancy. 1974. "Family Structure and Feminine Personality." In *Woman, Culture, and Society.* Michelle Zimbalist Rosaldo and Louise Lamphere, eds. Stanford, Calif.: Stanford University Press.

Colson, Elizabeth. 1969. "Spirit Possession among the Tonga of Zambia." In *Spirit Mediumship and Society in Africa*, pp. 69–103. John Beattie and John Middleton, eds. London: Routledge & Kegan Paul.

Crapanzano, Vincent. 1973. *The Hamadsha: A Study in Moroccan Ethnopsychiatry.* Berkeley: University of California Press.

1977. Introduction. In *Case Studies in Spirit Possession.* V. Crapanzano and V. Garrison, eds. New York: Wiley.

Culler, Jonathan. 1975. *Structuralist Poetics.* Ithaca: Cornell University Press.

Dandouau, André J. 1970. "Le Trumba." In *Early Kingdoms in Madagascar, 1500–1700*, pp. 324–9. Raymond K. Kent. New York: Holt, Rinehart and Winston.

Douglas, Mary. 1968. "The Social Control of Cognition: Some Factors in Joke Perception." *Man*, n.s. 3:361–76.

Dumont, Louis. 1970. *Homo Hierarchicus: An Essay on the Caste System.* Trans. Mark Sainsbury. Chicago: University of Chicago Press.

Faurec, Urbain, and Manicacci, Jean. n.d. "Histoire de l'île de Mayotte." Moroni.

Feuerbach, Ludwig. 1975. *The Essence of Christianity.* Trans. George Eliot. New York: Harper.

Garbett, G. Kingsley. 1969. "Spirit Mediums as Mediators in Korekore Society." In *Spirit Mediumship and Society in Africa*, pp. 104–27. John Beattie and John Middleton, eds. London: Routledge & Kegan Paul.

Geertz, Clifford. 1964. "Ideology as a Cultural System." In *Ideology and Discontent*, pp. 47–56. D. Apter, ed. Glencoe: Free Press. Reprinted in Geertz 1973b.

1966a. "The Impact of the Concept of Culture on the Concept of Man." In *New Views of the Nature of Man*, pp. 93–118. J. Platt, ed. Chicago: University of Chicago Press. Reprinted in Geertz 1973b.

1966b. "Religion as a Cultural System." In *Anthropological Approaches to the Study of Religion.* M. Banton, ed. A.S.A. Monographs 3. London: Tavistock. Reprinted in Geertz 1973b.

1972. "Deep Play: Notes on the Balinese Cockfight." *Daedalus* 101:1–37. Reprinted in Geertz 1973b.

1973a. "Thick Description: Toward an Interpretive Theory of Culture." In *The Interpretation of Cultures*, pp. 3–30. Clifford Geertz. New York: Basic Books.

1973b. *The Interpretation of Cultures*. New York: Basic Books.

Gluckman, Max. 1954. *Rituals of Rebellion in South-east Africa*. Manchester: Manchester University Press.

Goodenough, Ward H. 1965. "Rethinking 'Status' and 'Role': Toward a General Model of the Cultural Organization of Social Relationships." In *The Relevance of Models for Social Anthropology*. M. Banton, ed. A.S.A. Monographs 1. London: Tavistock; New York: Praeger.

Gray, Robert F. 1969. "The Shetani Cult among the Segeju of Tanzania." In *Spirit Mediumship and Society in Africa*, pp. 171–87. John Beattie and John Middleton, eds. London: Routledge & Kegan Paul.

Gueunier, Noel. 1976. "Notes sur la dialecte malgache de l'île de Mayotte (Comores)." *Asie du Sud-Est et Monde Insulindien* (ASEMI) 7, No. 2–3:81–119.

Haley, Jay. 1963. *Strategies of Psychotherapy*. New York: Grune and Stratton.

Harner, Michael, J. 1973. *Hallucinogens and Shamanism*. New York: Oxford University Press.

Hilgard, Ernest R. 1967. "Individual Differences in Hypnotizability." In *Handbook of Clinical and Experimental Hypnosis*. Jesse E. Gordon, ed. New York: Macmillan.

Huizinga, Johan. 1950. *Homo Ludens: A Study of the Play Element in Culture*. Boston: Beacon.

Huntington, Richard, and Metcalf, Peter. 1979. *Celebrations of Death: The Anthropology of Mortuary Ritual*. New York: Cambridge University Press.

Jakobson, Roman. 1960. "Linguistics and Poetics." In *Style in Language*. T. Sebeok, ed. Cambridge, Mass.: M.I.T. Press.

Janzen, John M. 1978. *The Quest for Therapy in Lower Zaire*. Berkeley: University of California Press.

Kelly, Raymond C. 1976. "Witchcraft and Sexual Relations: An Exploration in the Social and Semantic Implications of the Structure of Belief." In *Man and Woman in the New Guinea Highlands*. Paula Brown and Georgeda Buchbinder, eds. Washington, D.C.: American Anthropological Association, Special Publication 8.

1977. *Etoro Social Structure: A Study in Structural Contradiction*. Ann Arbor: University of Michigan Press.

Kennedy, J. G. 1967. "Nubian Zar Ceremonies as Psychotherapy." *Human Organization* 26, No. 4: 185–94.

Kent, Raymond K. 1970. *Early Kingdoms in Madagascar, 1500–1700*. New York: Holt, Rinehart and Winston.

Kiev, Ari, ed. 1964. *Magic, Faith, and Healing: Studies in Primitive Psychiatry Today*. New York: Free Press of Glencoe.

Kilson, Marilyn. 1972. "Ambivalence and Power: Mediums in Ga Traditional Religion." *Journal of Religion in Africa* 4, Fasc. 3:171–7.

Knappert, Jan. 1971. *Swahili Islamic Poetry*. Leiden: Brill.

Köngäs Maranda, Elli. 1967. "The Cattle of the Forest and the Harvest of Water: The Cosmology of Finnish Magic." In *Essays on the Verbal and Visual Arts*, pp. 84–95. June Helm, ed. *Proceedings of the 1966 Annual Spring Meeting of the American Ethnological Society*. Seattle: University of Washington Press for American Ethnological Society.

Koritschoner, Hans. 1936. "*Ngoma Ya Sheitani:* An East African Native Treatment for Physical Disorder." *Journal of the Royal Anthropological Institute* 66:209–19.

Kus, Susan, and Wright, Henry. 1976. "Notes preliminaries sur une reconnaissance archéologique de l'Ile de Mayotte (Archipel des Comores)." *Asie du Sud-Est et Monde Insulindien* (ASEMI) 7, No. 2–3:123–35.

Lambek, Michael. 1978. *Human Spirits: Possession and Trance Among the Malagasy Speakers of Mayotte (Comoro Islands).* Ann Arbor, Mich.: University Microfilms.

1980. "Spirits and Spouses: Possession as a System of Communication Among the Malagasy Speakers of Mayotte." *American Ethnologist* 7, No. 2:318–31.

Lambek, Michael, and Breslar, Jon H. 1982 Funerals and Social Change in Mayotte. In *Madagascar: Society and History.* Conrad Phillip Kottak, Aidan Southall, and Pierre Vérin, eds. Carolina Academic Press.

Leiris, Michel. 1958. *La Possession et ses aspects thèâtraux chez les Ethiopiens de Gondar.* Paris: Plon.

Lévi-Strauss, Claude. 1955. *Tristes tropiques.* Paris: Plon.

1963. *Structural Anthropology.* Trans. Claire Jacobson and Brooke Grundfest Schoepf. New York: Basic Books.

1966. *The Savage Mind.* Chicago: University of Chicago Press.

Lewis, I. M. 1971. *Ecstatic Religion: An Anthropological Study of Spirit Possession and Shamanism.* Harmondsworth: Penguin.

Ludwig, A. M. 1968. "Altered States of Consciousness." In *Trance and Possession States.* Raymond Prince, ed. Montreal: R. M. Bucke Memorial Society.

Martin, Jean. 1976. "L'affranchissement des esclaves de Mayotte, décembre 1846–juillet 1847." *Cahiers d'études africains* 61–62, No. 16:207–33.

Marwick, Max G. 1965. *Sorcery in Its Social Setting: A Study of the Northern Rhodesian Cêwa.* Manchester: Manchester University Press.

Messing, S. D. 1958. "Group Therapy and Social Status in the Zar Cult of Ethiopia." *American Anthropologist* 60:1120–6.

Métraux, A. 1955. "Dramatic Elements in Ritual Possession." *Diogenes* 11:18–36.

Milner, G. B. 1972. "Homo Ridens: Towards a Semiotic Theory of Humour and Laughter." *Semiotica* 5:1–30.

Modarressi, Taghi. 1968. "The Zar Cult in South Iran." In *Trance and Possession States,* pp. 149–55. Raymond Prince, ed. Montreal: R. M. Bucke Memorial Society.

Murphy, Robert F. 1971. *The Dialectics of Social Life: Alarms and Excursions in Anthropological Theory.* New York: Basic Books.

Nadel, S. F. 1946. "A Study of Shamanism in the Nuba Hills." *Journal of the Royal Anthropological Institute* 76:25–37.

Needham, Rodney. 1968gists. Review of *Seth, God of Confusion* by H. Te Velde. *American Anthropologist* 70:987–8.

Obeyesekere, Gananath. 1970. "The Idiom of Demonic Possession: A Case Study." *Social Science and Medicine* 4, No. 1:97–111.

Ottino, Paul. 1964. "La crise du système familial et matrimonial des Sakalava de Nosy Be." *Civilisation Malgache* 1:225–48.

1965. "Le Tromba (Madagascar)." *L'Homme* 5, No. 1:84–93.

1974. *Madagascar, les Comores, et le Sud-Ouest de l'Ocean Indien.* Tannanarive: Centre d'Anthropologie Culturelle et Sociale, Université de Madagascar.

Prince, Raymond. 1968. "Can the EEG Be Used in the Study of Possession States?" In *Trance and Possession States*. Raymond Prince, ed. Montreal: R. M. Bucke Memorial Society.

Radin, Paul, ed. 1964. *African Folktales*. Princeton: Princeton University Press.

Rappaport, Roy A. 1974. "The Obvious Aspects of Ritual." *Cambridge Anthropologist* 2:3–68. Reprinted in Roy A. Rappaport, 1979. *Ecology, Meaning, and Religion*. Richmond, Calif.: North Atlantic.

Ricoeur, Paul. 1971. "The Model of the Text: Meaningful Action Considered as a Text." *Social Research* 38:529–62.

   1976. *Interpretation Theory*. Fort Worth: Texas Christian University Press.

   1978. "Explanation and Understanding." Trans. Charles E. Reagan and David Stewart. In *The Philosophy of Paul Ricoeur*. C. E. Reagan and D. Stewart, eds. Boston: Beacon.

Rigby, Peter. 1968. "Some Gogo Rituals of 'Purification': An Essay on Social and Moral Categories." In *Dialectic in Practical Religion*. E. R. Leach, ed. Cambridge: Cambridge University Press.

Rusillon, Henri. 1912. *Un culte dynastique avec évocation des morts chez les Sakalaves de Madagascar: le "tromba."* Paris: Picard.

Sartre, Jean-Paul. 1948. *The Emotions: Outline of a Theory*. Trans. Bernard Frechtman. New York: Philosophical Library.

Snouck-Hurgronje, C. 1931. *Mekka in the Latter Part of the 19th Century*. Leiden: Brill.

Spiro, Melford. 1966. "Religion: Problems of Definition and Explanation." In *Anthropological Approaches to the Study of Religion*. M. Banton, ed. A.S.A. Monographs 3. London: Tavistock.

   1967. *Burmese Supernaturalism: A Study in the Explanation and Reduction of Suffering*. Englewood Cliffs, N.J.: Prentice-Hall.

Trimingham, J. Spencer. 1949. *Islam in the Sudan*. London: Oxford University Press.

   1964. *Islam in East Africa*. Oxford: Clarendon.

Turner, Victor W. 1967. *The Forest of Symbols: Aspects of Ndembu Ritual*. Ithaca, N.Y.: Cornell University Press.

   1969. *The Ritual Process: Structure and Anti-Structure*. Chicago: Aldine.

Van Gennep, Arnold. 1960. *The Rites of Passage*. Trans. Monika B. Vizedom and Gabrielle L. Caffee. Chicago: University of Chicago Press.

Verger, Pierre. 1969. "Trance and Convention in Nago-Yoruba Spirit Mediumship." In *Spirit Mediumship and Society in Africa*, pp. 50–66. John Beattie and John Middleton, eds. London: Routledge & Kegan Paul.

Vérin, Pierre. 1972. "Historie ancienne du Nord-Ouest de Madagascar." *Taloha* 5:1–174.

Walker, Sheila. 1972. *Ceremonial Spirit Possession in Africa and Afro-America*. Leiden: Brill.

Wallace, A. F. C. 1959. "Cultural Determinants of Response to Hallucinatory Experiences." *A.M.A. Archives of General Psychiatry* 1:58–69.

Wilson, Peter J. 1967. "Status Ambiguity and Spirit Possession." *Man*, N.S. 2, No. 3:366–78.

Zaretsky, Irving I., and Shambaugh, Cynthia. 1978. *Spirit Possession and Spirit Mediumship in Africa and Afro-America: An Annotated Bibliography*. New York: Garland.

Index

acceptance, 87, 89, 134, 144, 147, 171, 201 n4; *see also* belief
Achebe, Chinua, 207 n5
affines (*see also* marriage; spouses): after divorce, 23; and *mraba,* 20; spirits as, 80–1, 141–4, 202 n2, 202 n4
Africa: culture history of, 194 n2; laborers from, 3, 16; spirit possession in, 35, 193 n2, 194 n3; spirits from, 186
age groups, see *shikao*
agitated behavior; of *be tsiku,* 189–90; decline during cure, 103–4; of Habiba's spirit, 93, 99, 108–10, 112; individual variability of, 199 n6; of Kuraishiya's spirit, 136; of Rukia's spirit, 132; significance of, 102–4
aggression, 51
alcohol, 37, 41, 76–8, 125, 157, 162–4, 167–8, 206 n2
altered states of consciousness, 5, 32, 183–5, 191 n4, 206 n3
Althabe, Gérard, 203 n1
amorality, see morality
Andriantsuly: refuge in Mayotte, 15, 153; *trumba* spirit of ('Ndramaŋavakarivu), 153, 156, 158
annunciation (*see also* identity; names; Rukia's spirit): conditions for, 47, 189, 201 n6, 202 n8; examples of, 42, 135–6, 138; problematic nature of, 126, 134; significance of, 104, 117, 124, 126–7, 141, 144–7, 149–50
Antandroy, 189
asa (work, ritual) (*see also* rites of passage; ritual; *shuŋgu*), 9, 192 n10
Aujas, L., 203 n1
Austin, J.L., 145–6
authority (*see also* hierarchy; power): and age, 155; and spirits, 158, 205 n3, 205 n6; distribution between men and women, 24; distribution in village, 18, 19

azulahy (drumming ceremony), 186, 187
azulahy be (major *patros* drumming ceremony) (*see also* feasts, of spirits; *soma*) 89, 100, 124, 135–9, 165

Bako Ali, 95, 108–10, 136
Balandier, Georges, 70
Barclay, Harold B., 194 n3
Baré, J.F., 22, 70, 203 n1, 204 n2, 204 n9, 204 n11, 207 n1
Barthes, Roland, 10
Bateson, Gregory, 149, 199 n2
Becker, Alton L., 4, 8–9, 42, 183
belief (*see also* acceptance; dissimulation; possession, authentification of): complexity of, 30; contrast with acceptance, 201 n4; role in cure, 31; and skepticism, 45, 134, 185, 201 n4; in sorcery, 45; in spirits, 32
Benedict, Burton, 23
Bergson, Henri, 180
Biby Fatimah, 62
Bloch, Maurice, 193 n4, 205 n6
blood, 37, 39–40, 119, 120, 122, 125, 138, 201 n8
Boddy, Janice, 194 n3
Bourguignon, Erika, 5, 7
Breslar, Jon H., 37, 38, 137, 138, 186, 192 n1, 202 n8, 203 n5
bride, see weddings
Byrd, Emily, 149

Caplan, Ann Patricia, 193 n2, 194 n3
Carroll, Vern, 207 n4
cash crops, 16–17, 20, 92, 98, 200 n5
Changani (village), 90–3, 99–100
chicken, 37–8, 154, 204 n4
children: experience of trance in parents, 69, 176, 198 n 15; obedience expected from, 155; trance behavior in, 57
child spirits: class position of, 155, 159; compared to older spirits, 179; dietary

213